Everybody's Different

Praise for

Everybody's Different

Understanding and Changing
Our Reactions to Disabilities

"This is a great book. It provides us with a way to understand our feelings and move beyond fear and discomfort toward a greater tolerance and appreciation for all peoples. It's a must-read for anyone working or living with persons with disabilities. In fact, it's a must-read for everyone who cares about creating a more loving world."

—**Suzanne Mintz**
President and Co-founder
National Family Caregivers Association

"From the corporate boardroom to the classroom, this well-organized and thoroughly readable book will serve as a ready resource to anyone with occasion to interact with people with disabilities. . . . Its value lies in its lay language, practical tips, and most importantly in its appreciation of all human differences. Whether in the workplace or the marketplace, the reader will never regard people with disabilities with anything less than awareness, sensitivity, and confidence."

—**Richard G. Luecking**
President, TransCen, Inc.

"*Everybody's Different* is a critically important book because all of us will be touched by disability in our lives. Miller and Sammons clearly demonstrate how we can interact meaningfully and without fear. . . . They convey a deeper understanding and perspective rarely seen in print. . . . A truly significant book for the helping professions and direct care providers . . . [and] essential reading for all who want to live comfortably in our ever-widening diverse world."

—**Craig Winston LeCroy, Ph.D.**
Professor, Arizona State University, School of Social Work

"Nancy Miller and Catherine Sammons have created a charming prism that helps us focus on our reactions and interactions in everyday encounters with people who are different. This is a very carefully written, easily read book that informs and enlightens us about our own behavior in the face of difference. Although the book focuses on . . . physical differences and disabilities, the model has great power for thinking about our reactions to color, ethnicity, or national origin.

"It is very easy to take the lessons of this book to heart and to learn how to engage with others in a much more fruitful manner. The book is truly a delight."

—**Richard Goodman, D.B.A.**
Associate Professor, The Anderson School at UCLA

"By combining technical discussion with myriad individual perspectives and engaging activities, the authors provide a practical road map for personal growth and societal change. Stripping away the mystery which too often shrouds disability, they offer a clarifying lens through which to examine ourselves and the world around us. While consistently nonjudgmental in tone, the text insists upon an active response from the reader. Ultimately we are charged with the responsibility to take action, to make a difference. I enthusiastically recommend this book to anyone seeking to expand their horizons relative to disability."

—**Mark R. Donovan**
Executive Director, Marriott Foundation for People with Disabilities

Everybody's Different

Understanding and Changing
Our Reactions to Disabilities

by

Nancy B. Miller, Ph.D., M.S.W.

and

Catherine C. Sammons, Ph.D., M.S.W.

·P·A·U·L·H·
BROOKES
PUBLISHING C°

Baltimore • London • Toronto • Sydney

Paul H. Brookes Publishing Co.

Post Office Box 10624
Baltimore, Maryland 21285-0624

www.brookespublishing.com

Copyright © 1999 by Paul H. Brookes Publishing Co., Inc.
All rights reserved.

Typeset by Brushwood Graphics, Inc., Baltimore, Maryland.
Manufactured in the United States of America by
Edwards Brothers, Inc., Ann Arbor, Michigan.

Gender specifications alternate throughout the text.

Library of Congress Cataloging-in-Publication Data

Miller, Nancy B., 1939–
    Everybody's different : understanding and changing our reactions
to disabilities / by Nancy B. Miller and Catherine C. Sammons.
        p.   cm.
    Includes bibliographical references and index.
    ISBN 1-55766-359-9 (pbk.)
    1. Sociology of disability.   2. Discrimination against the
handicapped.   3. Handicapped.   4. Disability studies.
I. Sammons, Catherine C.   II. Title.
HV1568.M55   1999
362.4—dc21   98-51018
                                                                                CIP

British Library Cataloguing in Publication data are available from the
British Library.

Contents

About the Authors

Nancy B. Miller, Ph.D., M.S.W., Assistant Clinical Professor, Department of Psychiatry and Biobehavioral Sciences, UCLA, and private psychotherapist and consultant, Los Angeles

Nancy B. Miller is a social worker and anthropologist who has worked with children with disabilities and their families for more than 30 years. One of Dr. Miller's major interests has been the influence of American culture on attitudes about disabilities. She has been on the UCLA faculty for more than 25 years and has developed and taught courses in developmental disabilities in the School of Social Welfare, was Social Work Training Coordinator with the University Affiliated Program, which provides interdisciplinary training in disabilities for graduate students in a wide variety of disciplines, and was Social Work and Clinical Research Coordinator in the UCLA Department of Pediatrics Early Intervention Program. She was a consultant for UCLA Child Care Services for 20 years.

Dr. Miller is the author of *Nobody's Perfect: Living and Growing with Children Who Have Special Needs,* which received a *Child Magazine* Best Parenting Book Award for Excellence in Family Issues. She has numerous publications in books and journals, including several pioneering studies of siblings of children and adults with disabilities. She writes a regular family issues column for the online parent magazine, *Special Child* (www.specialchild.com).

Dr. Miller is a popular guest speaker nationwide, providing entertaining and inspiring presentations to parents and professionals on the topics of *Nobody's Perfect,* parenting issues and adaptation, and stress management for family caregivers.

As an active member of the Barrier Free Program at the Los Angeles County Museum of Art, she provides tours for adults and children with disabilities.

Catherine C. Sammons, Ph.D., M.S.W., Assistant Clinical Professor, Neuropsychiatric Institute and Hospital, and Social Work Training Coordinator, University Affiliated Program, UCLA

Catherine C. Sammons has worked with families of children and adults with disabilities as a psychotherapist, advocate, and educator for more than 20 years. She is social work training coordinator for the UCLA University Affiliated Program. She supervises and teaches clinical professionals in family support, sibling issues, and systems change. As an expert in mental illness and developmental disabilities, Dr. Sammons directs a statewide program, the California Mental Health and Developmental Disabilities Center (www.npi.ucla.edu/mhdd/).

Dr. Sammons has conducted numerous workshops and presentations throughout the United States. She has published in the journals *Social Work, Journal of the American Academy of Child Psychiatry,* and *Children Today* and has contributed to texts such as *Social Work Practice* (LeCroy, 1992, Wadsworth Publishing Company). Her psychotherapy and consulting practice is located in West Los Angeles.

After earning her Master of Social Welfare degree from the UCLA School of Social Welfare, Dr. Sammons held clinical social work positions in inpatient child psychiatry and at the UCLA Clinical Research Center for the Study of Childhood Psychosis. She participated in multiple research projects looking at the causes and course of autism in children and adults.

Dr. Sammons holds a doctorate from UCLA's Anderson School of Management, with a specialization in organization design and development. Her desire to improve staff working conditions and consumer responsiveness in human services agencies inspired her to conduct research, teach, and consult in the quality of work life, self-managed work teams, and innovative models for health and human services organizations.

The authors may be contacted at Post Office Box 49-2046, Los Angeles, CA 90049 or through nmiller@ucla.edu for information about *Everybody's Different* seminars and workshops for professionals, employees, students, and parents. The authors welcome readers' comments by mail, by e-mail, or through the Paul H. Brookes Publishing Co. World Wide Web site (www. brookespublishing.com).

Introduction

Everybody's Different is about *disability differences.* You're encountering more people with disabilities at work, at your place of worship, in your neighborhood, or while riding on the bus. If you're like most people, you have at least one family member with a disability. Perhaps you have a disability yourself.

This book is also about your *reactions* to disability differences: curiosity, confusion, inspiration, pity, and at times, discomfort or fear. When someone looks, moves, communicates, behaves, or learns differently, often you may not be sure of what to say, how to act, or even how to feel.

This book is also about your *interactions* with people who have disability differences: what you do, don't do, wish you'd done, or would like to do. It's about your facial expressions, words, and body language. You may wonder whether you should ignore a person's difference rather than give attention to it. Maybe you *feel* comfortable but *act* overly cautious because you don't want to say or do the "wrong thing." Perhaps you act overly friendly and realize that this does not seem very genuine. At times, you may feel uninformed—you may want to give the disability *no more and no less attention* than is relevant in a specific situation but are unsure of how to accomplish this goal. Many of us act on old habits and outdated beliefs because we don't understand our reactions, we avoid talking about them, and we lack the tools to try a different way.

Everybody's Different explains why you react the way you do (and maybe wish you didn't). You may not realize that your brain is "wired" to notice differences that initially seem unfamiliar, unexpected, or unsettling. Your beliefs and behaviors are also shaped by a lifetime of experiences and memories about differences and disabilities.

THIS BOOK WAS WRITTEN FOR YOU

This book is for you if you ever feel stuck in your preconceptions and misconceptions about disabilities and the people who have them. You may have grown up during a time when disabilities were still "in the closet" (or in that special classroom down the hall or that big brick building across town). Did you have the chance to know any children with disabilities in your school, neighborhood, or scout troop? Did your parents say, "Don't stare," when they saw you looking at a person with a different appearance? And, if you now have children of your own or work with children, how do you explain disability differences to them?

This book was written for *you...*

If you have a relative, friend, or co-worker with a disability and

- You're uncertain about how to think or act
- You aren't sure what to say or where to look
- You'd like to be supportive but not intrusive
- You'd like more information but don't want to be rude

If you work with clients who have disabilities and

- You'd like a fresh perspective to stay energized and current
- You're familiar with some kinds of disability differences but are serving new clientele
- You'd like a training text for direct support staff, students, new employees, and volunteers to enhance their comfort and effectiveness

If you are a business person providing products or services to customers who may have disabilities and

- You'd like to be better informed about disability differences

- You have limited time to really get to know your customers and want to have more positive and sensitive interactions with them

If you are the caregiver for a family member who has a disability and

- You'd like to understand why some people in your extended family, neighborhood, office, or social group are uncomfortable around you or your family member
- You sometimes feel uncomfortable about the reactions and comments of strangers in public places

If you have a disability and

- You're looking for insights about how others view you
- You sometimes feel uncomfortable with disabilities other than your own

WHAT YOU WILL GET FROM THIS BOOK

- *New awareness* of disability differences in others
- *Better understanding* of your internal emotional reactions to disability differences
- *Increased skills* for interacting with people who have disability differences

This is a time of dramatic change in our understanding of how disabilities are a part of everyone's life. All of us are more likely than ever to have a disability and to live or work with someone who has a disability. Stigmatizing attitudes toward people with disabilities are still prevalent in our society. We need to reexamine how we think about and interact with people who have disabilities, not only for our own comfort but also for the quality of community life.

Acknowledgments

It may take two authors to have an idea, but it takes a community to make it a book. Although we "gave birth" to the concept of *Everybody's Different*, it would never have matured into a finished book without the support and contribution of many individuals over a period of several years. First and foremost, our families stood by us right from the start, believing in our mission and understanding the huge amount of time and energy it required. Cathy is grateful for Trey's patience and loving support as well as his active participation—along with that of their children, Caitlin and Chase—in living the principles of this book in their daily family life. Her sister Gail was always there for her. Nancy thanks her husband Hans for his unwavering support and theoretical contributions. Nancy's sister Martha and best friend Dale have helped make these years an adventure in growth and humility that are beyond measure.

Special thanks to Theresa Donnelly for her enthusiasm in the early phases of this project. Heather Shrestha at Brookes has been the essence of clear direction and support in guiding our project through its evolution. And thanks to Mika Sam who has edited the manuscript with patience and precision.

Many colleagues and friends reviewed chapters, debated issues, asked questions, provided resources, and supported us in other valuable ways. We are grateful to all of them, including: Dale Atkins, David Berkey, Mary Cerreto, Aven and Martha Decker, Ralph Dennard, Nita Ferjo, Jim Finley, Arvin Fluharty, John Graham, Donna Ikkanda, Jan Larky, Douglas Lynch, Gay Macdonald, Robin Maisel, Mary Martz, David and Jan Mintz, Patty Moore, Teresa Reyes, John Schumann, Judy Segal, Robert Simon, Loretta Staudt, Sue Stoyanoff, Mark Tuvim, the UCLA Intervention Program staff and parents, Lynn Willmott, and Tracy Zemansky.

Although we had so much valuable help, the opinions in this book are solely our own. We realize that there are many more categories of disabilities than we could reasonably describe. We decided to, as much as possible, provide the reader with a representative, balanced summary of some of the more common or better-known disability differences. The decision to include or exclude any particular disability does not imply any judgment about the importance or impact of any disability.

Nancy B. Miller

Catherine C. Sammons

To my daughter, Kathy

NBM

To my parents, Cecile and Raemond Sammons,
and to Trey, Caitlin, and Chase, with love

CCS

Everybody's Different

1

Differences
in Everyday Life

Everybody's different. Some of us have differences that no one notices, while others are different in very apparent ways. We all look different from each other, sometimes by chance, sometimes by choice. Some people move on foot, while others use wheelchairs or other ways of getting around. We communicate in a variety of languages and dialects and also by using hand signs. Our behavior patterns have incredible variety, even within our own families. We all have unique physical strengths and limitations as well as different learning abilities, creative talents, and social skills.

Everybody reacts to differences. In the whole universe of differences, some attract us, some surprise or frighten us, and some aren't important to us at all. Our reactions to differences are sometimes complex and confusing. We often want to be open-minded and feel comfortable about other people's differences but find that some unfamiliar differences make us feel tense and judgmental instead. We are caught off guard when someone with an unexpected difference enters the room, and we may feel awkward as we try to appear unsurprised. When we see an unsettling difference, it can cause anxiety, uncertainty, and even a wish to avoid the other person.

Everybody evaluates differences. We admire some people for their differences and like to emphasize our own individuality at times. At other times, we work hard to avoid being different. We often see our own differences as "right" or "normal" and define differences in others as "wrong" or "deviant." At best, the phrase *everybody's different* implies a celebration of diversity. Sometimes, though, it seems we like the *idea* of diversity better than some of its realities!

In the 1990s, research in the neurosciences has revolutionized our understanding of how and why people react to differences. We now know that our first reactions are automatic reflexes, built into our brains. In fact, we *cannot avoid* reacting to differences. What we do after our first reaction, however, is based on our learning and choices. This chapter is about how and why differences are so important in our daily lives and why humans and animals need to have built-in mechanisms for detecting and evaluating differences. Our brains have evolved to do two things: to make predictions about what's coming next and to make a judgment about whether our experience matches or does not match what we expected. The story of how we experience and make judgments about mismatches from our expectations is the story of differences in everyday life.

HOW WE REACT TO DIFFERENCES

Defining Differences

There are many ways to define, describe, and discuss differences. This book focuses on three aspects of disability differences that are the most intense and least understood: the unfamiliar, unexpected, and unsettling.

Unfamiliar Differences

Unfamiliar differences are those that are new to *you*. You may find them attractive, interesting, frightening, or disgusting, or you may not be sure how to think or what to feel about them. Listening to people speak a language you don't recognize, attending a Native American powwow, going to a Chinese New Year celebration, or watching an opera all may be times when you react to unfamiliar sights and sounds.

Unexpected Differences

Unexpected differences are those that are familiar to you but are in a different setting or context. Some differences may surprise you because they reflect new social roles, such as the first time you worked with a male secretary or heard a female football announcer on television. Or, you may perceive an unexpected difference when a person's appearance or behavior doesn't fit your traditional expectation of his role, such as an opera singer who is blind, a slalom skier with one leg, or a television news reporter who uses a wheelchair.

Unsettling Differences

Unsettling differences are those that are disturbing to you. You may feel anxious, frightened, or even repulsed. You may see someone with an appearance difference that looks painful and imagine yourself in that situation, or you may connect a person's behavior difference to a long-ago frightening experience. Atypical body shapes or unpredictable movements are usually unsettling at first glance because of an automatic "survival" mechanism in your brain that reacts (and often overreacts) to differences.

Mixed Reactions

Differences may fit into one, two, or even all three of these categories. For instance, suppose you sit next to a woman using a portable oxygen tank at a meeting, and this is *unfamiliar* to you. Or, imagine that you see a man who is blind dining at a table next to you in a restaurant, and this is *unexpected*. Both of these situations may also make you feel *unsettled* because you are unsure whether the person is okay or whether you should be ready to react or help. You may want to stare with interest and curiosity but also think it would be rude. You may wonder how to interact without being seen as overly friendly and inappropriate.

Differences can be unsettling even when they are familiar; for example, you may feel unsettled every day as you drive by a person begging on the same street corner. Differences can be unsettling even when you're expecting them; for example, you may feel queasy when you visit an emergency room and see someone bleeding. In addition, both unfamiliar and unexpected differences can be unsettling. Atypical body shape, movements, behavior, or hard-to-interpret communication may unsettle us because these differences often set off automatic, primitive signals in our brain related to basic security and safety needs.

Awareness Activity

Defining Differences

1. Find a place to watch people, such as a sports event, a busy shopping mall, train station, bus, or fast-food restaurant. You may not be conscious of some of the differences that attract your attention, but you may have some of these reflexive initial reactions:
   - You gaze for a long time at an extremely attractive person.
   - You are surprised when you see a very tall woman.
   - You avert your eyes from a child with a facial scar.
   - You smile at someone who moves in an exceptionally fluid and graceful way.
   - You feel awkward when making eye contact with a woman in a wheelchair.
   - You stare at two people communicating in sign language.

- You are curious about two people speaking in an unfamiliar language.
- You feel frightened when a man begins shouting loudly at no one in particular.

Whenever you become aware that something about a person strikes you as "different," ask yourself the following four questions: *What* is the difference? *Why* did it draw my attention? *How* did I react? *Why* did I react the way I did?

As you practice your difference detection skills, you will become increasingly aware of the endless number and range of differences among people—and your wide range of reactions and evaluations of those differences.

Your Personal Comfort Zone

Everybody defines and reacts to differences differently. Beginning in early childhood, you developed your own comfort zone for others' differences. You became accustomed to differences that you saw frequently; ones that you saw less frequently surprised you. You learned how to *react* from your parents, siblings, teachers, religious leaders, peers, heroes, and the media. Today, your comfort zone continues to change and grow as you learn about and encounter new differences. You are continually revising your lists of what you consider different, expanding your comfort range about some differences and becoming less comfortable with others. Daily exposure to people, television, print media, advertising, and movies influences your perceptions about differences, as do your *own* experiences of being or feeling different from others in how you look, move, communicate, behave, or learn.

Most people look, move, communicate, behave, and learn in general patterns that we call "typical" or "average." In fact, we actually look for and expect familiarity in other people.

Our basic expectations (or *expected average*) of what is typical include the following:

- People will look generally symmetrical, have no missing body parts, and fall within a certain range for body size.
- People will move in coordinated ways, walk independently, and use their hands and bodies for specific tasks, such as eating and writing.
- People will communicate in ways that allow others to understand them, such as speaking clearly, writing in sentences, and using gestures, and they understand what others communicate to them.
- People will behave appropriately in social situations by blending in to crowds, standing in lines, taking turns, keeping certain social distances, and so forth.
- People will demonstrate their ability to learn by reading, following directions, using money, telling time, and working at a job.

Comparing Differences

Differences between people...are statements of relationships. . . . A difference cannot be understood except as a contrast between instances or between a norm and an example.[1]

—Martha Minow

When you detect a difference that is unfamiliar, unexpected, or unsettling, you try to make sense of it. Your immediate reaction tells you if this difference is within your comfort zone. If it isn't, then you compare the person's difference with an expected average, with yourself, with someone else, with a different time, or with your concept of an ideal.

- **Comparing with an expected average:** How is this similar to or different from what I am used to seeing or what I expect to see?

- **Comparing with yourself:** How is this similar to or different from me?
- **Comparing with someone else:** How is this similar to or different from other people I have known or know about?
- **Comparing with a different time:** How is this similar to or different from other times I have seen this person?
- **Comparing with an ideal:** How is this different from what I think of as "perfect"?

You Notice Some Differences More than Others

Everybody notices certain differences more than others. Perhaps you are related to several people who have very short stature. This is something well within your personal comfort zone, so you might pay little attention when you see someone with short stature in your office building. Or, your special affinity for people with short stature may lead you to notice them quickly.

A basketball scout knows a lot of people who are very tall. Instead of not paying much attention to strangers who are extremely tall, however, the scout readily spots young adults who are tall because he is always on the alert for prospective recruits.

If you rarely see people who are taller or shorter than your expected average, then you would undoubtedly react to someone of either extreme, short or tall. You notice some differences more than others because of two processes: habituation and sensitization.

Habituation: Getting Used to Differences

Some differences become so familiar that they become part of your personal comfort zone, your expected average. This is known as *habituation*. As time passes, the differences don't change, but you notice them less and less and evaluate them differently.

For example, suppose you live in southern California. An aunt visits from out of state, and you go for a walk on the beach. You see people with pierced navels and noses, mohawks, dreadlocks, and tattoos. At the beach, people surf, rollerblade, bicycle, and "hang out." You may barely notice these people because you have habituated to their differences, which have become part of your expected average for the beach. Your aunt, however, expresses surprise, humor, shock, and discomfort at the unexpected, unfamiliar, and maybe even unsettling display of deliberate human differences.

Here's another example: Your co-worker has a speech impairment resulting from a stroke. Both of you have had to make some accommodations related to her disability: You need to make sure to listen carefully to her slower speech, and your co-worker asks you to tell the server her order when you go to lunch together. Initially these were new and awkward behaviors for you, but you have habituated to them and now do them automatically. When a new client meets your co-worker, however, the speech difference may "leap" into your awareness again as you recognize the client's discomfort.

Sometimes a whole community habituates to a difference. For example, in the 1600s, a group of English immigrants settled on Martha's Vineyard, an island off the coast of Massachusetts. For the next two and a half centuries, the island had a strikingly high incidence of hereditary deafness, and both hearing and deaf people used sign language.

None of my informants remembered any formal teaching of sign language. It was...just a sort of instinct. You couldn't help learning it....Hearing children with no deaf immediate family members learned sign language by accompanying their parents on daily chores to the neighbors or the store, where they saw signs used regularly. They needed to learn the language to communicate with deaf adults as well as deaf playmates. . . . It was assumed that everyone in town was conversant with it.[2]

—Nora Groce

Sensitization: Tuning In to Differences

When you want or need to notice differences in greater detail than you do now, you must train yourself to see differences. To learn more, you sensitize yourself to specific details. *Sensitization* is the opposite of habituation. Every time you learn about a new topic, such as gardening, changing the oil in your car, or painting, you begin to see details that you have not seen before.

For instance, imagine that you are the new supervisor of a department with 20 employees. You need to learn their names and remember them. You scan the room and study each person's characteristics, such as gender, age, race, hair color, facial features, body size and shape, and voice. You are sensitizing yourself to differences that will help you remember each person.

You become sensitized to some kinds of differences in the course of daily living, depending on your current interests or needs. Have you ever noticed that after you buy a car, you see so many of that model on the road each day? An attorney selecting members of a jury panel becomes sensitized to how a prospective juror's interview behaviors might suggest how the juror will judge the client. A baseball coach observing a high school team can spot highly specific skills and subtle areas of weakness in the players. A mother whose child has asthma can detect several different kinds of coughs.

WHY WE REACT TO
DIFFERENCES: IT'S ALL IN THE BRAIN

Scanning and Orienting

You probably go through each day with a casual, disinterested awareness of similarities and differences you see in others. Most of them fit a typical pattern, and you may not even notice anything out of the ordinary. Their appearance, movement, communication, behavior, and learning generally match what you expect to see. Your brain, however, is taking nothing for granted. It continually scans the environment on constant alert for any deviation from your expected average range of familiarity. Your brain *always* orients to a difference that is as unfamiliar, unexpected, or unsettling. *Orienting* is giving something your full and undivided attention; it is different than casting a casual glance. Orienting happens faster than you can be aware of whenever there is a mismatch between what you expect to see and what you actually see.

A Brief History of the Human Brain

The human brain is equipped with a *difference detector*. Our modern-day capacities for detecting extremely subtle differences evolved through our hunter-gatherer ancestors, whose survival depended on knowing which people could be approached safely and which plants and animals would enhance or endanger their lives. Even today, we often leap to premature conclusions about potential threats after receiving very minimal and sometimes misleading cues.

The early human brain ensured survival by alerting our ancestors to avoid threatening differences. About 100,000 years ago, human brain structures and functions were nearly what they are today. The primitive functions remained intact, but by this time humans had gained some control over the primitive brain and could make better decisions as to how to handle its quick, initial reactions about what to approach or avoid.

Until about 40,000 years ago, our ancestors lived in groups of 50–500 people and rarely ever ventured farther than about 40 miles from home. The average village member saw fewer people in his lifetime than most of us see in a single day![3] The brain's evolved self-regulation ability made it possible for humans to expand their ways of thinking and communicating, extend the size and diversity of their social groups, and explore new territories.

We tend to see our distant past through a reverse telescope that compresses it: a short time as hunter-gatherers, a long time as "civilized" people. But civilization is a recent stage of human life, and for all we know, it may not be any great achievement. It may not even be the final stage. We have been alive on this planet as recognizable humans for about two million years, and for all but the last two or three thousand we've been hunter-gatherers. We may sing in choirs and park our rages behind a desk, but we patrol the world with many of a hunter-gatherer's drives, motives, and skills.[4]

—Diane Ackerman

We still have a basic survival need to be alerted to life-threatening events, and our primitive brain continues to be on the alert for us as a watchdog for possibly dangerous differences. Our primitive brain is our emotional brain, which reacts reflexively and protectively. Our modern brain is our reasoning brain, which can sometimes override the primitive brain's snap judgments with its power to learn, recall memories, consider options, and make decisions.

Some people may be unsettled at the thought of having such an active primitive brain, but it does help explain why we react to some disability differences in ways that we may not like. Our primitive brain's sometimes unwanted reactions may be hard to accept today because so many of us are striving to bring about personal, social, and political changes. We must honestly examine our internal, biological reactions, however, if we want to reshape our external actions and attitudes.

For better or for worse, our appraisal of every personal encounter and our responses to it are shaped not just by our rational judgments or our personal history, but also by our distant ancestral past.[5]

—Daniel Goleman

How Your Difference Detector Works Today

When you sense something (through sight, hearing, smell, taste, or touch) that doesn't match what you expect, that sensation first goes to your *thalamus*, a central receiving station in your brain. The thalamus then sends that sensory information to the fast-acting, primitive part of your brain known as the *limbic system*, for an emotional "fight-or-flight" appraisal. The information then is processed in the modern, reasoning part of your brain known as the *cerebral cortex*.

Your Primitive Brain

After receiving information about a perception from the thalamus, the limbic system determines the danger value and then reacts accordingly *before conscious choices are even possible.* Inside your limbic system there are a number of powerful structures, including the *amygdala* and the *hippocampus,* which make possible an instantaneous, automatic survival check of any sensory mismatch received from the thalamus.

The brain makes emotional, stop-or-go appraisals by virtue of its limbic system. Therefore, any time the survival check determines that a mismatch is possibly dangerous, the limbic system signals the action (motor) part of your cerebral cortex to freeze or escape from the person or situation. You didn't have to learn how to jerk away from danger: No one taught you, and you couldn't stop reacting that way if you tried. (The next time you are at the zoo, put your face close to the glass of the snake exhibit. No matter how "safe" your reason says you are, it would be virtually impossible to avoid jumping back if the snake were to strike at you.)

So, reacting to threatening or unsettling mismatches is innate and reflexive. Even when a specific difference, person, or event is not truly life threatening, at the instant of detection your brain doesn't yet realize that! You can and do override your limbic system's reactions. Understanding how this detection process works is the first step toward changing your uncomfortable reactions to differences in other people.

Awareness Activity

Your Senses and Your Primitive Brain

Here are some events that almost always trigger intense re-actions by your primitive brain. Try to imagine each event happening. What kinds of reactions do you have?

Sight

- A stranger approaches you on a dark street.
- Police lights blink in your rearview mirror.
- A small child dashes in front of your car.

Hearing

- An ambulance siren approaches.
- Your dog growls at the door when you are home alone at night.
- A child suddenly screams in the next apartment.
- You become aware of heavy footsteps behind you in an empty hallway.
- You are in a crowded elevator, and someone blurts out strange sounds.

Smell

- You smell a rotten odor when you open the refrigerator.
- You're in bed, and you smell smoke nearby.
- While flying on an airplane, you notice a strong gasoline odor.

Taste

- You've just taken a bite of very bad fish.
- You nearly choke on your food and regurgitate what you ate.
- You chew instead of swallow a very bitter pill.

Touch

- Your bare foot brushes against something slimy.
- You pick up a cup that you didn't know was hot.
- A stranger suddenly leans against you on a bus.

Your Modern, Reasoning Brain

Now that you know how difference detection occurs, you can understand that initial reactions to differences are instinctive and therefore "normal" in a purely biological sense. Our modern, reasoning brain, however, uses reasoning, planning, and evaluation to override these primitive limbic impulses.

If your initial survival check results in either a "wait-and-see" or "everything's safe" response, your cerebral cortex goes into action. It helps you to *compare* this difference with previous experiences and information, *evaluate* what is happening right now, and *decide* how to react. Within a few seconds your cerebral cortex allows you to preview your options and actually revise your initial reflexive reactions and feelings. You *can* learn ways to interrupt the automatic leap from detection to action, and you *can* choose how you would like to react to differences.

For example, imagine that you are about to enter a store and you see a person in a wheelchair coming out. Before you know it, you freeze for a fraction of a second. This encounter does not threaten your survival, so why should you react this way?

Here's why: Your primitive brain, or limbic system, gets your muscles and legs going before you have any awareness of what's happening. After about a half second, your cerebral cortex evaluates the reality and the seriousness of the situation. Your cortex can become dominant and override your reflex to retreat. In essence, your cortex decides, "This situation is different, but it's no problem," "Don't stare," "Be helpful," "Be patient," or "One day this could be you." The person in the wheelchair exits the store, and you enter without running away.

But there's more—your brain scorecard has just marked up one more example of "okay" outcomes about wheelchairs, and the next encounter you have with a person in a wheelchair will be more about a familiar event and less about an unfamiliar difference. Your personal comfort zone has expanded.

Now, imagine a second scenario. You work in a place where lots of people use wheelchairs. Because of this, wheelchair use is a difference that has become part of your expected average of ways people move. In other words, when you meet a person who uses a wheelchair, there is no mismatch between what you expect to see and what you do see.

Your Primitive and Modern Brains Work Together

Because your primitive and modern brains work together, deeply ingrained patterns continue to influence your behavior. Sometimes you react to differences in positive ways, and sometimes you react in confusing and inconsistent ways. Many of us have some stereotypes about people with disability differences that can be misleading and stigmatizing. Because of our stereotypes, we tend to react to people with disabilities in uncomfortable or negative ways. In order to understand and change these reactions, we *must* be able to rapidly evaluate the meaning and importance of any difference by using all sources of information available to us. In spite of our best intentions, we have

* A *biological* tendency to misperceive many differences as negative or threatening at first
* A *cultural* tendency to interpret differences negatively because of stereotypes we have learned and adopted from our families, peers, and the media
* A *psychological* tendency to be influenced by negative emotional memories, which cause us to react with fear or discomfort

Our attentional system constantly separates foreground from background and focuses on the foreground. If we don't consciously control the decision about what's important, the system will revert to survival needs—and we'll end up trampling beautiful flowers at our feet in a mad dash toward survival.[6]

—Robert Sylwester

Once our reasoning brain tells us that a difference does not put us in danger, the difference shifts to the background and *other* aspects of the person and the situation take the foreground. By understanding the tendencies of our primitive brain, we can consciously question, evaluate, and override our initial reactions. We can then use our knowledge, experiences, and best intentions to decide how we want to act. Reactions based on choices are usually better than reactions based only on instinct. The more we learn about how we detect and react to differences, the more successful our interactions will be.

Key Points

Detecting Differences

- You have your own personal comfort zone for differences in other people.
- Your brain constantly scans the environment for important deviations and mismatches from your expected average.
- You orient to differences instantly, often before you "catch yourself."
- During its survival check, your difference detector sometimes overreacts and equates differences with potential danger.
- Your modern, reasoning brain can override your initial, instinctive reaction to differences that are unfamiliar, unexpected, or unsettling.

- Your evaluation of differences involves a comparison of what you see with your expected average, with yourself, with someone else, with another time, or with an ideal.

Awareness Activities

Differences You See Every Day

The following activities are suggested ways of increasing your awareness of the many kinds of human differences that you may (or may not) notice in your daily life. Whenever you are aware that something is different about a person or situation, ask yourself the following questions:

- What is different about this?
- What is it about the difference that drew my attention?
- Was the difference unfamiliar, unexpected, and/or unsettling?
- What kinds of comparisons did I make?
- How did I evaluate the difference or the person with the difference?
- What did I learn from this experience?

Many of these activities are enhanced when you do them with a relative, a friend, or a colleague and then compare and contrast your observations and reactions.

People Who Look Different

Differences in appearance are the most obvious kind. The shape and size of another person are the first pieces of information we take in. Some people appear healthy; others ill. Some look happy; others appear depressed or angry. People have different body shapes and sizes, and some have missing body parts.

1. Find a place where you can observe a diverse group of people passing by, such as a shopping mall, an airport, a

train station, or a public library. What appearance differences draw your attention? Which are unfamiliar? Which are unexpected? Do any appearance differences make you feel unsettled? What kinds of comparisons about appearance differences do you find yourself making? Does anything about *your* appearance seem to draw attention from anyone?

2. Another time, settle in a place where you can observe a lot of people who look quite *similar* in many ways, such as a high school or college campus or the lobby of a corporate office building. Which differences stand out to you? Does it take longer to spot differences in this setting than it did in the first one?

People Who Move Differently

People move in many different ways, and nearly everything we do involves movement! More than 600 muscles in the body influence our movements. Consider all of the possible variations in human movement. Some people walk unsupported, while others have restricted mobility or unpredictable movements. Some people use assistance dogs, braces, canes, crutches, walkers, or wheelchairs to support or enhance their movement. Some people never stop moving—they gesture, twiddle their fingers, tap their feet, or have hand tremors. Some people sit without making any noticeable movement for a very long time.

1. In the same public place or another one, get comfortable and focus on how people move. Which movement differences draw your attention? Which ones are unfamiliar? Which are unexpected? Are any movement differences unsettling? What other reactions do you have to movement differences? What kinds of comparisons do you make about movement patterns? Does anything about the way *you* move draw attention from anyone? What do you learn about your own movement patterns by comparing yourself with others?

2. During a meal, during your morning routine, or as you carry out any other daily activity, pay attention to how your body moves. You'll probably notice that your body moves in ways that you've never thought about.

   First, focus on your breathing while you move. How fast are you breathing? Which body parts move as you breathe? Next, pay attention to your torso. Is it curved or straight? If you are sitting down, are you leaning to one side more than the other? Do you tend to sit still, or do you fidget? Do you have any mannerisms that other people might notice if they were observing you?

People Who Communicate Differently

Every day we interact with people who speak at different rates, use different vocabularies, and use different ways to emphasize their message. Our society has incredibly diverse methods of communication! Depending on where you live, people who speak languages other than English may cross your path frequently. We usually focus on the words a person is saying or writing and don't pay a lot of attention to communication style or other details unless these aspects interfere with our communication.

Some people are difficult to understand because they stutter, slur their speech, or have regional accents. Some people with tics may utter unusual sounds or inappropriate words. Some people communicate by lipreading or signing, voice synthesizers, communication boards, or other alternate methods. Everybody talks at different volumes and speeds. Some people are hard to hear when they talk; other people talk very loud.

1. Find a place to observe people who are talking or interacting a lot, such as a theater during intermission or a crowded delicatessen. Notice people's different styles of communication. What draws your attention about the ways people are communicating? Which communication differences are unfamiliar? Which are unexpected? Are any of them unsettling? What other reactions do you have to the com-

munication differences you observe? What kinds of comparisons do you find yourself making to the communication styles you observe? Did *you* communicate with anyone in a way that seemed to be unfamiliar, unexpected, or unsettling to them? What did you learn about your own communication patterns as you observed others?

2. Tune in to the news on television. Listen to the sports or weather announcer. Try to talk as quickly as he does.

People Who Behave Differently

It's often hard to articulate specific social rules for behavior, but we know immediately when one is broken! Many differences in public behavior are unsettling because they make us unsure about what's going on and/or uncertain of whether someone might lose control.

Some people behave in an orderly way, as if trying not to draw attention to themselves. Some people act unexpectedly or are inappropriately friendly. Some people stand very close to others; other people maintain too much distance. Some people make direct eye contact; others avoid it. Some people may appear unusually afraid of a certain object, person, or situation.

1. Watching the behavior of strangers is one way to sharpen your observation skills; another is to observe people you know, such as when you are at work in a staff meeting, a training session, or an informal situation, such as a coffee break.

   What kinds of behavior differences draw your attention? Which differences are unfamiliar? Which are unexpected? Are any unsettling? What other reactions do you have to various behavior differences? Did *your* behavior draw attention from anyone? What did you learn about your own behavior patterns from observing others?

2. Watch a television talk show on which people talk about their private problems and interpersonal conflicts. Which behaviors violate your personal comfort zone? How are the behaviors different from your expected average?

People Who Learn Differently

Every day you interact with or observe people who you may think are highly intelligent, not very smart, or somewhere in between. We tend to equate intelligence with education, even though it's often an error to do so. There are many kinds of intelligences and many kinds of education and training. Everybody has different skills and limitations.

Some people don't know how to balance a checkbook, some don't know how to change a tire, and some don't know how to cook a meal. Some people can't work unless they're supervised; others can only work alone. Some people are good at making creative decisions; others are good at carrying them out. Some people can't live alone; others can't live with anyone. Some people can read signs or figure out maps quickly; others need more time. All of us can make a list of things that we never learned to do because we thought they would be too hard.

For this activity, think about and observe your relatives and friends in their homes. Do they have difficulty mastering certain daily living activities? Is one person always behind on bill paying? Does that person never have a balanced checkbook? Does another person have trouble planning social events? Do you know someone who is stumped by his child's reading or math homework? Have you watched someone struggle to understand complex oral information or written instructions for assembling toys or furniture? Does anyone you know have a problem with keeping directions straight when driving or with learning the rules of a card game?

What learning differences draw your attention? Which differences are unfamiliar or unexpected? Are any unsettling? What kinds of comparisons do you find yourself making as you observe others? Were you reminded of *your* learning differences during this activity? What did you discover about your own learning styles and patterns?

PUTTING IT ALL TOGETHER

The disabled individual falls outside the ken of normal expectations, and the able-bodied are left not knowing what to say to him or her. . . . So pronounced and widespread is the aversion of eyes and setting of physical distance that I have never met a disabled person who has not commented on it.[7]

—Robert F. Murphy

Disability differences frequently confuse or frighten us. Most of us never admit these feelings out loud, but we wonder whether others also feel embarrassed or uncomfortable. It may seem that our primitive brains are working against us even as we try to interact comfortably. We can learn to get past this primitive protective act, however, by understanding how our brains function, by learning more about disability differences, and by seeking more contact with people who have disabilities. In Chapter 2 we take a closer look at disability differences today.

READINGS
AND RESOURCES

Books

The Stone Age Present: How Evolution Has Shaped Modern Life
W. Allman (Simon & Schuster, New York, 1994)

Descartes' Error: Emotion, Reason, and the Human Brain
A. Damasio (Putnam Berkley, New York, 1994)

*Your Child's Growing Mind: A Practical Guide to Brain
Development and Learning from Birth to Adolescence*
J. Healy (Bantam Doubleday Dell, New York, 1994)

*Making All the Difference:
Inclusion, Exclusion, and American Law*
M. Minow (Cornell University Press, Ithaca, NY, 1990)

The Right Mind: Making Sense of the Hemispheres
R. Ornstein (Harcourt Brace & Co., New York, 1997)

An Anthropologist on Mars: Seven Paradoxical Tales
O. Sacks (Alfred A. Knopf, New York, 1996)

*A Celebration of Neurons:
An Educator's Guide to the Human Brain*
R. Sylwester (Association for Supervision and Curriculum
Development, Alexandria, VA, 1995)

2

About Disability Differences

Everybody reacts to different disabilities in different ways. You may feel comfortable around some kinds of disabilities and unsettled around others. You may feel more at ease talking to someone who is blind than to someone who has mental retardation. You may be less surprised to see an older adult using a wheelchair than a child. You may want to "look past" or ignore a person's disability but find yourself distracted by his impairment. You may want to focus on a business transaction but feel self-conscious or worried about saying or doing the "wrong thing" and concerned that your discomfort will be perceived as insensitivity or rejection.

Because you initially orient to the unfamiliar, unexpected, and/or unsettling aspects of a disability, you may assume that discomfort is your "true" feeling and that insensitivity caused your reaction. Remembering that your *initial* reaction is not your *rational* reaction can help you move into more comfortable interactions.

This chapter helps you understand the assumptions you make about people with disabilities and show you some ways to expand your personal comfort zone for their differences. We all need more accurate information and more frequent exposure to the variety and degrees of differences we all have. We can then have more genuine exchanges of empathy for the impairments, inconveniences, frustrations, and challenges we all share in varying degrees at different times.

DEFINING DISABILITY

The words we use today to describe disabilities and people who have disabilities are different from the words that we heard and used as we grew up. One dramatic change has been the development of *person-first language*, which emphasizes the person rather than his disability. Instead of saying, "a handicapped person," "a retarded man," or "an autistic child," it is both more respectful and more accurate to say "a person with a disability," "a man with mental retardation," or "a child with autism." A disability is just one aspect of a person.[1] The following sections review some of the words, labels, and terms used to describe disabilities.

Impairment

An *impairment* is a missing, damaged, deficient, or weakened body part or function. A person who is deaf or has hearing loss has a hearing impairment. A person who is blind or wears glasses has a visual impairment. Someone who has chronic pain and stiffness from arthritis has impaired movement.

Disability

A *disability* is the inability to perform one or more major life activities because of an impairment.[2] *Major life activities* include the following:

- Caring for oneself in hygiene and homemaking

- Having full range of movement while standing, lifting, walking, and so forth
- Having intact senses (vision, hearing, touch, smell, taste, balance)
- Communicating with others (speaking, writing)
- Learning and working
- Using mental processes such as thinking, concentrating, and problem solving
- Interacting with others and developing and maintaining relationships

Disabilities are usually thought of in terms of a specific medical diagnosis such as spinal cord injury, cerebral palsy, or Down syndrome. That information is often important, but when you come into contact with someone with a disability, your attention is drawn toward a difference in how she looks, moves, communicates, or behaves. She may have a facial difference or an uneven gait, and you may wonder, "What's *wrong* with her?" Such information can be useful if it is relevant to your interaction, but in most social interactions, a specific label for the disability is often not important. It's more useful to ask yourself, "What's *different* about this person?"

Handicap

A *handicap* is any obstacle that lessens a person's chance of success. It is anything that makes a person's progress difficult or prevents him from doing something. Examples of handicaps include the following:

- *Social obstacles,* such as other people's negative attitudes and behaviors
- *Personal obstacles,* such as lack of information about one's own disability and resources
- *Physical obstacles,* such as inaccessible buildings, parks, or transportation
- *Resource obstacles,* such as insufficient money, insurance, personal care assistants, employment, training, housing, or recreation

These handicapping obstacles can shape a person's quality of life as much as or more than the limitations of a specific medical, physical, or learning disability.

Imagine, for example, that you have arthritis (an impairment) and cannot climb stairs (a disability). You want to go to a concert, but the theater has no elevator or ramp. You have a handicap because of the architectural inaccessibility of the theater. Similarly, a person who is deaf has a handicap while watching television without closed captioning; a person who is blind has a handicap in an elevator without braille signs; and a person who uses a wheelchair has a handicap when shopping in a store that does not have accessible parking, entrances, restrooms, and aisles.

We have been viewed too much in terms of our diagnoses and too little in terms of our personhood. . . . Most of our problems are caused not by our bodies but by a society that refuses to accommodate our differences.[3]

—Carol Gill

Resources and Accommodations

Resources include medical, educational, social, and other interventions and supports for people who have special needs because of their disabilities. These can include the following:

- Medical interventions for health conditions
- Individualized education programs (IEPs) in school environments
- Caregiving and personal assistance with daily living needs (e.g., dressing, shopping, driving)
- Job training and supported employment
- Therapies for improving physical strength and coordination, persistent emotional or behavior problems, and/or speech impairments
- Access to social and community programs, such as scout troops, sports programs, religious groups, and museums

- Assistive equipment to increase mobility, such as canes, crutches, scooters, walkers, wheelchairs, and cars with chair lifts, ramps, or adapted controls
- Financial supports, such as Medicaid and Social Security Disability Income

Accommodations are changes that people make in their interactions or physical environment to increase participation and equality. These can include

- Flexible work schedules for a spouse or a partner to fulfill caregiving duties
- Changes in lifestyle patterns to increase comfort or reduce fatigue
- Materials and aids to enhance daily functioning, such as adapted clothing, eating utensils, large-print books
- Adapted architecture, such as wider doorways, handrails, ramps, lowered countertops, stairway lifts, adapted public bathrooms, and accessible parking
- Communication devices, such as adapted telephones, communication boards, computers, and braille readers and writers
- Interactions that support community participation, such as bus drivers who announce stops, docents who are specially trained to assist museum visitors, and hotel employees who offer assistance
- Accommodations and equipment in airports, taxicabs, buses, trains, hotels, and tourist attractions, such as wheelchairs, lowered water fountains, lifts, and ramps

THE DIVERSITY OF DISABILITY

Disability is the one minority that anyone can join at any time, as a result of a sudden automobile accident, a fall down a flight of stairs, cancer, or disease.[4]

—Joseph P. Shapiro

Today there are more people of all ages with disabilities and more kinds of disabilities than at any other time in history. A greater variety of disabling conditions have been identified, including those caused by chemical toxins, HIV/AIDS, and work-related repetitive stress injuries. We also now know that many behaviors formerly branded "eccentric" or "just emotional" are caused by physical impairments. More people with disabilities and chronic illnesses are living longer because of advances in technology and medicine. As life expectancy increases, so does the risk of developing disabling conditions. More premature babies are surviving despite serious impairments. In the United States,

- A disability can be acquired at any time: in infancy, childhood, adolescence, or young, middle, or late adulthood. Fewer than 15% of disabilities are present from birth; the other 85% are acquired.[5] In 1995, more than 20% of the population had some level of disability. [6]
- In 1995, 8.8 million people had visual impairments and 10.1 million had hearing impairments.[7]
- More people are surviving disabling accidents, especially car, sports, and gunshot injuries. Each year 750,000 Americans become disabled, mainly through accidents.[8]
- Every 10 minutes, about 370 people acquire a disabling injury due to an accident.[9]
- Each year about 500,000 people experience strokes. Strokes are the leading cause of disabilities.[10]
- Arthritis is the leading cause of disability for people ages 65 and older; it currently affects 16 million people. After age 50, an estimated 80% of the population is affected by arthritis to some degree.[11]
- 12 million people experience asthma, the leading cause of absenteeism from school and work.[12]

Everybody's Life Is Eventually Touched by Disability

You may have had a physical or mental disability at some time in your life, or you may be close to someone who has. If you haven't yet, you probably will. Maybe your personal experience was a broken leg that kept you out of school for a month or a herniated disc that interrupted your ability to drive and play tennis for six months. Perhaps you have a permanent condition that affects some aspect of your appearance, movement, communication, behavior, or learning. Or, you may have a condition, such as diabetes or panic disorder, that is not immediately visible to others yet affects your daily activities. Perhaps someone close to you such as one of your parents or grandparents has arthritis, Alzheimer's disease, or Parkinson's disease. Your child may have difficulty walking because of cerebral palsy, your sibling may have a learning disability, your spouse may have limited mobility because of a stroke, or you may have a friend with a hearing impairment.

Disability Is Not an Us-or-Them, Now-or-Never, All-or-Nothing Condition

There are many permanent disabilities, motor, sensory, and mental impairments that require ongoing personal or technical assistance, such as hearing aids, wheelchairs, adapted computers, or personal care. But there has been a great increase in temporary disabilities that impose some limitations for a period of months or years and may improve through surgery, therapy, or medications.

We have traditionally thought of disability as a permanent status that, once acquired, stays with you forever. Our fear of having a disability is a terror of crossing a line that cannot be recrossed: from healthy to sick, strong to weak, "able" to "disabled."

Most of us think of "the disabled" or "the handicapped" as someone we don't know. Someone who's very different, maybe even "odd" in some way. When we know someone closely who happens to have some physical or mental problem, we most often say, "Oh, but he's not really disabled". . . . You can't be disabled and normal both, we figure.[13]

—M. Johnson

Disability is a continuum of differences. You may have a disability that limits most of your daily life activities, or you may have an impairment that makes a few activities harder to do. You may not be able to sit for long periods of time or read or drive without glasses, you may have to turn up the volume to hear the radio, or you may find that you can't digest spicy foods or dairy products. The shift from an inconvenience to a disability is often incremental, and even then it may fluctuate back and forth. You may be able to control pain with medication or ease stiffness with exercise. Sometimes people resist aid that can help them because the very act of accepting it feels like an admission of having a disability.

Some Disabilities Are Temporary or Episodic

Some people are temporarily disabled by injury, infection, or illness such as a back injury, pinkeye, or hives. *Temporary disabilities* may impose some limitations for a period of weeks or months, but they may be resolvable or may be greatly diminished through surgery, therapy, medication, and/or lifestyle changes.

Episodic and chronic disabilities include periods of usual activity interspersed with periods of disability. Symptoms of some disabilities can be predicted and minimized with preparation, such as symptoms of seasonal allergies, tinnitus, and some anxiety disorders, but others are unpredictable, such as symptoms of multiple sclerosis, fibromyalgia, migraine headaches, and lupus.

THE LIMITATIONS AND
CHALLENGES OF DISABILITIES

No one invites or welcomes the limited capacities that accompany a disability. No one chooses a diminished social status, with the discomfort and fear that are reflected in the reactions of other people. No one wants to struggle against an inaccessible environment that makes equal participation in the community difficult, if not impossible.

I have a significant disability. I don't minimize it. I've had to find unconventional methods to do my work and live my life. But that's the easy part. Human beings are imaginative and resourceful and can find ways to get things done. The harder part has been confronting institutionalized prejudice and discrimination.[14]

—Paul Longmore

Nonvisible Disabilities Create Other Daily Living Challenges

Our awareness of the diversity of disability expands as we consider the enormous number of people who have disabilities we can't see. Nonvisible disabilities often restrict a person's life choices, limit daily activities, and can require as much vigilance and care as any observable disability. Because there is no immediately noticeable evidence of impairment, a person with a nonvisible disability must often decide what to share about her disability because of uncertain reactions and consequences in social and work relationships. Some of the better known nonvisible disabilities include diabetes, heart disease, lupus, asthma, depression, chronic fatigue syndrome, and epilepsy.

People May Have a Disability in Some Situations But Not Others

A disability may affect an individual's ability to perform certain tasks in specific settings. For example, a man with a hearing impairment might not be able to understand the dialogue in a movie without subtitles. If he were watching a subtitled foreign film, however, he would be able to understand the dialogue as well as every other reading adult in the theater. A woman who does not read English would be handicapped during the same movie. Similarly, a man of very short stature might be handicapped in a typical grocery store but highly competent in his own modified kitchen.

Disabilities Matter More at Some Times than Others

A lawyer's job performance in her office and the courtroom need not be affected by the fact that she uses a wheelchair. When she is invited to a colleague's home for a dinner party, however, and discovers there are 12 steps up to the front door, she is handicapped. Social exclusion is still a common experience for many people who have disabilities. A high school student who is gifted in math and has a facial difference may be asked for homework help by a classmate but regularly excluded from social events. A corporate secretary with cerebral palsy may be included in coffee break conversations but never invited to social gatherings after work.

PERSPECTIVES ON DISABILITY

There are many different ways to think about disabilities. The following sections briefly describe four of these ways. The most familiar is the *medical perspective* because most physical impairments are defined and treated by medical professionals. Our personal attitudes are evaluated within a *societal perspective*. People who have disabilities have expressed their own perspectives about the meaning of disability through the *disability rights movement*. The *legal perspective* codifies and interprets standards for social and institutional behavior.

Medical Perspective on Disability

Disabilities result from impairments that occur before or during birth or result from injury or illness. Disabilities, therefore, are usually first identified by health care professionals. From a medical perspective, the emphasis is on describing a person's impairment, abilities, and limitations and the medical interventions that may help him improve his functioning. These might include surgeries, medications, prostheses, equipment, and various therapies. The medical perspective on disability focuses on:

- Listing symptoms
- Identifying what's broken (pathology)
- Naming the condition through interviews, examination, and testing (diagnosis)
- Searching for physical causes (etiology)
- Prescribing interventions, such as medications, surgeries, therapies (treatment)
- Making a prediction about change over time (prognosis)
- "Fixing" people (curing)
- Working to eradicate the condition (prevention)

Medical technology and research are heavily focused on preventing impairments, alleviating symptoms, and finding cures to arrest or reverse progressive conditions. Geneticists, pharmacists, neuroscientists, and physicians are steadily reporting breakthroughs in finding underlying causes and new treatments for a wide variety of disabling disorders.[15] In the past few years, the medical perspective has expanded its "comfort zone" to incorporate alternative, supplementary approaches such as meditation, acupuncture, herbal remedies, and hypnosis (among others) in the treatment of many disabilities.

Disabilities and Chronic Illness

Disabilities are associated with chronic illnesses. Some people consider themselves "sick" but do not think of themselves as having a disability, and many people who have disabilities are healthy and do not want to be thought of as "sick" or as patients. Many differences, such as short stature, missing limbs, facial differences, deafness, blindness, learning disabilities, and mental retardation, may be disabling but do not necessarily involve ongoing medical care. The paths of illness and disability often diverge following diagnosis or a specific intervention. So, even though you may see people using walkers or guide dogs, communicating with sign language, or having unusual mannerisms, it does not mean they are ill.

In our society most of us assume that people with disabilities need and want others' help and care. This assumption obscures the fact that we all—able-bodied and disabled alike—sometimes want and need such help. It encourages us to see, to think of, ill and disabled people as "receivers," and of the well as "givers."[16]

—J. Schneider

Sometimes an illness can cause a disability. Sometimes a disability can cause an illness. Sometimes the two coexist. Most chronic illnesses are disabling in one or more areas of a person's life. An acute illness such as meningitis or an injury from a car accident or severe burns can also result in long-term disabilities.

Disability is just one of many chronic disorders that is increasing. In 1995, approximately 99 million people had chronic conditions with persistent or recurring health consequences lasting for years. By the year 2030, nearly 150 million Americans are projected to have a chronic medical condition and about one-third of these will have limitations in their ability to live independently or work.[17]

—Pfizer Foundation

Societal Perspective on Disability

The experience of having a disability is feeling and being considered "different" in a very fundamental sense. All societies define the human qualities they value. They all have "expected averages" of appearance and ability. Society has three basic responses to an individual with a disability difference: to honor the person as an heroic or religious symbol, to accommodate her special needs within society, or to devalue and discard her. Unfortunately, history has given few examples of the middle ground. Ostracism has been the most common societal reaction.

Separating People with Disabilities

Throughout history, the separation of people with disabilities has been a common practice. Because disabilities were frequently thought to be linked with moral or spiritual failings, families typically felt a great deal of shame. Unexplained differences provoked fear, and society's tendency was to remove people from the mainstream of community life. At one extreme was the Nazi extermination plan, but the more pervasive policy was to segregate people with disabilities in facilities located away from the public eye. At the same time, the rationale developed that this solution was good for people who were outside society's comfort zone, that people with disabilities were "happier" around people of "their own kind," that they were protected from failure in the "normal" world, and that they were usually unable to be trained or educated and simply needed physical protection.

In spite of major changes in policies and programs, institutional separation still occurs, such as in schools and work or recreation programs. In more subtle ways, we continue to exclude people with disabilities: by avoiding conversations or social contacts because interactions are uncomfortable or inconvenient or by not wanting our child to play with a classmate whose appearance is unsettling. Many of us aren't even aware that we think or do these things, but some of us are becoming *aware* of our behavior and want to interact more often and more comfortably but are still *unsure* about how to do so without making "mistakes."

Awareness Activity

Your Reactions to People with Disabilities

When we consider that disability stigma has existed for so long, it is easy to understand why many of us are still confused and uncomfortable during this time of increasing interactions and evolving attitudes.

Below are quotes from people with various disabilities who have written about their experiences with other people. Think about whether any of these statements describe you. Some key words are emphasized in boldface for you to think about.

After you do this activity yourself, consider going through it again with some friends, family members, fellow students, or co-workers. Our reactions to people with disabilities is not a topic that comes up very often in everyday conversations— none of us likes to face our own uncomfortable and embar- rassing feelings. Knowing that our reactions are based on our life histories and realizing what needs changing, these exam- ples can serve as self-awareness starting points. When you share your thoughts and reactions, you learn that you're not alone in your questions and uncertainties.

- *People ask inappropriate questions when they encounter an unfamiliar difference:*
  Nondisabled people feel that our differentness gives them the right to **invade our privacy** and **make judgments** about our lives. Our physical characteristics evoke such strong feelings that people often have to express them in some way. . . . Many of us have experienced someone coming up and **asking us intimate things** about our lives. Our physi- cal differences makes our bodies public property. . . . It's **pity** that motivates that kind of reaction, **not empathy.**[18]
  —Jenny Morris

- *People make assumptions when they encounter disabilities in unexpected situations:*
  Upon meeting us, people would ask [my wife] how many years we had been married before my accident. This was something I would never get asked; she always did. **No one ever assumed that she might have chosen to be with me re- gardless of the wheelchair.** No one considered the possibil- ity that she did not think my accident was a tragedy.[19]
  —John Hockenberry

- *People may feel unsettled by some disabilities:*
  Disability makes people **uncomfortable** in a specific way. **It evokes primitive fears.** Many people do not like thinking

about disability because of an unspoken, perhaps unspeak-
able, fear that, if they do, they may themselves become
disabled or will have to confront the weaker parts of themselves. . . . **vulnerability, oppression, identity, unmet need,
dependency confusion, childhood hurts, and shame.**[20]
 — Mary Ann Blotzer and Richard Ruth

- *People sometimes give effusive praise—with underlying
judgments:*
Most nondisabled people . . . have gotten the message
that it isn't exactly politically correct to look me up and
down and burst out, "Oh, you poor thing! I feel so sorry for
you!" Instead, their response tends to take the form of
unmerited admiration. "You are so brave!" they gush,
generally when I have done nothing more awesome than
to roll up to the dairy case and select a carton of vanilla
yogurt.[21]

 —Nancy Mairs

- *Parents talk about how people react to their children who
have disabilities:*
Susie: It used to disturb me to see kids with mental retardation in the supermarket, and now here I am. I make it a
point to take Betsy because it's important she learn how to
behave in the market and to have that experience. But I
can understand how others feel. A lot of people are **afraid**
of people with mental retardation because sometimes they
look a little different or **have unpredictable behavior. We're
not taught** how to deal with that, and we fear what we
don't know.
Diane: Some people **look at us with pity** in their eyes. I
wish more people would think, **"Isn't it terrific that they're
out and getting around** and not letting their disability keep
them from doing things?"[22]

 —Susie Burmester and Diane G. Callahan

Including People with Disabilities

In the 1960s and 1970s, a dramatic shift in our society's philosophy led to the recognition that people with mental retardation needed and wanted to live in the community and participate in all aspects of daily life, including education, work, recreation, and voting. This movement, known as *normalization*, coincided with the Kennedy administration's support, the exposure of substandard institutional care, and the growing empowerment of parents who insisted on raising their children at home with essential services and supports. One leader of this movement was Wolf Wolfensberger who "provided the intellectual rationale, the moral grounding, and the indefatigable energy to the policy of deinstitutionalization."[23]

Many people who had grown up in institutions were moved into the community but felt like "strangers in a strange land." Relationships were understandably strained and uncomfortable all around. It became apparent that people who had left institutions to live in group homes weren't necessarily prepared to participate in daily community life, and their neighbors frequently lacked the skills and motivation for inviting them in.

In the 1980s and 1990s, people with disabilities, professionals, parents, and others have forged alliances to articulate the needs of people with disabilities and to work toward common goals of increasing social awareness, advocating for disability rights in education and employment, and making communities more accessible for people with special needs. This focus, known as *inclusion*, emphasizes that people with disabilities have the right to full community participation and that communities have the responsibility to ensure equal access to full community participation. Laws now mandate inclusion beginning in early childhood, and children are entitled to attend school in the least restrictive environment (LRE). The result is that increasing numbers of children with a variety of differences are being educated together.

This is the first generation of children with and without disabilities to grow up and be educated together. Consequently, within inclusive education we have come to entertain a cheerful optimism that the generation growing up now will be different than those of the past. We are hopeful that greater contact between children will begin to break down the barriers of misunderstanding and dispel the myths that have created society's response to disability.[24]

—Emma Van der Klift and Norman Kunc

Disability Perspective

People with disabilities have been at the forefront of changes in laws, funding, and services that began in the 1960s. They have had a major role in their own growing empowerment through group efforts such as the disability rights movement, defining a disability culture, and efforts in the 1990s to establish academic programs of disability studies. Many individuals with disabilities, through their writings, personal and professional achievements, and increased visibility, are having a major influence on public awareness and attitude change.

Disability Rights Movement

In 1962, Ed Roberts, a polio survivor with quadriplegia who used a wheelchair and an iron lung, managed to be admitted to the University of California at Berkeley even though officials strongly discouraged him. By 1967, he had entered a doctoral program, and Berkeley had admitted 11 other students with severe disabilities. Calling themselves "The Rolling Quads," they developed a group identity and began to articulate their needs for greater self-sufficiency and for improved campus and community access. By 1972, Ed Roberts, Judy Heumann,[25] and others provided unstoppable leadership in advocating for greater self-determination and community access in the establishment of Independent Living Centers throughout the country.

The medical model of disability measured independence by how far one could walk after an illness or how far one could bend his legs after an accident. But Roberts redefined independence as the control a disabled person had over his life. Independence was measured not by the tasks one could perform without assistance but by the quality of one's life with help.[26]

—Joseph P. Shapiro

Defining a Disability Culture

Although members of the disability rights movement encompassed a very diverse population, a group identity emerged. They became proactive—and effective—in defining their own needs, asserting themselves as consumers, not patients, and working to change legislation and attitudes. Increasingly, other people with disabilities—political activists, writers, artists, athletes, professionals, and educators—articulated their shared values, their common challenges in working for legal and social change, and their similar experiences of being stereotyped, stigmatized, and separated—both socially and physically—from the rest of society.

People with disabilities . . . share a common history of oppression and a common bond of resilience. We generate art, music, literature, and other expressions of our lives and our culture, infused from our experience of disability. Most importantly we are proud of ourselves as people with disabilities. We claim our disabilities with pride as part of our identity. We are who we are: we are people with disabilities.[27]

—Stephen Brown

Disability Studies

Disability affects everybody. We all have some direct personal connection with disability. Disability has an impact on our families in terms of relationships, caregiving, and gaining access to resources. Disability is a major economic issue for business, insurance, government, and health care organizations. Disability groups must continually raise large amounts of money to fund research and services. Our attitudes and actions toward people with disabilities reflect both our personal values and the ingrained values of our society about various disabilities. Disability affects every aspect of our society: political, social, personal, economic, moral, and legal. Because of the growing awareness of the impact of disabilities on society, interdisciplinary academic programs of disability studies are being established in many universities and colleges.

Legal Perspective on Disabilities

The legal perspective on disabilities is complex. Laws do not always keep up with the needs and demands of the people. Since the 1970s, the following laws have dramatically changed the legal position of people with disabilities by ensuring their rights and providing protection from discrimination for the first time in our history.

Rehabilitation Act of 1973

The Rehabilitation Act of 1973 was pioneering legislation that laid the groundwork for many laws to come.[28] It proposed a definition of disability that continues to be used and appears in the Americans with Disabilities Act of 1990.[29] The Rehabilitation Act prohibits employment discrimination in the federal government and federally funded programs on the basis of either physical or mental disability. Section 504 of the Rehabilitation Act prohibits the same discrimination in the provision of public services. Included in this law was a mandate for architectural accessibility of federally funded programs.

Individuals with Disabilities Education Act

The Individuals with Disabilities Education Act (IDEA) Amendments of 1997 is the current version of the groundbreaking Education for All Handicapped Children Act of 1975.[30] The

1975 law specified that every American child has the right to a
free and appropriate education in the LRE, regardless of her
disability. Prior to 1975, children were turned away from
schools for many reasons: Their wheelchairs could not be ac-
commodated on campuses, children needed personal assistance during the school day, for example, to use the restroom,
and teenagers with hearing impairments needed signing interpreters for high school classes.

Americans with Disabilities Act of 1990

The ADA was signed by President Bush in July 1990 and took
effect in 1992. Prior to the passage of the ADA, people with
disabilities were a marginalized population under the law.
The Civil Rights Act of 1964[31] prohibited discrimination on the
basis of race, religion, national origin, or gender, but people
with disabilities received no such protection. The ADA is a
unique piece of legislation because it has very few specific
provisions. Instead, it defines key terms to be applied on a
case-by-case basis.

When the ADA was passed, it immediately affected 4.5
million private-sector employees and 43 million people with
disabilities. It is estimated that one in seven Americans has a
disability as defined by the ADA. The ADA, which has three
sections (called *titles*), applies to people with alcoholism,
cancer, cerebral palsy, congenital abnormalities, diabetes,
epilepsy, facial disfigurements, hearing impairment, heart disease, HIV/AIDS, mental impairment, mental retardation,
muscular dystrophy, orthopedic problems, specific learning
disabilities, speech impairment, visual impairment, and other
disabilities. The ADA also covers people who are discriminated against on the basis of *a history* of having a disability or
because they are *regarded* as having a disability. The law also
extends to individuals and agencies and their employees who
have a relationship with or provide services to a person who
has a disability, including parents, spouses, and personal assistants.[32] The ADA also prohibits discrimination against people who use service animals.

Title I   Pertaining to all private employers with 15 or more employees, Title I mandates employers to provide "reasonable accommodation" to applicants and employees such as modified work schedules, changes to make facilities accessible, and provision or modification of equipment or devices, readers, interpreters, and assistants.

Titles II and III   Title II mandates nondiscrimination and reasonable accommodation in state and local government offices and agencies. Title III mandates the same in public places such as hotels, restaurants, stadiums, convention centers, theaters, bars, entertainment venues, stores, terminals, depots, and stations used for public transportation (other than airports), museums, parks, and other places of recreation, schools (public or private) or other places of education, child care centers, food banks and other social service centers, and gymnasiums and other places of exercise. Titles II and III specify that these entities may not deny a person with a disability necessary services, programs, or activities and must offer these in the most inclusive setting appropriate to the individual's needs.

Federal Family and Medical Leave Act

The Federal Family and Medical Leave Act[33] affects companies with 50 or more employees. It allows workers 12 weeks of unpaid leave within a one-year period for personal illness or to allow employees time to provide care for a family member.

PUTTING IT ALL TOGETHER

In our society, the experience of having a disability is the experience of feeling and being considered different in a very fundamental sense. Yet, everybody has, has had, or will have a personal experience with disability. Disability has an elusive, ever-changing definition. We all have degrees of difference in how we look, move, communicate, behave, and learn. We all share the same anxieties about change and loss in our abilities and appearance. Acknowledging our shared experiences of "differentness" and vulnerability can help us better accept disabilities as a natural part of human life.

Interacting comfortably and effectively with someone who looks, moves, communicates, behaves, or learns in ways that are unfamiliar, unexpected, or unsettling continues to be a challenge for many of us. It isn't always easy to change stereotypes and to expand our personal comfort zone for differences. But becoming aware of our reactions and attitudes is the first step toward positive change.

In today's world of "a slow but willing change of attitudes," it is likely that our reactions are increasingly based on "reticence or ignorance rather than real rejection."[34]

—Henry Betts

Attitude changes occur as we *learn more* about disabilities and *meet more* people with disabilities. People with disabilities are "out there" undoing the traditional limitations imposed upon them. We all can look forward to expanding our comfort zones for each other's differences and for our similarities as well.

For this to happen, we need to change more than our attitudes. We need skills for interacting, more opportunities for contact with each other, and more knowledge about each other. The next chapter describes some of the ways we learn how to think about and react to our own differences as well as the differences of others. As we become more sensitized to our own *feelings* and *reactions* about people who have disabilities, we can begin challenging and changing our *attitudes* and *actions*.

READINGS
AND RESOURCES

Books

With the Power of Each Breath: A Disabled Women's Anthology
S. Browne, D. Connors, & N. Stern (Cleis Press, Pittsburgh, 1985)

Bad-Mouthing: The Language of Special Needs
J. Corbett (Falmer Press, London, England, 1996)

Enforcing Normalcy: Disability, Deafness, and the Body
L.J. Davis (Verso, New York, 1995)

The Disability Studies Reader
L.J. Davis (Ed.) (Routledge Press, New York, 1997)

Born Different: Amazing Stories of Very Special People
F. Drimmer (Bantam Doubleday Dell, New York, 1988)

Interpreting Disability: A Qualitative Reader
P. Ferguson, D. Ferguson, & S. Taylor (Eds.) (Teachers College Press, New York, 1992)

Freaks: Myths and Images of the Secret Self
L. Fiedler (Bantam Doubleday Dell, New York, 1978)

Women with Disabilities:
Essays in Psychology, Culture, and Politics
M. Fine & A. Asch (Eds.) (Temple University Press, Philadephia, 1988)

Staring Back: The Disability Experience from the Inside Out
K. Fries (Ed.) (Penguin Books, New York, 1997)

Images of the Disabled: Disabling Images
A. Gartner & T. Joe (Eds.) (Praeger, New York, 1987)

Person to Person: A Guide for Professionals
Working with People with Disabilities
L. Gething (Paul H. Brookes Publishing Co., Baltimore, 1992)

Stigma: Notes on the Management of Spoiled Identity
E. Goffman (Simon & Schuster, New York, 1963)

Claiming Disability: Knowledge and Identity
S. Linton (New York University Press, New York, 1998)

Nobody's Perfect:
Living and Growing with Children Who Have Special Needs
N.B. Miller with "The Moms": S. Burmester, D.G. Callahan,
J. Dieterle, & S. Niedermeyer (Paul H. Brookes Publishing Co.,
Baltimore, 1994)

Pride Against Prejudice: Transforming Attitudes to Disability
J. Morris (New Society Publishers, Philadelphia, 1991)

No Pity: People with Disabilities
Forging a New Civil Rights Movement
J.P. Shapiro (Times Books, New York, 1994)

Inclusion: A Guide for Educators
S. Stainback & W. Stainback (Paul H. Brookes Publishing Co.,
Baltimore, 1996)

Legal Advocacy Organizations

Office of the Americans with Disabilities Act
Civil Rights Division, U.S. Department of Justice, Box 66118,
Washington, DC 20035-6118 (202-514-6193)

National Association of Protection and Advocacy Systems
900 Second Street, NE, Suite 211, Washington, DC 20002
(202-408-9514; TDD: 202-408-9521; fax: 202-408-9520)

3

Understanding Your
Reactions to
Disability Differences

In this chapter we invite you to look back on your life and think about some of the influences that helped shape how you react to disability differences today. As we describe in Chapter 1, your brain *requires* you to react to differences, but that's just the beginning. There are many other factors that have influenced *how* you react to disabilities:

- Your brain
- Your parents
- Your peers
- Your own appearance differences
- Your own ability differences
- Your own disabilities
- People you know who have disabilities

- What you know about disabilities
- Messages from society
- Awareness of your environment

The Awareness Activities in this chapter ask you to think about the ways you have learned to feel about disability differences and how your daily life is influenced by your beliefs and behaviors related to differences, including your own differences.

YOUR PARENTS

One of the many tasks of parenting is to teach children how to think about and relate to other people. Through your parents' instruction and by their example, you learned how to think and feel about the differences of your own family members and the differences of people outside the family. You were taught to compare other people with yourself and your family, to judge some differences as "all right" and others as "better than" or "not as good" as you. You probably learned about "us" and "them," good guys and bad guys, individuals and groups of people to fear, admire, avoid, envy, love, and hate. You developed attitudes about people who were richer or poorer than you, the people who worked for your parents, the people your parents worked for, and people who had a different skin color, who belonged to a different religion or faith, who were born somewhere else, or who had more or less education than you.

You also learned how to think about and react to people who had various kinds of disabilities that affected how they looked, moved, expressed themselves, or behaved. Most of us can remember at least one person in our family who had some type of disability. Perhaps your grandmother lived with your family following her stroke, or maybe your brother has cerebral palsy. You may have had an aunt who was deaf, or you may have a cousin who has mental retardation. You saw and heard how your family members talked about and treated relatives with disabilities, and you may have positive, negative, or mixed emotional memories about these experiences.

Your early education about disabilities expanded through contacts with other adults in your childhood. Some early experiences *enlarged* your personal comfort zone for differences: maybe your piano teacher stuttered, or the friendly woman next door walked with a cane, or your blind grandfather loved having you read to him. Other experiences may have *reduced* your comfort zone. You might have been confused by your grandmother because she never remembered anything you told her and yelled at the people taking care of her, or you may have been scared by the strange-looking man who wandered your neighborhood talking to himself, carrying a large sack that your brother warned you was full of dead cats. Memories about differences that made you feel frightened or unsafe are the first ones that pop up today when you encounter differences that make you feel the least bit unsettled.

Some families are comfortable with many kinds of differences and explore and discuss them with interest, giving messages such as "It's okay to ask questions," or "Let's find out more about it." Other families see some differences as threatening or uncomfortable and discourage unnecessary interactions, giving messages such as "Don't play with him," "Don't stare at her," or "Stay away from him."

Awareness Activity

Family Experiences with Disabilities

1. As a child, did any of your family members have a disability? How were these disabilities explained to you? How did family members talk about and interact with relatives who had disabilities?

2. What positive experiences did you have with relatives or neighbors who had disabilities? What problems or uncomfortable moments do you remember?

3. Which kinds of disabilities seemed comfortable for your parents, and which made them seem uncomfortable? Did

they encourage or discourage conversation about and interactions with people with disabilities? How did your family
members talk about disabilities and people who had them?
4. What similarities and differences do you notice between
your own attitudes about disabilities today and your parents' attitudes?

As you grew, you learned that differences are very important. With all of the messages your parents gave you about
differences in others, they were also giving you messages
about how *your* differences measured up. They compared you
directly or indirectly with their expectations for you, with
your siblings, with themselves, with your friends, and with
yourself—how you used to be, how they wished you could
be, or how you would grow up to be. Many of our attitudes
about differences in others began with our feelings about differences in ourselves.

Messages you heard (or thought you heard) about being
different became part of your self-image and your attitudes
about differences in others. These messages are evoked whenever you encounter a difference in someone that strikes a particular note of comparison with yourself. Comparing another
person's difference with your own may increase your comfort
and empathy but may also create discomfort if you *overidentify*
and assume that there is a similarity that does not exist. For
example, if you had a speech impairment as a child and grew
up feeling afraid of being teased, you might tend to assume
that other people with speech impairments also feel insecure
and self-conscious when talking.

YOUR PEERS

The Brain, the Bully, the Teacher's Pet

During your childhood, it wasn't long before your sphere of
influence shifted from your family to your peer group. You

started school carrying your new lunchbox and your family's beliefs and attitudes about differences. You and your peers also had vulnerabilities and fears about the outside world where you were on your own, without your parents' protective presence. You had to learn whether other people would help you feel safe from differences that were outside of your comfort zone and feel comfortable with your own differences. Some people made you feel this way—you may remember a best friend, a coach, or a teacher who saw your differences as unique and special.

Each of us has at least one childhood story about another kid who was favored, picked on, or teased because of some difference, whether it was related to a disability or because of his body size, his red hair and freckles, or the way he walked or talked. Some students could read as well as the teacher, and others couldn't keep up with their reading group. Many of us can remember feeling different in some way that made us feel rejected, stupid, ugly, or bad. Most of our experiences with being different as children were because of differences we had absolutely no control over.

Awareness Activity

Childhood Experiences with Disabilities

1. Did you have any kind of disability difference during your childhood? How was it explained to other people? How did others react to you and your disability?
2. Did any of your classmates have disabilities? How were their disabilities explained to you? Did you behave differently toward those classmates?
3. What memories do you have about name-calling as a child? Were you ever the target of name-calling? What names did you use against others?
4. Did you know any kids with disabilities in your neighborhood, church, camp, or other groups? What were you told

about them? How much interaction did you have with them?

5. Were you aware of "special" classes or schools in your community? What were you told, or what did you believe about them? How did you recognize kids in "special" classes?

6. Which of these experiences with disabilities have affected how you think about and react to people with disabilities today?

The Angst of Adolescence

Adolescence is a time of intense preoccupation with differences. It is a time of much trial-and-error learning, and great self-consciousness about your appearance. During adolescence the slightest difference can feel like (or actually be) a social stigma that may be temporary but feel eternal. How we *think* other people judge the way we look, move, talk, learn, or behave seems much more important than anything else in our world during adolescence. Recalling some of your memories from these experiences can help you understand how your comfort zone for differences has expanded and contracted, how your differences fit into the comfort zones of others, and how you saw others treated who didn't fit in. Some of the typical differences of adolescence include the following:

- Having feet so big you stumbled over them
- Having acne, pimples, or other skin problems
- Having breasts that you thought were too small or too big
- Wearing braces on your teeth
- Having an unusual facial feature or body part
- Feeling your voice cracking or your face flushing whenever you talked to someone you wanted to impress
- Feeling so socially nervous you would avoid any setting where you might have to make conversation
- Feeling like an academic failure in at least one subject or feeling set apart because school was so easy that you were called "a brain"

- Having a disability that seemed to make other people feel uncomfortable or avoid you

---

Awareness Activity

Adolescence and Awareness of Disabilities

1. Did you have a disability during your adolescent years? How did it affect your life in terms of friends, social life, attending school, and self-image?
2. Who did you know with disabilities during your middle and high school years? Were they classmates, teachers, relatives of classmates, peers in church or in your neighborhood, or members of clubs or groups outside of school? What are some of your memories about any of these people and their disabilities?
3. Did you have any close friends or date anyone who had a disability? How important was the disability to your relationship, and what did you understand about it?
4. What positive adolescent experiences with disabilities (your own or others') affected how you think about and react to disability differences today?

YOUR OWN APPEARANCE DIFFERENCES

Many disabilities involve differences or changes in appearance that may include loss of hair, scars, skin rashes or markings, unusual facial features, missing limbs or prostheses, or an irregular body size or shape. Seeing a person who looks different is unexpected, and the difference itself may be unfamiliar or unsettling to you. Your detection of a person's difference can trigger memories about your own appearance insecurities, and you might then easily assume that the other person feels the same way.

Appearance Adjustments You May Have Made

Everybody has some part of his face or body that he believes other people notice and react to. Many of our grooming/cosmetic behaviors are not for the purpose of drawing attention to ourselves but to hide features we dislike or think others will dislike. If you are not certain whether this is true about you, then consider what appearance adjustments you have made—or would like to have made—in the past week.

Daily Rituals

Everybody engages in some daily rituals to enhance their appearance, even if it's only running a comb through their hair. Women, for example, frequently apply some combination of foundation, powder, mascara, eyeliner, eye shadow, lipstick, and nail polish. Men experience greater hair loss, but women tend to spend much more time and money on their hair: first shaving, plucking, waxing, or cutting it and then coloring, curling, or straightening what is left. Most people use deodorants and/or fragrances to camouflage their natural body scent and moisture lotions to keep their skin looking "young."

Equipment and Extras

Some people wear glasses to see better; others use contact lenses to avoid how glasses make them look or to change their eye color. Some women wear contoured bras, shoulder pads, and other body shape enhancers or concealers. Some of us diet and exercise for our health; some of us do so for our appearance. Some people avoid wearing certain clothes because they think the clothes might make them look too fat, too old, or too young.

Surgeries

Reconstructive surgeries have made major advances in helping people improve their functioning and change their appearance when scars, burns, or birthmarks cause them personal and/or social discomfort. Most cosmetic surgery patients today, however, want to reduce signs of aging, enhance attractiveness, and feel socially and physically more desirable. We lift our eyelids, tuck our tummies, tighten our chins, enlarge or reduce our breasts, and change our noses. We smooth and tighten skin that sags. We implant, transplant, or remove body hair.

Awareness Activity

Appearance Anxieties and Adjustments

1. Have you ever looked in a mirror *without* having some opinion, positive or negative, about what you see? Do you own a magnifying mirror?
2. Which aspects of your appearance do you especially like? Which do you like the least? Which do you have no opinion about?
3. Who is your standard of comparison for specific aspects of your appearance? An "average"? A friend or relative? Yourself at another time? An "ideal"?
4. If you could change one aspect of your appearance, what would it be?
5. What are some appearance adjustments you make on a regular basis? Are there any that you would make if you had the courage, permission, time, or money?
6. If you had to go one month without making *any* adjustments in your appearance, how would you feel? How would other people react?

YOUR OWN ABILITY DIFFERENCES

Many disabilities involve differences or changes in ability that may affect movement, communication, learning, or behavior. Encountering a person who has one of these disabilities may be unexpected, and the difference may be unfamiliar or feel unsettling to you. Your detection of the difference may often trigger memories related to insecurities about some of your own ability differences.

You have enjoyed a number of ability achievements during your life. Some came to you easily, others you had to work hard for. Some of your abilities may have been more important to other people (such as your parents) than to you. Some of your abilities have been more important to you than to others.

There are many kinds of abilities: physical, academic, creative, communicative, and social. You may be extremely uncoordinated, or you may have a physical limitation that hinders your participation in active sports. That may be a source of major disappointment and frustration in your life, or you may not care at all. You may wish you had artistic talent and forever regret your lack of creativity, or you may love to paint by number, proudly framing the results.

Ability Achievements and Anxieties

While growing up, everybody has had the experience of being able to do some things but less able or unable to do others. How you have felt about your own abilities and inabilities can influence how you react to the abilities and inabilities of others today.

Awareness Activity

Your Physical Abilities and Anxieties

1. As a child, were you naturally coordinated, active, and drawn to physical activities, or did you have to be coaxed or forced to participate?
2. Were you ever unable to participate in any physical activities because of a health problem? If so, what was that like for you?
3. What did others say about your physical abilities and interests? Were you praised, criticized, shamed, or bragged about?
4. How did you compare with your siblings, other relatives, or your peers? How important was that to you then?
5. How much did your early experiences with physical activities become a part of your body image and feelings of physical competence today?

6. Are there some physical activities that you would like to take up today but believe you aren't capable of learning or being "good enough" at?

Your Learning Abilities and Anxieties

1. How "school smart" were you in the eyes of your mother, father, and teachers?
2. How did you compare to siblings or other relatives—and how important was that to you then?
3. What were your best subjects? Your worst? What came easily, and what did you never feel confident about?
4. Did you develop a sense of pride, shame, specialness, or averageness about your ability to succeed in school?
5. Was there any subject that you just couldn't learn, no matter how hard you tried?
6. Today, how smart do you feel compared with other people you know: your spouse, your siblings, your parents, your children, your friends, and your co-workers?
7. Do you have secret gaps in your knowledge, abilities, or intelligence that you try to hide from others?
8. As an adult, do you wish you had certain abilities but are too ashamed or embarrassed to take lessons or to ask for help?

Your Social Abilities and Anxieties

1. As a child, how easily did you make friends?
2. How often were you reprimanded by parents or teachers for being too loud or too quiet, too boisterous or too shy, insensitive or overly sensitive?
3. As a child, did you have any unusual behaviors or habits that annoyed other people? What was that like for you?
4. Did you have a best friend while growing up?
5. Today, how at ease are you in new social situations? Are you as content (or more content) with being alone than with being with other people?
6. What social skills do you wish you had today?

YOUR OWN DISABILITIES

If you have or have ever had a disability, your reactions to others' disabilities are affected by your own experiences. You may have met others with a similar disability through support groups, organizations, and programs or through mutual friends and felt the mutuality of the challenges you encounter and the power of combining information and resources. Meeting people with other kinds of disabilities also may have broadened your sense of group identity as you shared experiences of uncomfortable reactions from others, struggles with physical limitations, and the challenges of living in society with any kind of disability.

Everybody reacts to differences in other people that are unfamiliar, unexpected, or unsettling. If you have or have had a disability, then your expected average in other people may be very different from someone who has had limited exposure to people with disability differences.

Awareness Activity

Your Own Disability Differences

1. Do you think you have had more personal interactions and relationships with people who have disabilities than someone who does not have a disability?
2. Do you ever find that others expect you to be an "expert" about all disabilities because you have one?
3. Do you ever feel like other people cast you as a role model because of your accomplishments as a person with a disability?
4. Do you find that others' reactions to unfamiliar, unexpected, or unsettling differences apply to you?
5. Do you have a disability that is "nonvisible" that you hesitate to disclose?

6. If you acquired a disability as an adult, what have you learned about yourself in the course of adapting to this change? What have you learned about others?

PEOPLE YOU KNOW WHO HAVE DISABILITIES

If your spouse, child, sibling, or parent has or had a disability, then you have had the experience of watching others' reactions. If you are or have been a caregiver for a person with a disability, you have encountered reactions that make you particularly sensitized to how people with disabilities deal with their situations, and you are aware of the issues of daily living faced by many people with disabilities. You have also learned that other people are often uncomfortable interacting with you, the caregiver.

Learning from Your Own Reactions

What you know, how you feel, and how you react to people who have disabilities are highly influenced by your personal experiences with someone who has a disability. If anyone in your family has had even a brief illness or injury that required your participation in her care, then you know the mixture of feelings and reactions that can occur. You desire to provide physical relief and comfort for your family member as well as love and affection yet also feel fearful about her condition and the future. You may be concerned about whether you are doing too much—or not enough. You probably worry about meeting the needs of other family members and have concerns about some of your own needs. You may feel supported by some friends and relatives but feel that others have drifted away.

Learning from Other People's Reactions

In the next Awareness Activity, think about what you have learned about yourself and your reactions to disabilities from some of your own experiences. Also think about what you have learned from the ways other people reacted to you and your family member.

Awareness Activity

People You Know Who Have Disabilities

1. Have your direct experiences with someone who has a disability changed your personal comfort zone for disabilities in general? In what ways?
2. Has your relationship made you more aware of environmental obstacles? What obstacles have directly handicapped this person at home, at work, or in the community?
3. What were some of your experiences with other people's reactions to your relative's or friend's disability?
4. How have your beliefs and attitudes changed as a result of your relationships with people who have disabilities?

WHAT YOU KNOW ABOUT DISABILITIES

Information increases comfort. This is true about many things in life: operating a computer, playing a musical instrument, teaching a class, traveling, gardening, parenting, and learning about human differences.

There are many sources of information about disabilities, including personal experience with your own disability or with a family member's disability, reading materials, specialized college courses, television and movies, and conversations with friends or colleagues. The following Awareness Activity can help you to recall some of the ways you have already learned about disabilities and help you to develop ideas for gaining more information.

Awareness Activity

Learning About Disabilities

1. Visit a bookstore or library, and browse through the shelves. Books about disabilities can be found in many different sections, including health, self-help, parenting, special needs, psychology, sociology, education, and biography. An increasing number of bookstores have disability sections.
2. Think about movies and television programs that you have seen that focused on disability issues. How were the characters portrayed?
3. Pay attention to newspapers and magazine articles that have feature stories about people with disabilities and reports about breakthroughs in technology, legal issues, and medicine.
4. Have you ever visited a World Wide Web site, participated in an on-line chat, or received e-mail about disabilities? A number of World Wide Web sites you may want to visit are listed in the Resources sections of Chapters 5–10.

MESSAGES FROM SOCIETY

We are bombarded with messages from television, billboards, movies, magazines, and newspapers about how we should look and how many ways there are to achieve that end. We are taught to think that "beauty is only skin deep; it's character that counts," yet popular magazines portray attractive, physically fit people as role models for success and happiness in life. We tell our children to care about others, but the media push consumerism and material self-gratification. Many of us want children with disabilities to have every advantage—but in someone else's classroom, playgroup, or soccer team. We believe that people with disabilities should have access to the community, then resent their having the "best" parking places.

We have received so many conflicting messages about people with disabilities for so long that often we aren't really sure how we feel. Most of us want to be comfortable in our interactions and not have disabilities matter in our work and social relationships. Our confusion about all of these messages can overwhelm us and make us feel as though it's all too much trouble to change our attitudes and behaviors, or we can view our confusion as a healthy part of our personal and societal transition.

AWARENESS OF YOUR ENVIRONMENT

As an adult, you continue to be influenced by your friendships, adult education courses, career choices, volunteer work, movies you see, the books and magazines you read, and other media. Your attitudes about disabilities may be pretty well formed, but they can still change. The society you grew up in has been making some dramatic changes regarding disabilities since the 1960s.

People with disabilities have made themselves heard, have asserted their legal rights, and have moved out of group homes and institutions, and we have to decide how we feel about human differences. Each of us needs to reexamine our comfort zones for differences, confront our own ignorance, fears, and confusion, and act on our highest goals for a fully inclusive society.

Awareness Activity

Looking Around You

Does it seem to you that there are many more people in the community who have disabilities? There *are* more people with more kinds of disabilities than ever before (see Chapter 2), and there is increasing community accessibility. Look around your community and you will see the following:

- More ramps, curb cuts, accessible hotel rooms, bathrooms, movie theaters, and other public facilities
- More transportation vehicles equipped for people with disabilities, such as buses, trains, and vans
- Accessible parking spaces in every parking lot
- Public telephones with devices for people with hearing impairments
- Television sets with closed-captioning devices
- More magazines with articles about people with disabilities
- Magazines that focus on disability issues such as *Ability, Mainstream,* and *Exceptional Parent*
- In-depth television stories about new technology for people with disabilities
- More movies that include people with disabilities *without* focusing on their disability
- More people with disabilities in commercials and advertisements
- More autobiographies of people with disabilities
- More books about disabilities for parents and caregivers
- More nonfiction books about health issues and disabilities
- More children's books with characters who have disabilities

Awareness Activity

Personal Awareness and Action

1. Could a person with a wheelchair enter your home? Your bathroom? How about your office?
2. If you used a wheelchair, could you get around comfortably in your own home? Your favorite restaurant? Grocery store? Other places of business you frequent? As you go through your daily routines, look for accessibility and obstacles: the width of aisles, ramps or elevators in addition to stairs, parking lots, and bathrooms.

3. Have you ever mentioned an issue of accessibility to a store, restaurant, or theater employee?
4. Have you ever volunteered, donated money, or participated in events to support programs for people with disabilities?

PUTTING IT ALL TOGETHER

In Chapter 1, we describe why you react to differences: Your primitive, emotional brain detects differences in people that are unfamiliar, unexpected, or unsettling, and your modern, reasoning brain calls up your knowledge, memories, feelings, and beliefs to evaluate the situation at hand and decide how to react. In Chapter 2, we present an overview of disability differences in our society today. It is clear that disability touches everyone's life in a number of ways, yet many of us continue to be uncomfortable with interacting with people who have disabilities and even understanding our own attitudes. In this chapter, we describe how you developed your personal comfort zone for differences: a lifetime of influences from your family, peers, the media, and your own experiences with disability. In Chapter 4, we present our approach for helping you use your understanding of differences and of yourself to change your reactions to and interactions with people who have disability differences.

READINGS
AND RESOURCES

Books

Body Images: Development, Deviance, and Change
T.F. Cash & T. Pruzinsky (Eds.) (The Guilford Press, New York, 1990)

Minding the Body: Women Writers on Body and Soul
P. Foster (Ed.) (Bantam Doubleday Dell, New York, 1994)

Bodylove: Learning to Like Our Looks and Ourselves
R. Freedman (HarperCollins, New York, 1989)

*"Look at My Ugly Face." Myths and Musings on Beauty
and Other Perilous Obsessions with Women's Appearance*
S. Halprin (Penguin USA, New York, 1995)

*Prisoners of Belief: Exposing and
Changing Beliefs that Control Your Life*
M. McKay & P. Fanning (New Harbinger Publications, Oakland,
CA, 1991)

*The Cinema of Isolation:
A History of Physical Disability in the Movies*
M. Norden (Rutgers University Press, New Brunswick, NJ, 1994)

Making Changes: Family Voices on Living with Disability
J. Spiegel & P. van den Pol (Brookline Books, Cambridge, MA,
1993)

4

The 4D Approach

Most new people we meet either don't notice
[my daughter's] facial difference or are too
"polite" to mention it. Frankly, we wish people
would ask us, in a concerned or curious way,
about her condition. We welcome the opportunity to discuss it. What bothers us most is when
people stare at her and give us sympathetic
looks.[1]

—Hope Charkins

Chapters 1–3 explain some of the forces that shape your reactions to people with disability differences. But knowing where
your feelings come from is only the beginning—telling you
how you got here but not *where* you're going. The Action Tips
and Awareness Activities in this chapter will help you to feel
more confident in relating to people with disability differences. This chapter will help you do the following:

- Recognize disability differences more rapidly and accurately
- Understand your own feelings, attitudes, and reactions
- Feel more relaxed in these situations
- Identify more choices for how to act
- Better evaluate the interactions and new actions you've tried
- Feel more confident about future interactions

If you are looking for a comfortable, authentic, and more equal relationship with a person who has a disability difference, then you are well on your way to achieving it because a positive expectation eases the process.

Our *4D approach* can help transform your reactions and actions. You will be able to see situations more clearly and make informed and thoughtful decisions when you detect differences, thus expanding your options about what to do. Later on, we'll show you how your reactions and actions can change.

Relationships don't follow recipes. They evolve in ways that are unique and often unpredictable. They emerge from the synergy (blending together) of two people, their histories, and expectations. Your history, as you learned in previous chapters, is a combination of your family background, culture, and experiences. How you react and act will reflect you as an individual. But during every interaction, there are also influences from the other person. The person with a disability also has a unique history. Relationships are not determined by either person alone. We can't make a list of dos and don'ts because each person with a difference is a unique human being, and what works in one encounter might not apply in another.[2]

Your reactions and actions also will depend on the kind of relationship you have: neighbor to neighbor, co-worker to co-worker, teacher to student, parent to child's friend, salesperson to customer, and so forth. There are almost as many kinds of relationships as there are people! Your expectations for what the other person will say or do are highly dependent on the situation. Some interactions are encounters more than relationships, such as when you share a pew at church, speak to a hotel desk clerk, or play pickup basketball at the recreation center.

Both your encounters and ongoing relationships can be strained by the challenges of reacting to another person's disability difference. The next section provides a method for better handling situations in which the other person has a specific disability difference.

STEPS OF THE 4D APPROACH

There are four steps to the 4D approach:

- *Detecting:* noticing the other person's disability difference and your internal reactions (feelings and thoughts)
- *Deciding:* Deciding what the nature of the difference is and how relevant it is to the current situation, considering what your action options are, and choosing the ones that seem the most useful in the situation
- *Doing:* behaving according to your plan, perhaps acting in a new way
- *Debriefing:* afterward, reflecting on your actions, thinking about what worked and what didn't and what to try next time

DETECTING THE DISABILITY DIFFERENCE

Detecting means realizing or discovering. In the 4D approach, there are two steps to Detecting:

1. Detecting the other person's difference
2. Detecting your reactions to the difference

Let's look at the two parts of Detecting, which occur so close together in succession that they almost seem to happen at once.

Detecting the Other Person's Difference

When you notice that someone has a disability difference, you have detected something specific about that person. Using your senses of seeing and hearing, your brain's difference detector has noticed that something about the situation is missing, out of place, or different from what you expected to see (see Chapter 1). Remember, your brain is wired and programmed to anticipate patterns in your environment, including the typical shapes of other people's bodies and the ways they move, communicate, and behave. You'll also recall from Chapter 1 that your primitive brain searches for and notices differences and often flashes a danger signal. But the story does not stop there because your modern brain stores detailed information that you can draw on to decide whether that quick-check danger signal is a misperception or an overreaction. Your primitive brain's difference detector says, "Halt!" but your modern brain asks, "What's *really* going on here?" The main reason that relationships between people with disability differences and others are sometimes unsuccessful is that people often act on the first danger message instead of pausing and realizing that there's no real threat.

Noticing a difference is not a sign that you have a character flaw or prejudice. It is a natural process that is unavoidable and necessary. *Acting* on your first information, however, is often a mistake. Only your primitive brain is advising you! As you learn to pause in Step Two, Deciding, you'll feel more comfortable and take more appropriate actions.

Disability differences almost always cause people either to take a second glance—or to deliberately avoid looking. We may often try hard not to study the person using a wheelchair or walking with an assistance dog. But we also may have a sense of curiosity and wonder about how a person lives with a certain impairment.

Disabilities Are Unfamiliar

Is the difference new to you? Perhaps you've detected a difference because you've never seen a person using a ventilator or someone with extensive scarring on his face.

Disabilities Are Unexpected

Are you more uncomfortable when you see a person with a disability in a setting where you don't expect her to be? Perhaps you're used to seeing people with physical disabilities at a hospital or a day program for older adults. But when you first discover that your child's teacher uses a hearing aid or that your new supervisor has a prosthetic arm, you may be caught off-guard and do a double take.

Disabilities Are Unsettling

Is there something about seeing a person who looks, moves, communicates, or behaves in a different way that makes you feel uncomfortable or anxious? A particular disability can evoke emotional memories that trigger strong reactions.

Detecting Your Reactions to the Difference

Even though you may have an initial, split-second hesitation or negative reaction to a disability difference, that is usually *not* your *only* response. Let's explore all of the feelings and thoughts that occur in the milliseconds after your initial Detection.

The next sections help you Detect and handle your feelings when you are with a person who has a disability difference. At the heart of your encounter or relationship are your feelings and the other person's feelings. If you are dissatisfied with these interactions or if you've felt upset, scared, confused, or disappointed, then the first step toward improvement is to revisit your initial feelings.

Face Your Anxiety

Anxiety, nervousness, and distress can cause us to avoid interacting with a person who has a disability. We may not feel proud of this avoidance, and it can have a negative effect on the person who is being ignored. But avoidance helps us to tone down our anxiety.

A better way to deal with anxiety is to face it and manage it. A pounding heartbeat, muscle tension, sweaty palms, stomach jitters, and a quavering voice are just some of the physical sensations that go along with strong negative or distressing feelings. Some people blush or have difficulty making eye contact. If you detect a disability difference and then become very nervous, you will not be able to handle the situation effectively. Here's an illustration of how the 4D approach can get stalled when stressful feelings take over.

When your inner reaction is fear and you escape to avoid discomfort, then you

- Avoid people with disabilities
- Never learn more about them
- Miss out on meeting new people or relating better to people in your family, neighborhood, or workplace
- Feel like a failure and not the kind of person you want to be

It is really important to detect your distress level so that you can lower it and continue with the 4D approach. Try to rate your level of distress using one of the following descriptions:

- *Red Alert—Extremely Distressed!*   I feel panicky, immobilized, as though my feet were glued to the floor, or I have the urge to run away as far and fast as possible. I'm frightened.

- *Very Stressed* I'm clueless about the disability difference. I have no idea what the person will Do next. I'm looking for a way to exit without drawing attention.
- *Nervous* I'm pretty confused about the disability difference and what I should Do next. Maybe it's safer just to be polite and ignore the person.
- *Slightly Unsettled* I'm not sure about this difference. This seems like a new situation, but I don't feel threatened. I'll watch for clues from the other person about how to behave. Let me think of something safe to say or Do.
- *Calm* I feel okay, I'm fairly relaxed, and I'm interested in the situation. I'm ready to interact or respond in a variety of ways.

Relax

The key to becoming more relaxed and reducing your anxiety is to notice when you're *not* relaxed! Rating your distress using the scale just mentioned helps you take control of your reactions and actions. Rating also helps you notice and appreciate when your distress level is going down—either during a single encounter or during several encounters in an ongoing relationship. After you've rated your distress, there are two easy steps to relaxing:

1. *Think calming and encouraging thoughts.* We don't just experience the world; we also describe it to ourselves in our minds. Part of our uncomfortable feelings result from our self-talk or our thoughts. If you become aware of negative thoughts, then you can replace them with more positive ideas. Here are some soothing self-talk statements, but try creating ones that suit *you.*

- I need to relax.
- I'm going to calm down.
- It's going to be okay.
- I'll get through this situation.
- Take it one step at a time.
- Look for the positive.

- I'm going to relax my breathing.
- I'll turn off my worrying right now.

2. *Relax with deep breathing.* When you get worried, your breathing becomes fast and shallow. Deep breathing is one of the easiest techniques available anytime or anywhere that you need to calm down physically and emotionally. Deep breathing is simple to learn, quick to do, and easy to remember. This technique is helpful during a visit to the dentist's office, before giving a speech, or in any other stressful situation.[3]

Label and Accept Your Feelings

Labeling and accepting your feelings isn't as easy as it sounds. Few of us have a very rich emotional vocabulary, and many of us did not learn from our parents and teachers how to describe feelings with words. In fact, we were often taught to suppress or ignore many of our feelings, such as fear, envy, and anger.

Here is a long—but partial!—list of feelings that people may experience when they encounter a disability difference in someone else. Notice that some of them may be disconcerting to you, while others are comfortable or positive.

- Admiration—It's amazing how the human spirit can triumph!
- Anger—Why did this have to happen? Why don't people accept this person?
- Apprehension—Is this person dangerous?
- Apathy—I didn't even notice the difference. What's the big deal?
- Curiosity—I'd like to know more.
- Disappointment—Why can't science prevent or cure this disability?
- Discomfort—I'm uneasy; I'm feeling some strain.
- Disgust—It makes me sick; I can't look.
- Empathy—I can imagine how that person feels.
- Fear—Could that happen to me or to my child?
- Fixation—I can't take my eyes off that person.

- Frustration—I'll never be able to relate comfortably to that person.
- Guilt—Why am I "better off" than that person?
- Helplessness—Is there anything I can do to help?
- Inspiration—This person is so courageous.
- Interest—I'd like to get to know this person.
- Nervousness—I might say or do something wrong.
- Pity—That poor child!
- Relief—I feel lucky that it's not me.
- Resentment—I feel as though people with disabilities have more rights than other people.
- Resistance—I'd rather not sit next to this person.
- Sadness—What a loss!
- Shame—I'm ashamed that I can't bear to look.
- Shock—Oh no! What's *wrong* with her?
- Surprise—I wasn't expecting this!
- Sympathy—I feel sorry for this person.
- Tolerance—I feel okay with this.
- Uncertainty—I think I might say or do something wrong.

You can't make a good Decision about Doing something until you acknowledge your true feelings. When you detect a disability difference in another person, pausing to label your feelings is a way to change your unconscious reactions into conscious thoughts. Regardless of whether you label your feelings, they *will* shape your decisions and actions. Even when your actions are ineffective or unsatisfying, they are still driven by your feelings. So, becoming aware of your feelings is essential to understanding your past actions and making better decisions about your future actions.

Try to accept your feelings, even the ones you consider bad or wrong. When it comes to reactions to disabilities, we may feel guilty about some of our private thoughts and feelings. Maybe you realize that they are "politically incorrect" or that they are based on stereotypes or old-fashioned ideas. But when it comes to feelings, there are no "shoulds"—our feelings know no rules. We need to accept our feelings (and others' feelings) as they are. When some of our feelings are uncomfortable or distressing, we want to find ways to feel better. But these ways of feeling better should involve changing our thoughts or actions, *not* ignoring or denying our feelings.

In daily life we often experience several feelings at once. It can be difficult to sort them out. Many people find it easier to get angry or impatient than to express helplessness, fear, and other feelings that expose their vulnerability. So if you're upset during an interaction with a person who has a disability, then ask yourself, "What *else* am I feeling?"

Key Points

Detecting the Other Person's Difference

1. It's natural to notice disability differences.
2. Difference is in the eye of the beholder: If something *looks* different to you, it *is* different to you.
3. It's okay to have a negative impression of a difference—at first.
4. Disabilities can be
   - Unfamiliar—new to you
   - Unexpected—not anticipated in this setting
   - Unsettling—disturbing
5. After Detecting a difference, pause before acting on your first impression.

Detecting Your Reactions to the Difference

1. *Face your anxiety.* Distress will trap you in those upsetting feelings. Distress will block your Deciding and Doing.
2. *Relax.* Think calming thoughts. Take three deep breaths.
3. *Label and accept your feelings.* Describe them with words. Pay attention to all of your feelings, not just one.

There is no one best way to interact with or react to a person who has a disability difference. So, just as we should not stereotype people with disabilities by assuming that "the disability experience" is the same for everyone, we should not expect to have the same feelings about various disabilities. Our reactions are complex and varied. If we aren't initially at ease, then we can *become* more comfortable over time, after first processing our feelings. Let's move on to the next step in the 4D approach, Deciding.

DECIDING: EVALUATING THE SITUATION

Your difference detector has noticed the disability difference, and you've taken stock of your emotions, especially your anxiety level. After Detecting, the next step is to think about the difference so you can decide what to do next. The following three simple questions will help you Decide:

1. What kind of difference is this?
2. How relevant is the disability to this situation?
3. What are my action options?

1. What Kind of Difference Is This?

Now is the time to dip into the file cabinet (or CD-ROM) of your brain to consider what you know about the difference you've just encountered.

If your answer to this first question is, "Yes, I *do* recognize this difference," then you can move right on to the second question. You're fortunate that you recognize the disability, either because a family member or work associate has this disability or because you learned about it by watching television or reading.

If your answer is, "I *don't* recognize this difference," then pause for a moment to get a handle on this unfamiliar situation. In this book, we sort dozens of disabilities into six broad categories to help you react more quickly and appropriately in new situations. Consider which kind of difference the person has:

- An appearance difference
- A movement difference
- A communication difference
- A behavior difference
- A learning difference
- A nonvisible difference
- More than one difference

It may or may not be important for you to know which specific disability a person has, as you will see in Chapters 5–10. Your initial reaction, however, is based on a general category of difference: how a person looks, moves, communicates, and so forth. Here's why it's important for you to categorize the difference: When you're interacting with a person who has an unfamiliar disability, sometimes your uncomfortable feelings block or overshadow your ability to think calmly and rationally. When that happens, you move straight from Detecting to Doing and skip right over Deciding. There is a huge risk of making the disability *more* or *less* important than it really is. But if you pause to name the category of disability, then you are bringing the vague situation into clearer focus. It can be helpful to shift your frame of mind from the general population of "people with disabilities" (a category prone to stereotyping) to a smaller, more specific category. By guessing what the disability *is*, you're also deciding what it is *not*.

Categorizing the difference will also lead you toward useful action options. How can you decide how to behave if you are "clueless" about the other person's disability difference? By guessing the general type of disability, you'll guide yourself toward what you may need to say and Do in the situation. For example, suppose you're coming out of the dry cleaners, and you're curious about a man stumbling along the sidewalk. His movement reminds you of your uncle who has cerebral palsy. Because you've made a connection between this man and your uncle, you feel relaxed and ready for whatever may happen next. You can move on to Question Two, "How relevant is the disability to this situation?"

Imagine, however, that you've never heard of cerebral palsy. You observe the man for a few more seconds and start to feel nervous and cautious. The man looks pretty unsteady and unstable. One reaction would be to skip Deciding by grabbing your clean suit and dashing to your car to avoid crossing paths with the man—but you pause instead. You Decide that he has a movement difference. What's causing this difference? Several possibilities pass through your mind: he's drunk, he has a muscle problem in his legs, he has *some* kind of disability. After a few more seconds of observation, you realize that his left arm and leg seem to be very well coordinated, and only his right arm and leg are not. His movement doesn't look like the random stumbling of someone who is intoxicated. Then you hear the man speak to the barber standing in front of his shop; because you see the man move his mouth and tongue with great effort, you Decide he has a communication difference as well. You have categorized the differences that you observed and can now move on to Question Two.

Changing our reactions to people with disability differences does *not* require that we know about every kind of difference. Most people know a little about several disabilities; some people with direct experience know quite a bit about one disability but almost nothing about others. It is a common mistake to expect a person with one disability difference to be well-informed about other disability differences, but the disability community is more diverse than similar. No person should have to apologize for not knowing about a particular disability difference—a willingness to learn more is the most important thing.

> Disabilities always create curiosity on the part of the observer. What is the disability? How profound is it? Can I see it, touch, know it? How did it happen? What does it interfere with? What would life be like if I had that impairment? . . . The question demands an answer. I must tell you the status of at least some portion of my body. . . . The question never has to be put because it is always actively in a default mode—it is always already asked.[4]
>
> —Lennard J. Davis

As you Decide which kind of difference the person has, keep in mind that sometimes a person with a disability experiences an observer's curiosity as intrusive. This is similar to the intrusive curiosity that many pregnant women feel when strangers grill them with personal questions: When are you due? Are you having a boy or a girl? Is this your first? Some strangers go so far as to pat the woman's stomach, an action that certainly would be considered unacceptable if the woman weren't pregnant!

2. How Relevant Is the Disability to This Situation?

After you've identified the difference, you can move on to the second question that guides your Deciding. *Relevance* means how pertinent the disability is, and it depends on three things: time frame, role expectations, and activities.

Time Frame

At the beginning of every interaction, you have a sense of how long you will be relating to the other person. Will your contact be fleeting, brief, intermittent, or ongoing? To return to the example of the man near the dry cleaners, you might have only a fleeting encounter as he walks by and you exchange smiles. Or, if you're headed for a haircut, you might have a brief conversation because the man is already talking to the barber. If

Time frame	What's expected

Fleeting
   Example: passing someone
   on the street
	Making momentary eye contact,
	smiling, or nodding

Brief
   Example: standing behind
   someone in line or sitting next
   to someone on a plane
	Making small talk

Intermittent
   Example: seeing other par-
   ents from your child's soccer
   team at the weekly game;
   visiting your optometrist for
   an annual exam
	Seeing a person again for short
	periods of time
	Possibly having a short conversation

Ongoing
   Example: interacting with
   family members, close
   friends, and co-workers
	Being with a person for long periods
	of time more than once
	Possibly mentioning conversations or
	activities from your last encounter
	Making plans for the next time you
	see a person

you discover that the man has just moved into your apartment building, then you can look forward to intermittent contact. If he is your new co-worker, then you'll be having ongoing contact.

Then, figure out what expectations are linked with this time frame. The table above lists time frames and associated expectations, and you can add your own examples as well.

Understanding the time frame expectations of the interaction will guide you as you Decide what to say or Do next. For example, reminding yourself that the time frame is fleeting or brief can help you relax and can take the pressure off. You will know that you don't need to perform a great social feat. Even if you make a blunder, no one may notice, and you can learn from the experience. If the time frame is longer, then this is your signal to take more time Deciding what to Do. You will have the time to improve your actions, whatever they may be. You will have the opportunity to get to know the other person, and she can guide you as you learn more about her disability difference.

Role Expectations

Although you may think of a role as a job for an actor, the fact is that we all use roles every day. In the 4D approach, a *role* is a set of expectations you have for another person. Your role expectations include

- Your goals for the interaction (its purpose)
- Your desire or need to continue the interaction
- Your motivation for the encounter to succeed
- Your obligation to stick with this encounter

Just as your brain has a set of expectations about how other people will appear to you, you also have expectations about how they will act or behave. Just imagine approaching daily life without any expectations of other people's behavior. Think about all of the people you interact with: family, friends, co-workers, neighbors, shopkeepers, tollbooth or parking garage attendants, security officers, receptionists, waiters, and so forth. If each of us didn't have some pretty detailed expectations about the people who occupy these roles, then we'd be very nervous and constantly "on the alert" about what they might do next. But instead, we can relax most of the time and assume that others will behave according to our role expectations. We become vigilant and notice when people *don't* act according to our expectations. Sometimes, meeting a person with a disability difference in an unexpected role challenges our expectations, and we have to reexamine our assumptions about roles and behavior.

After you've Detected and identified the difference, ask yourself which roles you and the other person are playing. What expectations are associated with each role? You may want to consult the table on the next page, but there are many kinds of roles, so you'll probably come up with some answers not listed here. Quickly taking stock of roles will help you plan your actions. Here are some sample roles and the behaviors that are typically expected from them.

The list of roles in the table is long because there are many, many kinds of roles. Your gender, age, cultural back-

Role	What's expected
Strangers	You expect to be ignored by most strangers, such as those on the subway.
	On the main street of a small town, you might expect a smile and a hello.
People making a commercial/business transaction	You might expect a friendly glance from people whom you see every day but have never met, such as people at the gym or cashiers at the supermarket.
	You might expect a few pleasant words or small talk about the weather or sports.
	A product is given for payment; and you and the other person move on.
Professionals (co-workers, doctors, teachers, lawyers, and so forth)	Professional behavior should reflect specific standards and ethical codes: For example, disclosure of personal information is discouraged or kept to a minimum.
	The professional is expected to direct the interaction and give advice.
Neighbors	If your neighbors are a part of your life, you might expect that they're there to help you.
	Or, you might expect them to just smile and wave from across the street.
Friends	Longtime friends may listen patiently to your problems and pleasures, whether day-to-day or momentous; you count on them to be there for you over the years.
	You will share warmth and support with certain friends only in particular settings, such as work or clubs.
Family members	Expectations of family members can be quite varied; husbands, wives, siblings, parents, cousins, aunts, grandparents, and others all have different role expectations.
	In most families, there is an expectation that relatives will be interested in your well-being, available to you, and loyal.

ground, and other factors shape your role expectations. Only *you* can list all of the ones that are pertinent to *your* life at a given time. When you pause to consider role expectations, you'll have your own list in mind.

The key point about time frame and role expectations is that when the other person has a disability, you still need to respect roles (yours and his). If the person is a receptionist in the lobby of an office building, then you wouldn't need to comment on his leg braces. The interaction would be formal, brief, and commenting on body parts or medical devices is not appropriate to the role and time frame.

Activities

When you've identified the roles and time frame for your interaction, the disability difference comes into focus. But the crucial part of deciding relevance is considering the activities that are or will be taking place. One of the common mistakes that people make when interacting with others who have disability differences is to make *more* or *less* out of the disability than the situation calls for. Disabilities, however, do not have the same meaning and importance in every situation. There is no such thing as "universal relevance." Because of this, you and the other person are the experts on what the situation calls for, even if you are not an expert on the disability itself. Think about what you and the other person will be Doing; what actions, activities, and behaviors would be taking place—regardless of the disability. Then Decide how relevant the disability is to these specific activities. Relevance is a combination of specific disability, time, roles, and activities. You'll have to put all the elements together and Decide how relevant the disability is in *this* specific situation.

You can think of relevance on a scale from one to five. Here are some examples to help illustrate some points on this imaginary scale.

If a deaf person is sitting next to you on a park bench, and your only activity is sitting, then the disability is probably of incidental importance to the interaction (Level One).

If the same deaf person is a customer in your department store, and she has an interpreter with her, the relevance of her disability goes up to Level Two: You'll need to adapt your communication style, but this won't be difficult because an

In this situation, the disability difference

1
is incidental

    2
    requires simple
    accommodations

        3
        is fairly important and
        requires more extensive
        accommodations

            4
            is a major focus

                5
                is the only reason
                or the primary reason
                for the interaction

interpreter is available. The sales interaction can continue as expected, and you two can perform the roles of salesperson and customer with no disruption and a small amount of accommodation.

Suppose you are a college professor with a deaf person in one of your classes. The difference moves closer to the center of the interaction scale and probably requires more extensive accommodation (Level Three). You will need to adapt a number of your teaching techniques because he uses a hearing aid and lipreads. Other students will need to accommodate his communication requirements; for example, he will need a seat with a good view of the instructor's face, and speakers should look directly at him.

If the deaf person is your wife and she has just lost her hearing as a result of an accident, surgery, or medication, then the disability is likely to be a major focus in your relationship for a long time to come (Level Four). Both you and your wife will embark on a path of tremendous emotional and behavior change, which will affect a variety of activities when you are together.

If you are a speech-language pathologist and have weekly therapy with this person, or if you are a graduate student advocate from the university's office of students with disabilities, then her disability is the primary reason for your interaction (Level Five).

Here are more examples in which disabilities have varying degrees of relevance to the situation:

- The nurse taking your blood pressure has a facial difference. (Level One)
- A guest at a birthday party wears leg braces and uses crutches. (Level One)
- As you approach the door of a restaurant, you note that the woman behind you uses a walker; instead of just passing the door to her, you step to the side and hold the door for her. (Level Two)
- A guest at a wedding reception is blind and asks you to describe the type and location of buffet table foods. (Level Two)
- The balloon man at a carnival looks at you with a quizzical expression after you've made a complicated order for several balloons. He gestures that he has a hearing impairment and also does not speak. You jot down your order on a tablet. (Level Two)
- The person next to you on an airplane is making gestures and jerking his head in ways that startle you; you're a little fearful but you've heard of a neurological condition called Tourette syndrome that can cause atypical movement. You make small talk to get more comfortable while deciding what to do next. (Level Three)
- You volunteer to learn how to guide visitors with disabilities through a local art museum. (Level Three)
- A close friend has just learned that his three-year-old child has autism; you often visit this family, and you're finding out more about this disability difference and how you can develop a relationship with the child. (Level Four)
- Your mother is recovering from a stroke and has lost her ability to speak; you've taken for granted weekly tele-

phone calls with her and now have to figure out new ways to stay in touch with her. (Level Four)

- A new photocopying technician at your office speaks in an overly loud voice and seems emotionally sensitive. Lately he's done a number of your orders incorrectly, especially the rush requests and telephone orders. You learn that he has mental retardation and Decide to explain your orders in a different way. You invite him to lunch to get to know him better and talk about more effective ways to place orders. (Level Four)
- As a visiting nurse, you provide services to people who use ventilators to breathe. (Level Five)
- As a school psychologist, you assist children with special needs as they move from segregated special education classes to inclusive classes. (Level Five)

Keep in mind that even after you Detect a person's difference, there will be many more things that you won't know about the other person. Even if you know that a person has a difference, you still might not know the following:

- The reason for the difference
- The person's unique strengths, talents, interests, or special needs
- The person's significant life experiences and values
- The person's adaptation to and attitudes about his difference
- The person's expectations, hopes, and fears about interacting with you

3. What Are My Action Options?

After you have considered your disability knowledge, the role and time frame expectations, and the relevance of the difference, you are ready to make a short mental list of a few action options. In each situation, the range of action possibilities is quite long. But you've been actively Deciding, so you've already honed down the choices to a few that make sense and are likely to work for you and the other person in this situation.

Your action options fall into three categories and you'll probably use all of them:

- Looking
- Saying
- Behaving

Looking

Looking can take many forms. Most people do not like to be stared at, and people with disabilities are no exception. Sometimes we think that any looking is the same as staring, so we avoid looking altogether. *Regarding* someone, however, is different from staring. Regarding acknowledges the person's disability in a nonjudgmental way. It's similar to glancing at his clothing, car, or baby. Staring, however, is a long, direct examination that implies an evaluation or judgment. It recasts the person as a curiosity. By contrast, turning away means the person is being ignored. Staring and looking away are thus both extreme behaviors that convert the person with a disability into an object of scrutiny or make her feel invisible.

Whether or not I talk with strangers depends on the way they look at me. They often get a strange expression and I can tell that my nose makes them sick. They make a funny face or cast their eyes aside. If this happens I look down or turn my head. But if a person looks squarely into my eyes without glancing at my nose, it makes me feel at ease and I can answer questions or talk without feeling self-conscious and ashamed.[5]

—Frances Macgregor

You have to look somewhere! It's rarely a problem simply to look into the other person's eyes. If the other person is blind, then still look into her eyes as you talk because it will make a difference in how she hears your voice. If she is in a wheelchair, then lower your face to get at her eye level, and sit down, if possible. Consider looking at the disability difference itself only when it fits the situation. Try smiling! That's almost always a safe behavior.

Remember, *with each person you encounter, the disability is only one of his characteristics.* Practice thinking about the impairment as just one attribute among many others. Suppose a co-worker has a paralyzed arm and also dresses well, has a friendly smile, and a sharp sense of humor. Or, she may use foul language, wear rumpled clothes, and be rude to her secretary. The more you know about her other characteristics, the less focus you put on her arm.

Awareness Activity

Watching People Looking at People

The next time you're in the park, at an airport, or in another public place, watch people looking at other people! Observe the ways in which they do or don't look at each other. Notice the difference between staring and regarding. Is there also an "admiring look"? Watch for people who look but then look away. Is anyone "looking through" other people? Do you see anyone looking shocked or disapproving?

Saying

People often get stalled in their encounters with others who have disabilities because they think there's only one right thing to say—but there is never only one right thing to say! Searching nervously for the "perfect" words will only frustrate you! Remember, what you say depends on how much you know about the disability, the time frame and roles, and activities in the situation. If the disability isn't pertinent to the roles, if there's little time, or if the disability isn't related to the situational activities, then it probably isn't a good idea to comment on it. For example, think back to the relevance in Question Two. The shape of the nurse's face isn't relevant to the task of taking your blood pressure, so there's no need to comment on it. In situations that call for quick and easy accommodation, such as holding a door for a person who uses a walker or explaining the type and location of foods at a buffet for a person who is blind, there's also no need to talk about the difference. You might think that it would be rude to ignore the person's disability—but you wouldn't ask questions about his other characteristics, such as personality, hair color, or shoe size, when these features aren't relevant to the situation.

When the disability *is* relevant to the situation, however, you have a lot of choices about what to say. Your action options include acknowledging the difference, asking for information, and asking whether assistance is needed.

Acknowledging the Difference Acknowledging the difference means that you mention it during your interaction. The only cardinal rule here is to use person-first language, which means not equating a person with her disability. For example, saying that a person has epilepsy is better than saying, "She's an epileptic." Also, you should avoid terms that evoke pity, such as "wheelchair-bound" or "afflicted with mental retardation." "Uses a wheelchair" and "has mental retardation" are better choices of words.

A person is not defined by her impairment or difference. Labels in themselves don't create or cure disabilities. The differences described in Chapters 5–10 may be evident to you even if you do not have the specific vocabulary to describe them. When you lack specific, respectful terms to describe a disability, however, your reactions may be more negative because the unfamiliar, unexpected, and unsettling aspects of the disability become the focus of the interaction. Understanding basic terminology can increase your comfort and enhance your actions.

Terminology shifts with the times, and labels go in and out of fashion. This is not because labels are trivial—just the opposite is true. *Labels are potent symbols*, not of the features of specific disabilities, but of society's attitudes and values about the people being labeled. Terminology changes are like evolution: gradual progress toward a more accurate and dignified vocabulary of differences.

In Chapters 5–10, we provide the terms professionals use when discussing disability differences. A person with a disability, however, may have specific opinions about self-identification and how he refers to his difference. You should take your cue from the person with whom you are interacting. When you know that person well enough and when it seems relevant to the situation, you should ask what *his own* word preferences are.

You can acknowledge a difference in several ways:

- By making a direct comment, such as "I see you're using a communication board"
- By making an indirect comment that accompanies an adaptation in your own behavior or to the environment, such as by saying, "Would you prefer a straw?" to a person whose arms appear paralyzed

Asking for Information　Even when a person's disability is relevant to the situation, it can be difficult to ask for information in a sensitive way. Here are some ways you can ask for information and still respect a person's privacy:

- Preface your request, such as by saying, "Please let me know if I'm prying."
- Explain why you're asking for information (i.e., why it's relevant to ask about the disability), such as by saying, "I'd like to know more about your disability, so we can do ___ better."
- Try asking the person about another aspect of himself, rather than his disability.
- As with acknowledgments, use person-first language.
- Ask, "Is there anything specific that you think is important for me to know about your _____?"

Offering Assistance　Always wait for an answer before you go ahead and provide assistance. When you touch a person or her equipment without asking first, she is likely to feel frightened or annoyed. With unwanted assistance, you risk appearing patronizing or intrusive. The following are examples of offers of assistance:

- "Would you like some help reaching that book?"
- "Would you like me to read this political petition to you?"
- "Do you want to trade desks so that yours faces the door and you can see people entering?"

Behaving

As you choose your actions, remember that there is not just one right way to handle a situation. But there are a few general guidelines to keep in mind:

- *Do* provide assistance if your offer was accepted.
- *Do* accommodate differences whenever you can (see Chapters 5–10 for specific ideas).
- *Do* focus on the other person's abilities and strengths.
- *Do* include the other person in the social situation, rather than exclude her.
- *Do* focus on the task or purpose of the situation, not the difference!

The Deciding process takes only a few moments, but it ensures that you're more in control of your actions and that your actions reflect your goals and values, rather than your sometimes uncomfortable or negative first-impression internal reactions to differences.

Key Points

Deciding What to Do

1. First, ask yourself, "Do I recognize this difference?" If you don't know, then try to categorize the difference (appearance, movement, communication, behavior, learning, or nonvisible).

2. Then ask yourself, "How relevant is the disability to *this* situation?" Consider the time frame, roles, and activities.
3. Finally, ask yourself, "What are my action options?" Possibilities include
   - Looking without staring
   - Acknowledging the disability using person-first words, asking for more information, or offering assistance
   - Assisting if your help is welcome, accommodating however you can, focusing on abilities, including instead of excluding, and getting on with the task of the situation

---

DOING: TAKING ACTION

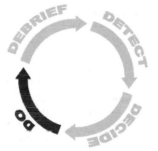

Doing, the third step of the 4D approach, is putting your decision into action. Most of us want to Do the "right thing." There is no way to guarantee success, but you can stack the deck in your favor. Here are some points to remember:

- If you accurately Detected the disability difference and your own feelings, then you're on the right track.
- If you spent a few extra seconds Deciding what to do, then you're more likely to succeed.
- Use the anticipation to guide you, not as a way of avoiding the situation—just *Do* it!
- If you know what you should do but lack confidence, then imagine that your child, your niece or nephew, or a

friend's child is watching you. What kind of role model do you want to be for them?

- Keep in mind that if you have an ongoing relationship with the other person, you'll have many chances to try other ways of interacting.

What happens when you're uncomfortable with the action you've decided to take? That is, what happens when you know what you should do but are nervous about doing it? Try to remember your relaxing skills from Detecting, the first step in the 4D approach. Relaxed breathing takes just a few seconds and enables you to think and act more effectively (see Endnote 3).

Awareness Activity
Doing

Observe a person with a disability interacting with family or friends. In a restaurant, at a public swimming pool, a concert, or an airport, notice people with disabilities and the people who accompany them. What do you notice about those *other* people?

- How are they *looking* at the person with the disability?
- What are they *saying* to the person? How often is the disability itself mentioned and in what contexts? How is assistance offered?
- How are they *behaving*?

Key Points
Doing

1. Don't skip Detecting and Deciding.
2. It's better to attempt interaction than to ignore or flee.
3. Observe what happened after you acted.

DEBRIEFING: MAKING IT BETTER NEXT TIME

You Detected a disability difference in someone, you Decided what to Do, and you went ahead and Did what you planned to Do. Now you can move on to the fourth step in the 4D approach, Debriefing, which means looking back and reflecting on the interaction and then looking forward to the next encounter with that specific person or to a similar encounter in the future. The next Awareness Activity may help you debrief. Answer these questions privately, in your thoughts, or talk them over with someone else who was present in the encounter.

Awareness Activity

Debriefing

1. **Think about what happened this time.**
   - Did I Detect the difference accurately?
   - Did I Detect and manage my own emotional reactions?
   - Did I relax and Decide what my action options were?
   - Were my actions consistent with my Decisions? If not, why not?
   - Was the purpose of the interaction accomplished?
   - What worked well? What didn't work well?
2. **Figure out what went wrong.** If the situation went well, then congratulate yourself—and keep up the good work! If the

situation did not go so well, then try to figure out why. Ask yourself whether any of these pitfalls occurred:
- I focused on the difference too much.
- I acted as though the difference weren't relevant at all, but actually it was.
- I got stuck in stress and forgot to relax.
- I got stuck in pity and didn't focus on abilities.
- I worried too much about "the right thing" to do, so I Did nothing.

3. **Think about what could happen next time.** Ask yourself what you could do differently next time.
   - Detect the disability and my feelings, and relax.
   - Decide more carefully, or consider more action options.
   - Look at the person or disability by regarding, not by staring.
   - Talk to the person with person-first words, ask for information, offer assistance, and so forth.
   - Interact differently by including instead of excluding and by focusing on the person and his *abilities*.

PUTTING IT ALL TOGETHER

The first few times you try the 4D approach, you might feel frustrated that you don't achieve complete comfort and control over the situation. This approach is not a precise recipe but rather a group of key ingredients that, when applied in good faith and in the recommended order, are likely to improve your understanding and interactions.

Suppose you try the 4D approach but still feel a great deal of discomfort interacting with people who have disabilities. You may need some additional strategies to increase your comfort with a specific disability difference. You might try

- Spending more time with people who have that difference
- Asking more questions, if the time and place are right
- Reading books and watching movies about the difference
- Contacting the appropriate self-advocacy organization

- Reflecting back on your childhood experiences with your own or others' differences to better understand why this specific disability is so unsettling

Chapters 5–10 show you how the 4D approach applies to specific disability differences. They begin where you are: observing, meeting, encountering, or relating to a person with a disability. These chapters are arranged using the categories and labels that you might use when first Detecting another person's difference. We often first notice differences in others by observing their *appearance, movement,* and/or *communication. Behavior* and *learning* differences can be subtle or obvious. Some disabilities are *nonvisible.* Each disability difference chapter

- Explores cultural myths, assumptions, and beliefs
- Helps you understand what the difference might feel like
- Explains some of the reasons why this difference occurs
- Describes typical interventions and supports
- Shares some experiences of people who have that difference
- Provides suggestions for interacting
- Offers facts at a glance
- Suggests readings and resources for more information

Most people do not think in terms of a diagnosis or medical label when they're at the shopping mall and see someone with a facial difference. Our first concern is *not* coming up with technical terms when a new co-worker stutters. Medical vocabulary can be very helpful when educating ourselves and speaking to professionals, but often people are in a situation in which they don't even know how to *ask* the medical question, much less answer it.

We often assume that a person has just one disability, when she actually may have two or three. But the following chapters address different kinds of disabilities separately because we can react most thoughtfully by considering just one category of disability at a time. Speech impairments may accompany a movement disability, such as cerebral palsy. Behavior differences may coexist with learning disabilities. It's very difficult to generalize about these combinations because there is more variety than similarity among people with disabilities. Even when a person has more than one disability, your attention is usually drawn to one difference at a time. For example, when a store clerk is assisting a customer who uses a wheelchair and also has a speech impairment, the speech difference will probably take "center stage." But when the customer leaves the store and wheels out to the bus stop, the bus driver's primary focus might be the vehicle's wheelchair lift.

5

People
Who Look Different

All societies establish cosmetic prescriptions for conformity to socially valued appearance and "beauty." In our society few compromises are allowed in meeting these prescriptions. Those persons who do not fit societal expectations in any major regard may anticipate a lifetime of challenges.[1]

—Joan Ablon

More than the wisdom of age, the knowledge of education, or the achievement resulting from hard work, our society worships appearance. We tend to judge ability by appearance, we judge character by appearance, and we even judge worth by appearance! These judgments influence our reactions to and interactions with people who look different from what is typical or expected.

MYTHS, ASSUMPTIONS, AND BELIEFS

Belief: The Face Symbolizes the Person

When you sit next to a stranger at a meeting or are introduced to a person at a party, your first connection is with his face. People look into each other's eyes for multiple signals of safety and information about whether—and how—to interact. We make a lot of assumptions about other people (and they do the same about us) in a split second.

The importance of the face in defining a person is evident in the words commonly used to describe facial differences, by the symbolism of the face in film and literature, and by the experiences of people with facial differences. People with facial differences are sometimes described as "disfigured," "damaged," "deformed," or "distorted," all words that carry stereotypes that extend beyond the physical difference.

In all human relationships, it is the face that is the symbol of or synonymous with the person. Intimately connected with communication, both verbal and nonverbal, and the region where the sense of self is located, it is the focus of attention whenever people meet. Because of its social significance, any condition that distorts it and makes it ugly or unsightly to look at can take precedence over all other personal and social traits and insidiously become the most important thing about that person.[2]

—Frances Macgregor

Myth: Appearance Influences Happiness and Success

"The body beautiful" is presented to us by the media and beauty industry as our ticket to happiness, success, and sexual fulfillment. Although we may think many of these campaigns are superficial and misleading, we go to great lengths and spend large amounts of money and time to disguise, minimize, conceal, and remove what we perceive to be appearance "flaws." Our personal daily grooming habits and our reactions to how other people look reflect our preoccupation with and anxiety about appearance.

People stare, and people make job determinations and reject persons with facial scars, those with severe spinal curvatures, shut and blinded eyes, limps, or paralyzed limbs. The public reacts in terms of how upsetting a disfigured person is to them. People spontaneously and quickly flinch away from disfigurements that scare them. . . . If people are deformed, they may be converted into things and treated in an altered manner.[3]

—Norman Bernstein

Beauty and ugliness are subjective concepts, but standards for both exist in every culture. We all have our own ideas of what we consider beautiful and ugly, and we all have yearnings and anxieties about our appearance. Research suggests that there are some universally desirable characteristics, such as facial and body symmetry, which are attractiveness concepts that cross racial and cultural boundaries. The differences between the words *irregular* or *atypical* and *disfigured* or *deformed* reflect an attitude about which kinds of appearance differences are stigmatizing.

Most of us agree that there are times when a person is less attractive. For example, chicken pox, a severe bout of eczema, or hair loss following cancer treatments may change a person's appearance in ways that make others feel unsettled.

What if a woman's face is permanently scarred from a severe burn, or a man's leg has been amputated, or a child's facial features are atypical? What about the wrinkles and sags due to aging? Do we truly accept a person's right to participate fully in community life and appear the way she truly is? Maybe it's time to question our beliefs that a person whose appearance falls outside of a basic standard should "do something" to look "better." Our society may be very sympathetic to a person's distress, but there is also an unspoken rule that he should stay out of the public eye or disguise his unsettling appearance to protect the rest of us from some sort of aesthetic shock.

It's hard to have a facial difference when the world would have you believe that a pimple is a crisis.[4]

—Hope Charkins

WHAT IT FEELS LIKE

We all have had appearance differences either from birth or acquired from an illness or injury. You probably remember people reacting to your appearance with extreme curiosity, staring, ridicule, or avoidance. Some of your differences may have been temporary; others permanent. You may have had braces on your teeth or crooked or missing teeth, hair growing or showing in unwanted places or no hair where you wanted some, eyeglasses or an eye patch, a skin condition such as moles, warts, scars, or birthmarks, or body features that you thought were too large, too small, too crooked, or too ugly.

During pregnancy, your hands and legs might have become very swollen. Your feet might have been so puffy you couldn't wear regular shoes. Everywhere you went, you felt as though people stared at your feet, legs, and hands. Or, perhaps one morning you awoke to find your eyes swollen and red. An allergic reaction had made your eyelids puffy, but you had some pressing tasks at your office, so you went to work anyway. Co-workers were sympathetic to your distress but obviously felt unsettled by your appearance.

Have you ever seen your reflection in a funhouse mirror? How did you react? And how do you react when you see a photograph of yourself? If you feel awkward or self-conscious about any aspect of your own appearance, then do you assume that other people who have appearance differences feel the same way? This may not be true, but it can be a helpful assumption *if* it motivates you to "look past" the difference and focus on the person and your interaction.

APPEARANCE DIFFERENCES YOU MAY ENCOUNTER

Most appearance characteristics fall within your personal comfort zone, so you instinctively notice people who have unfamiliar, unexpected, or unsettling facial features or body shapes. For example, seeing a man without arms might be unfamiliar to you. Seeing a person with an oxygen mask and tank is unexpected at a park but not in a hospital lobby. And seeing a woman with no hair might be very unsettling if you imagine her to be seriously ill or in pain. Reactions of admiration, curiosity, interest, surprise, shock, fear, or disgust can all increase your urge to grab a second look at someone even as you feel an urge to look away.

Facial Differences

Some people are so aesthetically repelled and even threatened by the sight of an abnormality that, despite genuine feelings of sympathy and compassion, they are unable to cope with or maintain a face-to-face situation. Others find interaction difficult because they are distracted or "put off" by a defect, even a relatively mild one such as a scarred lip or crossed eye, areas that happen to be those by which we most actively send signals to one another.[5]

—Frances Macgregor

Facial differences significantly influence our assumptions and interactions with others. Facial differences are quite varied and include the following:

- Asymmetry such as unbalanced eyes or ears at different heights
- Irregular features of the nose, chin, or jaw
- Skin variations such as birthmarks, scars, rashes, or discoloration
- Mouth variations such as crowded or missing teeth, or lip differences

- Prosthetic facial parts such as eyes, ears, a nose, or cheeks
- Hair characteristics such as baldness, missing eyebrows or eyelashes, or an unusual hairline
- Eye-related differences such as eyeglasses or patches, non-seeing eyes, or eyes that focus in different places

If you look at my eyes, you can see they're different. It is this visible difference which, especially during childhood, was the object of ridicule: I didn't realize that there was anything wrong with me until I started getting picked on by the kids. . . . When I started school, [I was] suddenly being called names! And then there were a lot of practical jokes. Glue in my hair, hiding my books, tripping me, stuff like that. It was rough growing up.[6]

—Marilynn Phillips

Body Differences

Atypical or Missing Body Parts

When we detect that someone looks different, we size her up for "wholeness." We expect to see two eyes, two ears, two arms and legs, and 10 fingers and toes, and we orient to missing, extra, or atypical body parts.

One of the most dramatic and traditionally unsettling examples of unusual body form is conjoined twins (sometimes called "Siamese twins"). The April 1996 cover of *Life* magazine featured the glowing faces of six-year-olds Abigail and Brittany Hensel, who are conjoined twins. The upbeat, compassionate article emphasized the girls' similarity to typical children.[7]

Atypical Body Size

We see certain body size differences more often than others. For instance, unusually obese or extremely thin people tend to draw our attention, although the average range of body weight often varies across age and cultural groups. It is common to see very tall or very short adults, but some height differences are unexpected. In a basketball game, we expect to see very tall men or women; in a horse race, short ones. Sometimes we do a double take to be sure that a very short adult is not a child who looks older than he really is.

Dwarf characters popularized on television, in films, and in children's games present dwarfs as creatures in caves, exotic "sidekicks," or persons with special or magical abilities. Smallness in size is a disvalued characteristic in our society, and may carry with it expectations of persons who are perennially childlike. The fact that dwarfs are ordinary persons with normal intelligence who work, play, and manage families and the business of daily life is less known to the general public.[8]

—Joan Ablon

Skin Differences

We are accustomed to seeing a range of skin colors related to race or ethnicity. Some people think freckles are cute but dislike birthmarks and skin blemishes. We expect a person's skin to have a uniform appearance, so we rapidly detect differences in skin texture, such as scars or unusual markings.

Psoriasis keeps you thinking. . . . You are forced to the mirror, again and again; psoriasis compels narcissism, if we can suppose a Narcissus who did not like what he saw. In certain lights, your face looks passable; in slightly different other lights, not. . . . I cannot pass a reflecting surface on the street without glancing in, in hopes that I have somehow changed.[9]

—John Updike

Awareness Activities

Appearance Differences

1. In Chapter 1, we asked you to observe the variety of ways people look, move, communicate, behave, and learn. Now that you have read more about appearance differences, we invite you to observe appearance differences again. This time, look carefully at the diversity of human appearance differences: the shapes of facial and body parts, the symmetry and irregularity of specific characteristics. Note which differences you find attractive and which make you feel unsettled. Which appearance differences are "built-in" to the person, and which differences are chosen—such as clothing, makeup, and adornment?

   As you observe people, become aware of the assumptions you make about them and the stereotypes you have based on their appearance.

2. Keep track of movies and television shows you watch during a given week, and look at the appearance characteristics of the characters. Actors are specifically chosen to portray certain character traits. How do the appearance differences of characters fit or challenge our stereotypes about heroes, villains, victims, and everyday people?

3. On a given day, do something to alter your appearance by wearing a sling, an eye patch, or a large bandage on your face. Pay attention to how people react to you, what they say to you, and how you feel about looking different.[10]

REASONS WHY PEOPLE LOOK DIFFERENT

Appearance differences *are not* disabilities; they are simply part of human diversity. But appearance differences are included in the Americans with Disabilities Act if they are considered to be a disability by others and if people are discriminated against because of their appearance. Appearance differences may be *related* to a disability, such as Down syndrome, cleft palate and lip, or missing limbs, or to an illness, such as cancer or scleroderma. Appearance differences have numerous causes, including events before or during birth, illnesses and medical conditions, injuries, and aging.

Events Before or During Birth

Even before a person is born, genes, hormonal imbalances, exposure to toxic substances, quality of prenatal care, and many other unforeseen factors and events may influence appearance and body shape. Differences such as Down syndrome and cleft palate and lip develop before birth, as do some variations in limb and facial features. Fetal alcohol syndrome, which causes both appearance differences and developmental disabilities, results from a mother's alcohol use during pregnancy.

Illnesses and Medical Conditions

Illnesses can cause a variety of appearance differences, such as skin changes and variations in body shape and weight. Several illnesses can result in changes in skin appearance: Scleroderma causes hardening of the skin, with swelling, stiffness, and pain in the joints, and rosacea causes a persistent redness or flushing of the face. For example, chicken pox can leave scars, and Kaposi's sarcoma, which may accompany AIDS, produces skin lesions and discoloration. Alopecia is an autoimmune condition that causes hair loss. Curvature of the spine can result from osteoporosis.

Sometimes an illness or injury does not change a person's appearance, but the side effects of medication and treatments do. Common examples are hair loss from chemotherapy or weight gain from steroids. Limb amputation may be necessary due to complications from diabetes.

Injuries

Appearance-changing injuries can occur at any age. Children and adolescents are particularly prone to injuries from bicycle, automobile, and motorcycle accidents, fires, fireworks, and gunshot wounds. In addition, adults may be injured in military combat or sports, household, or job-related accidents. Healed injuries can result in facial and body scars and altered limb and body shape.

Aging

Societal stereotypes about aging, appearance, and ability create reactions that range from ambivalence to extreme negativity toward normal signs of aging, such as graying or thinning hair, facial wrinkles, sags, or spots, and stooped posture. The reluctance to embrace aging often results in a parallel resistance to being considered disabled when the normal aging process causes hearing, visual, and memory impairments.

Visual Impairments

Visual impairments can result from a number of causes: prenatal influences, oxygen deprivation at birth, illnesses such as diabetes, injuries, or aging. They present themselves in many different ways. *Partially sighted* is a general term that refers a person with some sight. Mild impairments, or those that can be largely correctable with glasses, are often nonvisible.

Blindness is the lack of clarity or field of vision. A person who is considered *legally blind* has less than 20/200 vision in the better eye or a field of vision less than 20 degrees. *Low vision* is present if a person cannot read a newspaper at a normal viewing distance, even with glasses. A *cataract* is a cloudy covering of the lens inside the eye, which causes a progressive loss of vision. It occurs most frequently as people age. Regular exams can detect cataracts in the early stages of growth, and they can be surgically removed. *Glaucoma* is a disorder in which abnormal pressure within the eye results in decreased vision and blindness. Glaucoma is one possible side effect of diabetes. With early diagnosis of glaucoma, progressive vision loss can be slowed with prescription eyedrops.

Blindness usually is apparent in the way a person moves: with a Seeing Eye dog, a white cane, or both. Even though people with visual impairments don't look different in terms of body differences, our first awareness in an interaction is often the absence of typical eye contact. We connect to and interact with others through mutual gazes that convey our attention, emotions, understanding, and intention. When this gaze is absent, we often don't know where to look or how to interpret the other person's part in the communication.

INTERVENTIONS AND SUPPORTS

Most appearance differences do not require interventions because they are not truly impairments but rather *variations*. People with atypical height and body shapes have few intervention options.

Medical Interventions and Assistive Technology

A person's appearance can draw our attention because of the presence of a wheelchair, crutches, walker, cane, hearing aid, or eyeglasses. Many of us react to the "high tech" equipment that is becoming increasingly common. We are both fascinated by and fearful of devices such as voice synthesizers, ventilators, portable oxygen tanks, and artificial limbs.

Reconstructive surgery is one intervention to restore appearance and to improve functions such as breathing, eating, or walking. Surgical procedures for facial differences such as cleft palate and lip can restore the expected symmetry of facial features. Surgeons are now able to use artificial skin with burn survivors and can cover large scarred areas of the body.

Appearance-changing medical devices can be as subtle and common as teeth braces or as unusual as a tube connected directly to a person's throat or stomach.

Medical devices such as prostheses for limbs or facial parts are increasingly common as more people survive severe accidents and illnesses. The technology for prostheses has advanced to producing artificial skin and computerized limbs that operate with maximum efficiency and minimal differences in appearance. Prosthetic and transplanted body parts are increasingly available for legs, feet, hands, arms, fingers, and parts of the face.

People with small or damaged airways can now breathe through tracheostomy tubes, which are evident by the presence of a "plug" that is inserted surgically in the throat. Growth hormone treatments are being used (with some controversy) for some children with short stature.

Appearance-Enhancing Products

There is a growing array of products for people who have both temporary and permanent appearance differences including hairpieces, hair transplants, and head coverings for people with hair loss and specifically tailored clothing for women with mastectomies. Special makeup minimizes scars, uneven skin tone, and texture.

Visual Supports and Equipment

People who are blind or have specific visual impairments may look different because of the supports they use, such as white canes, Seeing Eye dogs, dark glasses, or thick eyeglasses. In some situations, you may observe a person making tentative steps or using his hands or fingers to detect markers in the environment. People with visual impairments have access to reading materials in braille or large print, books on tape, descriptive videos, and computers that read braille.

INTERACTING WITH PEOPLE WHO LOOK DIFFERENT

Person-First Words

Remember, a person is not defined by her impairment or difference. The appearance differences described in this chapter may be evident to you even if you do not have specific vocabulary to describe them. When you lack specific, respectful terms to describe a disability, however, your reactions may be more negative because the unfamiliar, unexpected, and unsettling aspects of the disability become the focus of the interaction. Understanding basic terminology can increase your comfort and enhance your actions.

As you interact with people who have appearance differences, remember to use person-first language. Avoid using negative words such as "disfigured," "defective," or "deformed." Here are some preferred terms:

- He has an appearance difference.
- She has a facial difference.
- He has a missing limb.
- He has short stature. (Some people of short stature prefer to be called "dwarfs" or "little people." The word "midget" is not appropriate.)
- She has a visual impairment.
- He has limited vision.
- She is blind.

Detecting Appearance Differences

You react to appearance differences that are unfamiliar, unexpected, or unsettling. You may not know why someone has short stature, a facial difference, or a missing limb, but at the instant of detecting it doesn't matter why. Your perception is that something about the person is atypical and is possibly outside your personal comfort zone.

Many appearance differences are simply variations of the range of human diversity and are not disabilities. Their social meaning often leads people to react to appearance differences with fear, repulsion, disgust, or pity. Fairy tales and films have repeatedly used appearance differences to portray evil and horror, encouraging unsettling reactions to people with appearance differences.

An appearance difference may be associated with a disability. It can be important to detect some related disabilities because you may need to alter more of your behaviors to accommodate the other person or to understand him better.

Deciding

1. What kind of appearance difference is this?
2. How relevant is the appearance difference to the situation?
3. What are my action options?

Understanding the social impact of an appearance difference can be very helpful in your interactions with someone who has a difference that is usually detected as unfamiliar or unsettling. It alerts you to anticipate uncomfortable reactions and to accommodate the person's special needs in the physical environment and in social situations.

Remember that there is more than one way to communicate and interact effectively. The Action Tips that follow are not prescriptions but rather possibilities for you to consider. It's better to try *some* action than to ignore or avoid the other person.

Action Tips

Appearance Differences

Most appearance differences are often *no more* than that. Don't assume that the person has any kind of ability difference unless there is some evidence. But because of our society's great emphasis on how people look, some appearance differences are stigmatized and become handicaps. Some differences in how people's faces or bodies are formed almost seem to be in a spotlight. When you have contact with someone with an appearance difference, you may feel two opposite urges: wanting to stare and wanting to look away. You may want to look at the difference to get used to it or to understand it better. You may want to look away because you don't want the person with the difference to feel uncomfortable or see your discomfort. To ignore the difference or to focus on another part of the person may make you feel even more uncomfortable. It takes practice to *not* display every distressing reaction to differences that are unfamiliar, unexpected, or unsettling.

- You can learn to "get past" an appearance difference by focusing on two things: the person, not his appearance, and the situation at hand. If your encounter is brief and impersonal, put aside your impulse to stare or ask questions. Your curiosity about a person's difference is not permission to inquire about it! If your interaction is more extended but the person's appearance is not relevant, focus on the purpose of your interaction. If the difference *is* relevant to the situation, then ask for relevant information. If not, wait for the other person to make reference to the difference before you bring it up. Don't claim you didn't even notice the difference if this isn't true.
- Remember that the other person may be waiting for a sign from you to find out whether you are interested or intrusive, compassionate or pitying, or relaxed or anxious. He may also want to find out whether you are able to see past the difference.

People with Visual Impairments

- If the other person is blind or has a significant visual impairment, be sure to identify yourself when you approach. If you want to shake hands, you can let her know this by asking, "May I shake your hand?"
- Nonverbal communication such as pointing, nodding, or smiling may go undetected by a person who cannot see your features, so accompany any gestures you make with words, such as "The waitress is here to take our order" or "Yes, I agree with you."
- Tell him if another person joins you or walks away.
- Even though you may not be able to have mutual eye contact, your speech will be easier to hear and understand if you look at the person's face.
- If you are walking together, describe any stairs or changes in ground texture ahead. Be sensitive and describe relevant sights and sounds in the environment.

- If the person has a Seeing Eye dog, suppress any desire you may have to pet it—even if you mean well. The dog is working and should not be distracted.

Doing

Despite your surprise at someone's appearance difference, you'll probably find that most of the time the difference has very little, if any, relevance to the interaction. Even when you're not sure what to say or how to behave, your motivation for the interaction to succeed is the most important message you can convey!

Whenever you interact with someone who has an appearance difference, there is not just one right thing to do. It does help, however, to remember these general pointers:

- Focus on the other person and his abilities and competencies.
- Include the person in the social situation. Don't talk around the person—always address him directly.
- Provide assistance if asked or if your offer was accepted.
- Get on with the task or purpose of the situation!

Debriefing

You Detected an appearance difference in someone, you Decided what to Do, and you went ahead and Did what you planned to do. Now you can move on to the fourth step in the 4D approach, Debriefing, which means looking back and reflecting on the interaction and then looking forward to the next encounter with that specific person or to a similar encounter in the future. The questions that follow can help you Debrief. You can answer them privately, in your thoughts, or talk them over with someone else who was present during the interaction.

Debriefing

1. **Think about what happened this time.**

- Did I Detect the difference accurately?
- Did I Detect and manage my own emotional reactions?
- Did I relax and Decide what my action options were?
- Were my actions consistent with my decisions? If not, why not?
- Was the purpose of the interaction accomplished?
- What worked well? What didn't work well?

2. **Figure out what went wrong.** If the situation went well, then congratulate yourself—and keep up the good work! If the situation did not go so well, then try to figure out why. Ask yourself whether any of these pitfalls occurred:
   - I focused on the difference too much.
   - I acted as though the difference wasn't relevant at all, but actually it was.
   - I got stuck in stress and forgot to relax.
   - I got stuck in pity and didn't focus on abilities.
   - I worried too much about "the right thing" to Do, so I Did nothing.

3. **Think about what could happen next time.** Ask yourself what you could do differently next time.
   - Detect the disability and my feelings, and relax.
   - Decide more carefully, or consider more action options.
   - Look at the person by regarding, not by staring.
   - Talk to the person with person-first words, ask for information, or offer assistance.
   - Interact differently by including instead of excluding and by focusing on the person and his *abilities*.

Appearance Differences

At-A-Glance

Number of Americans with Appearance Differences

- One in 17,000 infants is born with some type of albinism, with varying degrees of absence of pigmentation in eyes, skin, and hair.[11]

- 3.3 million cosmetic surgeries were performed in 1996 (three quarters were for women). In 1996, 1.5 million pounds of fat were liposuctioned out of nearly 300,000 adults.[12]
- The most common birthmark, a port wine stain, appears in three out of 1,000 infants.
- Psoriasis affects 6.4 million people, with 150,000–260,000 new cases every year; 10%–15% of people with psoriasis are younger than the age of 10.[13]
- Rosacea affects 13 million people.[14]

People with Appearance Differences

Jim Abbott, baseball pitcher
Billy Barty, actor
Andrea Bocelli, opera singer
Chang and Eng, conjoined twins who were sideshow performers
Ray Charles, jazz musician
W.C. Fields, actor
Mikhael Gorbachev, former Russian premier
Linda Hunt, actress
Daniel Inouye, U.S. Senator
Helen Keller, author
Matt Luke, baseball player
Ved Mehta, author
Gheorghe Muresan, actor
Tom Thumb, sideshow performer
John Updike, author
Bree Walker, television news anchor
Stevie Wonder, singer

READINGS
AND RESOURCES

Books

More than Meets the Eye:
The Story of a Remarkable Life and a Transcending Love
J. Brock & D.L. Gill (HarperCollins, New York, 1994)

Body Images: Development, Deviance, and Change
T.F. Cash and T. Pruzinsky (Eds.) (The Guilford Press, New York, 1990)

Children with Facial Difference: A Parents' Guide
H. Charkins (Woodbine House, Bethesda, MD, 1996)

Born Different: Amazing Stories of Very Special People
F. Drimmer (Bantam, New York, 1991)

"Look at My Ugly Face!" Myths and Musings on Beauty
and Other Perilous Obsessions with Women's Appearance
S. Halprin (Viking, New York, 1995)

Second Sight
R. Hine (University of California Press, Berkeley, 1993)

On Sight and Insight: A Journey into the World of Blindness
J. Hull (One World Press, Oxford, England, 1997)

Planet of the Blind
S. Kuusisto (Dial Press, New York, 1998)

Face to Face
V. Mehta (Oxford University Press, Oxford, England, 1978)

The Me in the Mirror
C. Panzarino (Seal Press, Seattle, 1994)

An Anthropologist on Mars: Seven Paradoxical Tales
O. Sacks (Alfred A. Knopf, New York, 1995)

Face Value
L. Shafritz (1994; Available by writing the author, Post Office Box 45-5854, Los Angeles, CA 90045)

You Don't Have to Be Blind to See
J. Stovall (Thomas Nelson Publishers, Nashville, TN, 1989)

Self-Consciousness: Memoirs
J. Updike (Alfred A. Knopf, New York, 1989)

Films

The Best Years of Our Lives (1946)

The Miracle Worker (1962)

Phantom of the Opera (1962)

Tell Me that You Love Me, Junie Moon (1970)

The Elephant Man (1980)

The Hunchback of Notre Dame (1982)

Mask (1985)

Edward Scissorhands (1990)

Beauty and the Beast (1991)

Scent of a Woman (1992)

Lorenzo's Oil (1993)

Man Without a Face (1993)

Frankie Starlight (1995)

Powder (1995)

My Giant (1998)

The Mighty (1998)

Video

Living with Facial Disfigurement
Program Development Associates, 5620 Business Avenue, Suite B,
Cicero, NY 13039 (800-543-2119)

Self-Advocacy/Support Organizations

About Face USA
Post Office Box 93, Limekiln, PA 19535 (800-225-3223;
e-mail: abtface@aol.com)

American Foundation for the Blind
11 Penn Plaza, Suite 300, New York, NY 10011 (212-502-7661;
www.afb.org; e-mail: afbinfo@afb.org)

Cleft Palate Foundation
104 S. Estes Drive, Suite 204, Chapel Hill, NC 27514 (919-933-9044;
www.cleft.com

Little People of America, Inc.
Post Office Box 9897, Washington, DC 20016 (800-243-9273)

National Association for Visually Handicapped
22 West 21st Street, New York, NY 10010 (212-889-3141;
e-mail: staff@navh.org)

National Down Syndrome Society
666 Broadway, Suite 800, New York, NY 10012-2317
(800-221-4602; www.pcdtd.com/ndss/)

National Limb Loss Information Center
900 East Hill Avenue, #285, Knoxville, TN 37915-2568
(423-524-8772; www.amputee-coalition.org)

National Organization for Albinism and Hypopigmentation
1530 Locust Street, #29, Philadelphia, PA 19102 (800-473-2310;
www.albinism.org)

National Psoriasis Foundation
6600 Southwest 92nd Avenue, Portland, OR, 97223
(800-723-9166; www.psoriasis.org)

National Rosacea Society
800 S. Northwest Highway, #200, Barrington, IL 60010
(888-662-5874; www.rosacea.org; e-mail: rosaceas@aol.com)

Phoenix Society for Burn Survivors
11 Rust Hill Road, Levittown, PA 19056-2311 (800-888-2876;
www.lewisville.com/nporgs/phoenix)

United Scleroderma Foundation
89 Newbury Street, #201, Danvers, MA 01913 (800-722-4673;
www.scleroderma.com)

6

People
Who Move Differently

If I can't run, I might be an inferior messenger if
time is critical. However, my inability to run might
just as likely have stimulated me to address time
more creatively or to develop ways to send
messages swiftly that are as efficient as running,
or vastly superior.[1]

—Carol Gill

We are a moving, doing society. Physical strength and agility
are second only to appearance in our society's emphasis on
what is important about the human body. We believe that our
bodies define us, that they are *who* we are. How good we look
and how well we move are foremost in our evaluations of ourselves and others.

We equate mobility with independence, self-control, moving forward, and getting ahead. "Making great strides," "choosing the fast track," and "moving up in the world" are symbols of American energy and success. Many people share some common stereotypes about movement differences, and, like most stereotypes, they are often hard to change.

MYTHS, ASSUMPTIONS, AND BELIEFS

Assumption: Problems with Movement = Problems with Thinking

Many people assume that someone who has restricted movement or who uses an assistive device such as a wheelchair or a walker also has problems learning and understanding—that a slow body is a sign of a slow mind. Indeed, some movement disabilities are related to other differences, including cognitive, communication, behavior, and appearance differences, but it is not correct to assume without evidence that other differences exist.

Because it's common to assume that there's a connection between movement and thinking, you might initially feel anxious or fearful when you meet someone with unusual or atypical movements, such as tics or impaired coordination and balance. You might be afraid that you're witnessing a loss of behavior control. You may feel unsettled when you meet a person who is paralyzed because you don't know what to expect about his thinking ability.

Myth: Standing and Walking = Independence, Strength, and Success

The phrases "Stand up for yourself," "Stand and be counted," and "Walk like a man" are commonly used to invoke images of strength, independence, and leadership. In our society, all of these are virtues. When a person's motor control falters—

even a bit—the common stereotype is that the person becomes dependent, weak, and even a failure. In our tradition of worshipping cowboys, superheroes, and jocks, the implications of limited movement often weigh more heavily on men than on women.

Myth: Fast Is Good. . . . So Faster Is Better

Our society's values about productivity and efficiency are manifested in our pace of living. You've probably heard a few of these phrases: "Get a move on," "Time is money," and "Take the fastest route from A to B." Speed is equated with success and progress. The faster you move, the more you will get done, and the more successful you will be. Most of us have a hard time being slowed down by others: slow drivers on the freeway, the indecisive person in front of us at the fast-food take-out counter, or the person in the crosswalk using a cane. In our society of instant communication via cellular telephones, pagers, call waiting, faxes, and e-mail, we are increasingly conscious of our fast pace of movement and often become impatient with those who get in our way.

When the pace of life increases, stamina becomes more important to participation in every aspect of society. . . . Everyone who cannot keep up is urged to take steps (or medications) to increase their energy, and bodies that were once considered normal are pathologized. . . . I have noticed that it has become increasingly unacceptable to "slow down" as one ages, when not long ago it was expected.[2]

—Susan Wendell

WHAT IT FEELS LIKE

We all have trouble from time to time with our movement. If you have ever had an arm or leg in a cast or have had to lie in bed while recovering from major surgery, then you know what muscle weakness is like. If you have had tennis elbow, tendonitis, or carpal tunnel syndrome in your wrists and fingers, then you have experienced pain with the slightest arm movement. If you have ever suffered the stiffness resulting from whiplash in a car accident, you learned how important movement is in everyday activities such as taking a shower, driving a car, or shopping for groceries.

If you have experienced impaired movement, you learned how much of your daily living environment you take for granted and how much you need your environment to support you. If your condition was temporary, you coped in one way or another, assuming you would recover at least some of your functioning. If you have a long-term condition that restricts your daily activities, you have had to find ways to adapt, learn new skills, modify old ones, and give up others. You have had to change your environment to fit your new needs, such as obtaining special aids and equipment, adapting your car, or adding ramps or handrails in your home. Possibly you need assistance from others for some activities of daily living.

MOVEMENT DIFFERENCES YOU MAY ENCOUNTER

You see a young man coming down a hallway, entering your business, or sitting next to you in a class. If his movement varies from your expectations, your first reaction is to check to see whether all of his body parts are there. You notice his large-muscle movements: the position of his torso, how he holds his head, and what his arms and legs are doing. You make a quick, sweeping review of how they are working together. You expect that his muscles *will* do what they are supposed to do and that they *will not* do anything they aren't supposed to do. So, any movement difference you detect will be unexpected. Some movement differences may also be unfamiliar to you and may be unsettling, such as seeing a woman with precarious balance, a child who has uncontrolled movements, or a man who seems to move with discomfort or pain.

Unpredictable Movements

Unpredictable movements result from muscles that do what they're not supposed to do. Unpredictable movements are frequently seen with spasticity and tics. Although *spasticity* is stiffness of the muscles due to increased reflexes and can make movements appear jerky, it is not a "jerky" movement itself. *Tics* are unexpected facial or body movements, throat sounds such as humming, or the blurting out of words, common in Tourette syndrome (see Chapter 8).

Uncoordinated Movements

Uncoordinated movements include difficulty using large muscles (upper arm and leg muscles), which may result in balance problems and an uneven gait, or difficulty using small muscles (hand, finger, and facial muscles), which may result in problems with eating, speaking, writing, and other fine motor tasks.

Repetitive Movements

Repetitive movements include *tremors* (continuous shaking), which are often apparent in hand, arm, and neck muscles and are common in Parkinson's disease. Repetitive movements are similar to the sounds coming from a broken record: The same action is repeated over and over. A person with compulsive behaviors may feel the urge to repeat certain movements such as straightening her desk, washing her hands, or walking through a doorway several times before moving forward (see Chapter 8).

Restricted Movement

Restricted movement includes facial or body parts that have limited or no movement due to paralysis, muscle weakness, or stiffness and movements that a person limits to minimize pain. Restricted movements can range from stiffness in the neck from a car accident to quadriplegia, which is paralysis of the upper and lower body due to spinal cord injury.

Movement Changes that Can Occur with Age

Getting older is not a disability, but physical changes, illnesses, and injuries that occur later in life may result in movement limitations that eventually become disabling. These changes do not occur for everyone; and with health maintenance, nutrition, and exercise, the frequency and intensity of some of these limitations can be reduced. Some of the following movement differences may occur with age:

- Physical reaction time may slow down and impair ability to drive or handle machinery.
- Accuracy of vision and hearing may decline, and often the person will not be aware of or is reluctant to acknowledge the change. Reduced vision or hearing may cause a person to compensate by moving more slowly but may also increase risks for accidents while crossing streets or driving.
- Reduced strength, energy, and stamina may require shorter periods of work or concentration and more frequent rest breaks.
- Walking may become more difficult because of changes in posture, balance, and gait along with changes in vision and hearing.
- Accidents that affect movement, such as falls, may occur more easily or may require longer healing time, especially with conditions such as osteoporosis (reduction of bone density).

Awareness Activity

People Who Move Differently

1. The next time you visit a museum, ask at the admissions desk whether a wheelchair is available; if so, experience

the exhibits from a seated perspective. How do you see the exhibits differently? How do other visitors react to you? Note the accessibility of restrooms, exhibits, gift shops, and dining areas. You can also do this activity with a friend. Take turns using the wheelchair while the other pushes or walks alongside. Observe how other visitors react to each of you and how that affects your feelings about each role.

2. Wear a sling on one arm—not your writing arm—for a half day to experience movement restriction. Then switch the sling to your writing arm for several hours to feel even more limitations. Compare the two experiences in terms of the kinds of activities you cannot do independently. Make a list of modifications that would have made certain tasks easier, such as household chores, self-care, eating, and working.

3. Plan a day when you do everything at a slower speed: dressing, eating, driving, walking, shopping, and working. Notice your positive and negative reactions to moving slower. How do other people react to your slowed pace of movement?

4. To experience difficulty with coordination, peel an orange with one hand. Does this task become frustrating to you? Think of possible solutions that would make the task easier for someone who experiences this kind of challenge regularly.

REASONS WHY PEOPLE MOVE DIFFERENTLY

Everything you do is caused by a muscle contraction—even breathing! More than 600 muscles and 206 bones help your body to function. This chapter is about the working muscles of the body: the large muscles that control your posture and movement of your head, trunk, arms, and legs, and the small muscles that control tiny movements of your face, throat, hands, and feet.

People gesture and move in myriad ways and rhythms. These different ways of moving are *learned* differences that may be a cultural trait or individual style. Our focus here, however, is on movement differences that are related to a *motor impairment* such as cerebral palsy, an *injury* to the spinal cord, or an *illness* such as arthritis. Movement differences are most detectable when a person cannot use or has difficulty moving his extremities—arms, hands, legs, and feet—or lacks the strength to walk, grasp, or lift objects. For a person to carry out any movement as intended, four things have to happen:

- The brain must be able to send a specific message to the spinal cord.
- The spinal cord must be able to convey the message through the nerves to the muscles.
- Bones, joints, and nerves must be in good working order.
- Muscles must be able to receive and act on the message.

The Brain Must Be Able to Send a Specific Message to the Spinal Cord

All movement begins in the brain: The *motor cortex* initiates and controls movement, and the *cerebellum* coordinates and fine tunes action and speech. If there is any damage to the motor cortex or the cerebellum, movements may be disordered. Some of the more familiar disorders are caused by cerebral palsy, stroke, Parkinson's disease, and amyotrophic lateral sclerosis (ALS).

Cerebral Palsy

Cerebral palsy is a condition caused by damage to the brain before, during, or soon after birth. It is not hereditary and is not progressive. Some people who have cerebral palsy may have difficulty speaking clearly. Intelligence may be but is not always affected. Many people, however, mistakenly assume that people who have cerebral palsy also have mental retardation, especially when their speech is difficult to understand.

Depending on which part of the brain has been damaged, muscles are affected in different ways. Some people with cerebral palsy may have muscles that are stiff and tight, causing restricted movement. Some people may experience uncontrollable movements of their facial, trunk, and limb muscles. Other people with cerebral palsy have a disturbed sense of balance and depth perception. Cerebral palsy can affect some or all of a person's limbs. Sometimes only one side of the body is affected.

Think of your cerebellum (motor coordination center) like a miniature computer. Whenever you want to make a move, the cerebellum sends out a message to the part of the body that you want to coordinate. Well, my cerebellum sends out a message that may or may not get there the way it should. Messages from my cerebellum are kind of like interdepartmental memos—they go out, but you never know if they will get there and what effect they will have on people when they arrive.

My main difficulties are with fine motor skills. That is why I'm able to operate a vehicle [which uses] 80 to 90 percent gross motor skills. I have trouble doing up my top button, threading a needle, and eating some types of food like soup. . . .

Have you ever noticed the difference between eating soup and eating a sandwich? When you are eating a sandwich you are not using as many of your fine motor skills. But when you are eating soup, you use many more fine motor skills. So when I have soup, everybody has soup.[3]

—Lee Bussard

Stroke

A *stroke* is a sudden block of blood flow to the brain, caused by a blood vessel that has become clogged. Strokes can also result from brain injuries or aneurysms, which occur when a weakened blood vessel bursts. The brain damage from strokes usually causes some degree of body paralysis, difficulty speaking and moving, memory problems including distractibility and short attention span, and visual perception problems that can affect balance and distance judgment. Transient ischemic attacks (TIAs) are "mini-strokes" that often precede a major stroke. Common symptoms are sudden onset of confusion, ataxia, and memory loss.

[Since my stroke] I have become friends with slowness, both as a concept and as a way of life. In the past, I was noted for the [impressive] speed with which I could accomplish things. At first, the contrast was a source of great frustration. I had to learn to be patient. . . . Six months ago, I could slip across the street to post a letter in the time it takes to type this sentence. Now I would have to raise myself up from my chair, find my cane, limp to the front door (say, three minutes), negotiate the steps to the street, and make my way to the corner (roughly five minutes), and then hobble back and collapse, exhausted, on the sofa, as though I had just run a marathon. Every day, I am acutely reminded that there is a world out there, a world I cannot be part of in quite the same way. One tangible effect of my illness, however, has been a more Zen-like response to the pressures and anxieties of the world, and in my new mood of self-examination I am inclined to say, "So what?"[4]

—Robert McCrum

Parkinson's Disease

Parkinson's disease is a progressive disorder caused by the brain's inability to manufacture a chemical that signals the muscles to move. Symptoms include involuntary tremors, movements that appear stiff, and balance problems. Speaking may become slower and slurred due to stiffening of muscles in the throat and face, but cognition is not directly affected. Balance problems during walking often occur.

For years, [Muhammad Ali] was terrified privately at what Parkinson's had sometimes wrought—tremors, a mask-like face, an unsteady gait. And, most traumatic for him, a hushed voice which no longer made the world listen up. . . . His once-brash proclamations and poetry all but silenced, Ali lowered his profile because of his impairment. He feared rejection, warily viewed the media; live television interviews were out of the question. . . . The [Olympic] torch lighting gave him courage and more self-confidence to face the camera and the public. . . . "I wondered why people cried when I lit the torch. . . . Some disabled people had given up—they didn't care. . . . But when they saw me on TV, standing before the whole world, some said, 'If he can do it, why can't I?' "

After the torch lighting, a woman called Ali's office and cried as she told the story of how her husband, beset with Parkinson's, hadn't left their home in years—until he watched Ali on TV. The next day, the man stopped everyone on the street and proudly informed them: "I've got 'Muhammad Ali disease!' "[5]

—John Saraceno

Amyotrophic Lateral Sclerosis

ALS, a progressive disorder, is also known as Lou Gehrig's disease. Nerve cells send motor messages from the brain, to the spinal cord, to the muscles. If these nerve cells die, movement messages cannot be transmitted to the spinal cord, and muscles gradually deteriorate. The disease can affect any set of muscles in the body, including those used for walking, talking, breathing, swallowing, bowel and bladder control, and other bodily functions.

Before my condition [ALS] had been diagnosed, I had been very bored with life. There had not seemed to be anything worth doing. But shortly after I came out of hospital, I dreamt that I was going to be executed. I suddenly realized that there were a lot of worthwhile things I could do if I were reprieved. In fact, although there was a cloud hanging over my future, I found to my surprise that I was enjoying life in the present more than before.[6]

—Stephen Hawking

The Spinal Cord Must Be Able to Convey the Message

For a message to travel from the brain to a muscle, it has to pass through nerves in the spinal cord. All motor and sensory messages travel from the brain to the body and back again by way of the spinal cord. If there is any damage to the spinal cord, then motor messages may not reach the muscles, resulting in paralysis or extreme muscle weakness. Spinal cord interruptions that affect movement include multiple sclerosis (MS), polio, and spinal cord injury.

Multiple Sclerosis

MS is a progressive disease that results from deterioration of the protective layer surrounding the nerves in the spinal column and causes increasing muscle weakness. Other symptoms include blurred vision, tremors, fatigue, and loss of feeling or paralysis in the arms or legs. MS usually begins in young adulthood and follows a very individualized and unpredictable pattern for each person, with varying degrees of severity, remission, and progression.

As my MS has worsened over the 30 years that I have had it, each new set of symptoms demanded creative changes in my living environment and in my social and professional life. For a while I tried to cover up my symptoms, even though my bouts of dizziness while I was walking and my stumbling gait sometimes made me look like I was drunk. I avoided walking where people could watch and stare.[7]

—Shaena Engle

Polio

Also known as infantile paralysis, *polio* is a viral infection that attacks the spinal cord. It can cause paralysis from the neck down or paralysis of the lower extremities only. Paralysis of the upper body usually requires the support of a ventilator, whereas lower body paralysis requires braces and crutches or a wheelchair. Until the mid-1950s, when vaccines were developed, polio often spread in epidemic proportions. New cases have practically disappeared, but many adults who contracted the virus as children continue to have postpolio effects. Former president Franklin Roosevelt had polio, but his motor impairment was concealed from the public eye because of the stigma of having a disability.

My paralysis made gestures impossible, and I was amazed at how profoundly that compromised my ability to communicate subtlety. I could no longer convey mixed meanings or mute aggression by hand signals, and many jokes were completely impossible to tell without them. It is also hard to find a substitute for pointing to clarify direction, and it is hard to show resolve without standing firmly. As a result, I feel awkward when I speak now, almost as though I were tongue-tied.[8]

—Arnold Beisser

Spinal Cord Injury

Spinal cord injury usually results from trauma such as automobile or sporting accidents and gunshot wounds. Sometimes the spinal cord does not develop properly before birth, and the newborn baby has a condition known as *spina bifida*. The severity and location of impairment on the spinal cord determine which muscles are affected. The higher along the spinal cord, the higher in the body paralysis occurs. Injury resulting in upper and lower body paralysis is called *quadriplegia. Paraplegia* refers to paralysis of two limbs, most commonly the legs.

When they told me what my condition [spinal cord injury] was, I felt that I was no longer a human being. . . . Then Dana came into my room and knelt down to the level of my bed. We made eye contact. I said, "Maybe this isn't worth it. Maybe I should just check out," and she was crying and she said, "But you're still *you* and I love *you!*" and that saved my life. . . . All that self pity comes in the beginning. And it does recur. But what you begin to say to yourself is, "What life can I build?" "What life do I have?" and the answer, surprisingly, is "more than you think."[9]

—Christopher Reeve

Bones, Joints, and Nerves Must Be in Good Working Order

Other parts of the body may also interrupt the path of a movement message from the brain to a muscle. Any damage or weakness in bones, joints, or the nerve pathways between the spinal cord and muscles can distort or prevent movement. For example, arthritis and osteoporosis are two diseases in which bone and joint interruptions cause movement differences.

Arthritis

Arthritis is a disease that causes swelling, pain, and restricted movement in the joints. *Rheumatoid arthritis* prevents movement because of excess fluid buildup resulting in joint swelling and pain, especially in the knees, elbows, hands, and feet. *Osteoarthritis* involves the degeneration of cartilage that protects the bones. It frequently occurs in singular sites, such as the hips or knees. Common symptoms of arthritis, such as muscle stiffness and fatigue, range from mild to severe and may come and go. Arthritis affects movement in various ways. For example, muscle stiffness may affect walking, climbing stairs, driving, and sports activities; muscle stiffness in arms and hands may affect housework, writing, sewing, typing, and hobbies. Fatigue from arthritis can prevent or slow performance of daily tasks at home and work.

Osteoporosis

Osteoporosis is a bone disease resulting from reduction in bone mass and occurs most frequently in older women. The disease has no symptoms until a bone fracture occurs and does not heal properly. A person with osteoporosis is prone to more fractures, chronic pain and weakness, height loss, and curvature of the spine.

Muscles Must Be Able to Receive and Act on the Message

Muscle problems that interfere with movement include low, high, or changing muscle tone and muscular dystrophy.

Low, High, or Changing Muscle Tone

A person's movement may be different because his muscles are too loose, too stiff, or fluctuate between being loose and stiff. With reduced muscle tone, a person may not be able to grasp or lift objects and may have difficulty sitting up or even holding his head up. Too much muscle tone causes muscles to be stiff and creates trouble with walking or other movements.

Muscular Dystrophy

Muscular dystrophy is a general term for several genetic muscle diseases in which voluntary muscles degenerate. There are nine major types of muscular dystrophy, which may be apparent at birth or may not appear until adulthood. The most common form causes slowly progressing muscle weakness in adults beginning with the face, neck, feet, and hands. The most common form of muscular dystrophy, *Duchenne muscular dystrophy,* appears between 2 and 6 years of age, and a wheelchair is usually needed for mobility by 12 years of age.

INTERVENTIONS AND SUPPORTS

There is no cure for most movement disorders, but there are therapies and medications to reduce or control symptoms. Children and adults with movement differences can sometimes strengthen existing motor skills and maintain mobility by using a wide range of rapidly evolving equipment and technology. Adaptations in the environment can make a major difference in providing alternative ways of functioning in everyday life.

Adapting the Environment

People with long-term movement disabilities and their advocates have encouraged manufacturers to create and adapt furniture, tools, and sports and recreation equipment. Many of the innovations are designs that provide more convenience and comfort for *everyone* and are now known as universal design. For example, ramps, elevators, larger public bathrooms, wider doorways, curb cuts, and lower water fountains make life easier for parents with young children, older adults, and many others.

Home adaptations include wider doorways, entrance ramps, and lower kitchen and bathroom counters. Many new homes and major remodeling projects are increasingly incorporating accessible modifications as standard features. Offices, stores, and other public buildings are now required by the Americans with Disabilities Act to include such features as lowered drinking fountains, elevators and/or ramps, wider doorways, and adapted restrooms. In Great Britain, builders are required to incorporate universal design for accessibility in all new homes.

When a movement impairment affects speech, a number of communication devices can be used. People who have limited or no use of their hands can use adapted telephone systems and computers that are activated by voice, by mouth movements, or by eye blinks (see Chapter 7).

The right "assistive device" can turn passive patients into independent consumers, able to go to school, work, rear families, and live on their own. Machines now speak for the voiceless, see for the sightless, and move and touch for those who cannot move their own muscles.[10]

—Joseph P. Shapiro

Mobility Support

Walking

Walkers, canes, crutches, braces, and prostheses assist people with walking. People who use these devices also have increased comfort, stability, and balance and reduced fatigue and pain. These aids allow people to manage their lives and have more control, choices, and access to the community. They can walk longer distances, travel more easily, and navigate stairs and slopes. People with visual impairments walk with white canes to check their path and signal to others that they are moving with limited vision.

Transportation

Cars and vans have many available adaptations, including special controls for drivers with paralysis or lower body weakness and lifts and ramps for easy entry. Methods of public transportation such as buses and trains also incorporate lifts or ramps for easier access.

Wheelchairs

A wheelchair is one of the first images many people have when they think of a person with a disability, and it is used as the international symbol for disability—the official white-on-blue design signaling accommodations such as parking spaces, restrooms, ramps, and automatic doors. Many of us have traditionally thought of wheelchairs as cumbersome pieces of medical equipment, and people who use them have been thought of as "crippled" or elderly. Because of these stereotypes, many people who could greatly increase their mobility with a wheelchair resist using one. Most wheelchair users, however, view this equipment as a *solution* to a mobility limitation.

Some people who use wheelchairs also walk with braces and crutches, such as a person who has postpolio paralysis. Some people use wheelchairs following surgery and to alleviate chronic back or hip pain. Using a wheelchair can prevent or reduce fatigue and strain, a major benefit for people with heart or breathing problems, back or leg weakness, or general frailty from aging or recovery from illness. For people with balance problems, a wheelchair reduces the chance of falling.

Design and technology are advancing steadily, and wheelchairs have become sophisticated mobility tools. Manual or self-propelled chairs require reliable upper body strength, or assistance from another person. Electric chairs use batteries that power a directional switch box usually operated by an arm or hand or by a "sip and puff" mouth device. There are sports chairs for tennis, basketball, racing, and cross-country riding, and there are full-size tricycles for recreation. Chair designs include a variety of colors and options for comfort or convenience, including a wide selection of chairs for people of all ages. Electric scooters, similar to small golf carts, have three wheels and are especially convenient in retirement and other residential communities.

It took years of being in a wheelchair before I could be truly amazed by what it could do, and what I could do with it. On a winter night in Chicago, after a light snow, I rolled across a clean stretch of pavement and felt the smooth frictionless glide of the icy surface. I made a tight turn and chanced to look around and back from where I had just come. The street lamp cast soft icicle rainbows that arched over and highlighted the white surface with bursts of color. Tracing out from where I was I saw two beautiful lines etched in the snow. They began as parallel and curved, then they crossed in an effortless knot at the place where my wheelchair turned to look back. My chair had made those lines. The snow was the signature of every turn I had ever made, revealed by the wintry template of newly fallen snow. It was the first time I dared to believe that a wheelchair could make something, or even be associated with something, so beautiful.[11]

—John Hockenberry

Aides and Assistants

Aides and Personal Assistants

Some people with movement differences need help from another person to carry out some activities of daily living, such as dressing, eating, getting from place to place, shopping, driving, housekeeping, and cooking. Sometimes this assistance or caregiving is provided by a family member, such as a parent, a spouse or partner, or a sibling. Friends, neighbors, and others from the community may also volunteer to assist people with disabilities, and some organizations deliver meals or provide transportation for people who are homebound and request the service. A person who is paid to provide assistance or health care services is usually called an *aide* or a *personal assistant*.

Assistance Dogs

Traditionally, assistance dogs were trained to work with blind people but are now being trained for people who have other disabilities such as hearing impairments, cerebral palsy, spinal cord injury, and seizure disorders. Assistance dogs (also called guide dogs, working dogs, or service dogs) are trained to perform a wide range of specific tasks: to alert a deaf person to telephones and doorbells, transport objects to and from people with movement limitations, turn switches off and on, and sense the onset of seizures and alert family members or aides. Less commonly, other animals such as monkeys are trained to provide assistance.

Therapies and Medications

Intensive rehabilitation therapy can be effective for many people, depending on the severity and location of the person's impairment. Exercise and physical therapy can help a person with a movement difference to maintain muscle and joint tone. Physical therapists develop individualized exercises to develop range of motion and strength, and they create movement regimens to target specific impairments. Meditation and deep-breathing routines can help maintain respiratory strength and reduce tension. Medications are available to slow muscle degeneration, but the side effects of some medications may occasionally create other physical problems.

INTERACTING WITH
PEOPLE WHO MOVE DIFFERENTLY

Person-First Words

Remember, a person is not defined by her impairment or difference. The movement differences described in this chapter would be evident to you even if you did not have specific vocabulary to describe them. When you lack specific, respectful terms to describe a disability, however, your reactions may be more negative because the unfamiliar, unexpected, and unsettling aspects of the disability become the focus of the interaction. Understanding basic terminology can increase your comfort and enhance your actions.

Here are some preferred terms for people with movement differences:

- A person *has a physical disability*—don't say he is "crippled" or "lame."
- A person *uses a wheelchair*—avoid saying he is "confined to a wheelchair" or "wheelchair-bound."
- A person has an *atypical gait* if she limps or has a balance problem with walking.
- A person has a *tremor* if he has small, shaking movements in the hands, neck, or head.
- A person has a *tic* if she makes jerking or other unusual, repetitive movements or sounds.
- A person is *uncoordinated* if he has difficulty getting all of his muscles to work together smoothly.
- A person has *paralysis* if she has no movement or feeling in part of her body.
- A person has *spasticity* if his movements are stiff and uncoordinated—avoid calling him "spastic."

Detecting Movement Differences

When you detect a movement difference that is unfamiliar, unexpected, or unsettling, you may want to stare at the person to get more information and figure out what is different with the way she walks, uses her hands, or guides her wheelchair. You may be wary of a man with balance problems, or spasticity, unsure whether he has a physical or mental problem or is inebriated. You may want to watch the person out of curiosity or interest but may also want to avoid seeing any unsettling movements that could create an awkward or embarrassing situation. As with appearance differences, you may be uncertain about where to look and whether you should pretend you don't notice the difference. You may wonder whether the person was born with his movement difference or whether he was in an accident.

A movement difference may or may not be associated with another disability difference. A man who has had a stroke may also have problems with speaking (see Chapter 7). A woman with cerebral palsy may have uncoordinated arm and head movements and appearance differences as a result of altered muscle development.

In many situations, especially brief encounters, you don't need to know why a person has a movement difference in order to have a successful interaction. When you have an ongoing relationship with someone who has a movement difference, however, you will learn how to anticipate environmental accessibility and obstacles.

Deciding

1. What kind of movement difference is this?
2. How relevant is the movement difference to the situation?
3. What are my action options?

Understanding that someone you know has a movement difference can be very helpful. It alerts you to think about his accommodation needs in the environment and can help you plan ways you may need to adapt your plans or behavior.

Remember that there is more than one way to communicate and interact effectively. The Action Tips that follow are not prescriptions but rather possibilities for you to consider. It's better to try *some* action than to ignore the other person or leave.

Action Tips

Movement Differences

- **Make a quick check of the environment.** Are there any obstacles such as stairs, uneven pavement, or poor lighting that will make the person's movement difficult or impossible? Are there places to sit as needed? Does she have the equipment and supports that she needs, such as a wheelchair, a walker, or a cane?
- **Ask yourself whether you are an obstacle.** If you are, then move or reposition yourself. Some people with movement differences talk or eat at a slower pace. Be prepared, if necessary, to slow your pace of talking, and to increase your listening patience! (For more tips on interacting with people who have communication differences, see Chapter 7.) When walking or sharing a meal with a person who has a movement difference, slow down your pace accordingly.
- **Offer help that is appropriate to your relationship and interaction.** If you do not know the person well, and he is having difficulty buttoning a coat, cutting meat, or turning pages in a book, ask him to let you know whether you can help in some way. Taking over the task without asking can make the other person feel demeaned and embarrassed.
- **If the person uses a wheelchair, always remember that the chair is part of her personal space.** Do not lean on it. When-

ever possible, sit down in order to be at eye level for communication. If you are going somewhere together, be alert to physical obstacles. Remember that her field of vision is waist-high compared with people who are standing and that this restricts her view and conversation in a group of standing people.

- **If the person has an assistant, look for cues about how much the assistant remains in the background or is needed to help the person communicate or move.** Don't talk to the assistant "about" the person with the movement difference unless you are requested to do so—talk directly to the person.
- **If a person has a service animal, do not talk to it, pet it, or play with it without the owner's permission.** Your friendly gesture may distract it.

Doing

Despite your surprise at another person's movement difference, you'll probably find that many times the difference has very little, if any, relevance to the interaction. Even when you aren't sure what to say or how to behave, your motivation for the interaction to succeed is the most important message you can convey!

Whenever you interact with someone who has a movement difference, there is not just one right thing to Do. It does help, however, to remember these general pointers:

- Focus on the other person and his abilities and competencies.
- Include the person in the social situation. Don't talk around the person—always address him, not his assistant or interpreter.
- Provide assistance if asked or if your offer was accepted.
- Get on with the task or purpose of the situation!

Debriefing

You Detected a movement difference in someone, you Decided what to Do, and you went ahead and Did what you planned to Do. Now you can move on to the fourth step in the 4D approach, Debriefing, which means looking back and reflecting on the interaction and then looking forward to the next encounter with that specific person or to a similar encounter in the future. This activity may help you debrief. You may answer these questions privately, in your thoughts, or you may talk them over with someone else who was present during the interaction.

Debriefing

1. **Think about what happened this time.**
   - Did I Detect the difference accurately?
   - Did I Detect and manage my own emotional reactions?
   - Did I relax and Decide what my action options were?
   - Were my actions consistent with my Decisions? If not, why not?
   - Was the purpose of the interaction accomplished?
   - What worked well? What didn't work well?
2. **Figure out what went wrong.** If the situation went well, then congratulate yourself—and keep up the good work! If the situation did not go so well, then try to figure out why. Ask yourself whether any of these pitfalls occurred:
   - I focused on the difference too much.
   - I acted as though the difference wasn't relevant at all, but actually it was.
   - I got stuck in stress and forgot to relax.
   - I got stuck in pity and didn't focus on abilities.
   - I worried too much about "the right thing" to Do, so I Did nothing.
3. **Think about what could happen next time.** Ask yourself what you could do differently next time.

- Detect the disability and my feelings, and relax.
- Decide more carefully, or consider more action options.
- Look at the person or disability by regarding, not by staring.
- Talk to the person with person-first words, ask for information, or offer assistance.
- Interact differently by including instead of excluding and by focusing on the person and his *abilities*.

The social change that is occurring is clear: As more of the community becomes accessible, more people can participate in community life. We will see wheelchairs and assistive devices more often and become habituated to them. This will help us interact and become more comfortable with people who have movement differences, and the stigma of having a movement difference or using an assistive device will diminish.

Movement Differences

At-A-Glance

- Arthritis is the leading cause of disability for people ages 65 and older, affecting an estimated 16 million people. Osteoarthritis is the most common form of arthritis. After age 50, an estimated 80% of America's population is affected with osteoarthritis to some degree and may experience pain and stiffness. By the year 2010 when the first wave of baby boomers are in their mid-60s, it is predicted that more than 70 million people will have osteoarthritis.[12]
- 500,000–700,000 people have cerebral palsy, with about 5,000 infants diagnosed each year.[13]
- Approximately 333,000 people have multiple sclerosis.[14]

- 25 million people have osteoporosis, 80% of whom are women. Approximately one in two women and one in eight men older than 50 will have osteoporosis-related fractures.[15]
- Parkinson's disease affects 1 in 250 people older than 40 years of age.[16]
- There are approximately 183,000–230,000 people with spinal cord injury alive today, with about 10,000 new injuries each year. Auto accidents cause 37%, and violent acts account for 26%. Males between 16 and 30 years old are the most frequent victims.[17]
- Strokes are the leading cause of disability; 500,000 people have strokes every year.[18]
- According to the 1990 U.S. census, 1.8 million people use wheelchairs. Approximately 5.2 million people use a cane, crutches, or a walker for at least six months.[19]
- In 1960, the first International Paralympics Games had 400 participants. In 1996, the International Paralympics Games took place in Atlanta during the 1996 Summer Olympics, and 3,500 athletes from 120 nations competed in 17 medal events. Categories of disability included visually impaired and blind, amputee, cerebral palsy, quadriplegia and paraplegia (wheelchair), and others.

People with Movement Differences
Muhammad Ali, boxer
James Brady, former Presidential press secretary
John Callahan, cartoonist
Johnny Cash, singer
Chuck Close, artist
Robert Dole, former U.S. Senator
Chris Fonseca, comedian
Michael J. Fox, actor
Annette Funicello, actor
Billy Graham, religious leader
Stephen Hawking, astrophysicist
Joseph Heller, author
Katherine Hepburn, actress
Judith Heumann, Assistant Secretary of Education

John Hockenberry, journalist
Pope John Paul II
Ron Kovic, disability advocate
Paul Longmore, historian and author
Nancy Mairs, author
Itzhak Perlman, violinist
Christopher Reeve, actor
Janet Reno, U.S. Attorney General
Franklin Delano Roosevelt, former U.S. president
Mary Verdi-Fletcher, dancer

READINGS
AND RESOURCES

Books

Flying Without Wings:
Personal Reflections on Loss, Disability, and Healing
A. Beisser (Bantam Doubleday Dell, New York, 1990)

A Problem of Plumbing and Other Stories
J. Bellarosa (John Daniel & Company, Santa Barbara, CA,
1989)

Don't Worry, He Won't Get Far on Foot
J. Callahan (Random House, New York, 1989)

Taking the Lead: Dancing with Chronic Illness
L. Giroux (Transcontinental Printing, Louisville, Quebec,
Canada, 1998)

Moving Violations: War Zones,
Wheelchairs, and Declarations of Independence
J. Hockenberry (Hyperion, New York, 1995)

What Happened to You?
L. Keith (The New Press, New York, 1996)

Waist High in the World: A Life Among the Nondisabled
N. Mairs (Beacon Press, Boston, 1996)

Stop Osteoarthritis Now! Halting the Baby Boomers' Disease
H. McIlwain & D. Bruce (Fireside Books, New York, 1996)

Under the Eye of the Clock
C. Nolan (St. Martin's Press, New York, 1987)

The Cinema of Isolation:
A History of Physical Disability in the Movies
M. Norden (Rutgers University Press, New Brunswick, NJ, 1994)

Growing Up with Joey
S. Papazian (Fithian Press, Santa Barbara, CA, 1997)

A Paralyzing Fear: The Story of Polio in America
J. Smith (TV Books, 1998)
Also a PBS documentary

Look Up for Yes
J. Tavalaro & R. Tayson (Kodansha America, Inc., New York, 1997)

Films

Pride of the Yankees (1942)

Sunrise at Campobello (1960)

Tell Me That You Love Me, Junie Moon (1970)

Coming Home (1978)

Touched by Love (1980)

Modern Problems (1981)

Duet for One (1986)

Gaby: A True Story (1987)

Born on the Fourth of July (1989)

My Left Foot (1989)

Passion Fish (1992)

Good Luck (1997)

The People vs. Larry Flynt (1997)

The Waterdance (1992)

Everything That Rises (1998)

Magazines

Ability Magazine
Post Office Box 10655, Costa Mesa, CA 92627

Exceptional Parent Magazine
555 Kindermack Road, Oradell, NJ 07649 (www.e-parent.com)

Mainstream Magazine
Post Office Box 370598, San Diego, CA 92137-0598
(www.mainstream-mag.com)

New Mobility Magazine
Post Office Box 15518, North Hollywood, CA 91615-9773
(800-543-4116, x480)

Videos

People in Motion
Films for the Humanities and Sciences, Post Office Box 2053,
Princeton, NJ 08543 (800-257-5126; www.films.com)

Six videotapes. Part I includes *Ways to Move*, *Ready to Live*, and *Redesigning the Human Machine*. Part II includes *A New Sense of Place*, *Breaking the Silence Barrier*, and *Without Barriers or Borders*.

Self-Advocacy/Support Organizations

American Paralysis Association
500 Morris Avenue, Springfield, NJ 07081 (800-225-0292;
www.apacure.com)

Arthritis Foundation
(800-283-7800; www.arthritis.org)

Muscular Dystrophy Association
3561 East Sunrise Drive, Tucson, AZ 85718 (602-529-2000)

National Ataxia Foundation
2600 Fernbrook Lane, Minneapolis, MN 55447 (612-553-0020;
www.ataxia.org)

National Easter Seal Society
230 West Monroe Street, Suite 1800, Chicago, IL 60606
(800-221-6827; TDD: 312-726-4528; www.seals.com)

National Handicapped Sports
451 Hungerford Drive, Suite 100, Rockville, MD 20850
(301-393-7505)

National Multiple Sclerosis Society
733 Third Avenue, New York, NY 10017 (800-344-4867;
www. amss.org)

National Parkinson Foundation
1501 Northwest 9th Avenue, Miami, FL 33136 (800-327-4545;
www.parkinson.org)

National Spinal Cord Injury Association
8300 Colesville Road, Silver Spring, MD 20910 (301-588-6959)

National Wheelchair Athletic Association
3595 East Fountain Boulevard, Suite L1, Colorado Springs, CO
80910 (719-574-1150)

Special Olympics International
1350 New York Avenue, NW, Suite 500, Washington, DC 20005
(202-628-3630)

Spina Bifida Association of America
4590 MacArthur Boulevard, NW, #250, Washington, DC 20007
(800-621-3141)

Spinal Cord Hotline
(800-526-3456)

Spinal Cord Information Network
University of Alabama Pain Rehabilitation Center, 1717 6th Avenue S, Birmingham, AL 35233-7330 (205-934-3330; www.spinalcord.uab.edu)

United Cerebral Palsy Associations, Inc.
1660 L Street, NW, Washington, DC 20036-5602 (800-872-1827; www.ucpa.org)

7

People Who Communicate Differently

"Did you know that the t-two things people fear
most are d-death and speaking in p-p-public?"
I ask. "All my life I would have died rather than
speak in public. What if they found out I stuttered? What if they found out there was something wrong with me? What if they found out I
wasn't perfect? I would die of embarrassment."
I look straight at the audience. "Right now I am
totally embarrassed. Am I dead yet?"[1]
—Anne H. Mavor
performing her show "Mouth Piece"

Communication is an essential part of being human. The ability to express feelings, needs, and preferences is usually taken

for granted. Only when we lose the ability to talk—even temporarily—or when we notice that someone else has difficulty
communicating, do we realize how much we depend on communication. It is hard for most of us to imagine a day without
talking and nearly impossible to consider a life without some
form of communication. Communication is at the heart of our
relationships and interactions. With casual acquaintances we
communicate through greetings and small talk. In intimate relationships we reveal our inner feelings through nonverbal
communication as well as words. Of course, it would also be
extremely difficult to work without using language because
most jobs require exchanging a lot of specific information,
making plans, and negotiating.

Communication is also at the heart of our cultural expression. How could we have literature, songs, plays, and all of
the other manifestations of our national heritages without language? Some people believe that language is the true essence
of humanness.[2] Language not only communicates to others
what we're thinking, it also alters and shapes our thinking.
That is, to some extent, our ability to organize our private
thoughts depends on our language ability.

MYTHS, ASSUMPTIONS, AND BELIEFS

Many people believe you can tell a lot about a person by the
way she talks. Regional accents signal where she has lived.
People who speak loudly may be considered ill-mannered;
those who speak softly may be considered shy. If someone
speaks slowly, then listeners may assume he *thinks* slowly.
There are many misconceptions about communication.

Myth: Smart People Are Also Well-Spoken

We are often impressed by articulate speech that flows and is
full of long sentences with a rich vocabulary. We tend to
equate this kind of communication style and skill with overall
intelligence. So, when we communicate with someone whose
speaking is slower, perhaps difficult to understand, or just

simpler, we assume that he can't be very smart. A similar assumption is that a person who can't hear and can't talk is likely also to have mental retardation. Our typical expectation has been that communication skill is synonymous with learning skill. But this is not an accurate picture of learning *or* communication, which are two abilities that are often independent. Especially since the advent of *augmentative and alternative communication devices,* we are learning to separate *what* a person says from *how* she says it.

Myth: Stuttering Is a Psychological Problem and a Sign of Extreme Shyness

Teasing and laughing are common responses to people who stutter. Movie characters who stutter are commonly depicted as extremely ill-at-ease, poorly socialized individuals. In fact, stuttering is not the *result* of psychological problems, but it can often *cause* interpersonal problems when it is poorly understood by family, friends, and work associates.

Myth: People with Hearing Impairments Usually Can't Talk

The vast majority of people with hearing impairments can and do use oral language; thus, "deaf and dumb" is an inaccurate term. When individuals use hand signing, we often misunderstand this mode of communication. We don't realize that hand signing isn't just pantomime; it's a language in its own right. Actually, signing refers to a *group* of languages. There is no universal sign language used around the world.

Myth: People Who Don't Talk Can't Communicate

Perhaps the most serious myth of all is that people can communicate only through talking. When you encounter someone who does not talk, never assume she does not communicate. Observe her as you attempt to communicate, and also ask her and her assistant or caregiver for tips. You may be surprised at the variety of communication methods people use: signing, writing, typing, pointing to images on a board or computer, using electronic voice synthesizers, and many more. And don't forget the oldest form of communication: body language. People also communicate through facial expression, voice tone, and body movement.

WHAT IT FEELS LIKE

Most of us have had a glimpse into the world of communication differences. Have you ever stretched out on your couch to watch a favorite television show and found that your remote control battery is dead and the volume is too low to hear clearly? You hear a few of the words, but you can't catch all of them. This is similar to having a *hearing impairment*. If you've ever had wisdom teeth extracted and your mouth was swollen and packed with cotton, then you've experienced a *speech impairment*. Or, perhaps you've traveled to another country and tried to order from a menu written in a foreign language. The waiter was impatient. You started off speaking English, but he looked at you blankly. Then you attempted to speak the local language, and the waiter only frowned at you. You felt the frustration of not being understood.

COMMUNICATION
DIFFERENCES YOU MAY ENCOUNTER

When you cannot understand what another person is saying or when you can't make yourself understood, you may feel frustrated and annoyed. You may even feel helpless if you haven't faced this situation before and can't think of a different way to handle the interaction.

Differences in Communication *Style*

You probably recall listening to someone who repeats part of a word ("p-p-please") when talking. Or, you might have heard someone whose pronunciation is unclear. You might know other people who communicate with their hands, using sign language, or with the aid of a device that displays words and pictures or emits an electronic voice.

Differences in Communication *Content*

Some people have communication differences that are harder to describe. They may pronounce their words clearly, but something is different about the meaning. Perhaps a person's topics seem repetitive, irrelevant, or odd. Sometimes you have difficulty following his train of thought. Some people's communication is altered because they can't recall names of familiar objects and are frequently at a loss for the word they need.

Awareness Activities

Communication Differences

Nonverbal Communication

Place an X of first-aid tape over your mouth and spend an evening at home without speaking. Afterward, talk about the following questions with your family or roommates:

- What nonverbal communication methods did you use?
- Were there moments when you or your relatives/friends became frustrated? Why?

Speech Impairment[3]

Select a newspaper article. Close your jaw without clenching your muscles tightly. Without moving your jaw, read the selected passage aloud to a friend or co-worker. Afterward, talk about the following questions:

- How did your speech change? Did you talk more slowly?
- How did you feel when your friend had difficulty understanding you?

- Ask your friend some factual questions about the article. Did she misunderstand some of the facts? How did she feel trying to understand you?

Hearing Impairment

Although no activity can truly capture the experience of a hearing impairment or deafness, these two might give you some idea of the sensory difference.

1. Insert good-quality earplugs in your ears, and wear them for several hours at home. Notice the reduction in environmental sounds and clarity of other people's speech. Then, with someone else to listen for cars or other dangers, take a walk in your neighborhood. Consider the personal safety sounds that you would miss if you had a significant hearing impairment. For example, how would you notice a racing car approaching you from the side as you crossed the street, someone calling for help from inside an apartment, or a police siren approaching rapidly? How would you assist a friend with a hearing impairment if you heard these sounds during a walk together?

2. If you have two televisions in separate rooms, ask a family member to watch a news broadcast in one room. In the other room, watch the same show with the volume turned off. Concentrate on the reporter's face and body language. Use the video segments and graphics as clues. At the end of the show, tell your family member the news—as you saw it. Think about the challenge of lipreading. (Keep in mind that most people who want to develop this skill *do* receive specialized instruction.)

REASONS WHY PEOPLE
COMMUNICATE DIFFERENTLY

Some people's communication differences are caused by lack of experience with a language (such as people who are learning English as a second language). Although these communication differences have an impact on people's lives, they are changeable, fixable, and sometimes temporary. The focus of this chapter, however, is on communication differences that are enduring and usually caused by physical or neurological impairments.

One way to think about communication differences is to begin with the basics of oral communication, the most common form. There are three essential parts to oral communication: hearing, speaking, and understanding. We learn oral communication by

- Hearing what our parents and others are saying
- Speaking
- Understanding what is said to us and preparing what we will say to others

Although vision and gesture are not absolutely essential during oral communication, we often watch others' body cues, such as facial expressions, and we may gesture to emphasize our point.

Impairments in hearing, speaking, or understanding can cause communication differences. The next sections review some of the common causes of differences within each category.

Deafness and Hearing Impairments

Hearing is a complex process that involves the outer ear, which catches sound and funnels it down the ear canal; the middle-ear bones, and the inner ear, where fluid and nerves send sound impulses to the brain. Impairment of any part of the ear can cause hearing loss or deafness. People with some *hearing loss* may *also* be referred to as *hard of hearing* or as having a *hearing impairment*. Hearing loss is very common; you probably know a number of people with this difference.

Deafness is defined as the inability to hear. Technically speaking, many deaf people do hear certain sounds, but the term usually refers to a person who cannot hear human speech. People with congenital deafness do not typically experience a "silent" world in the sense that they do not feel the *loss* of sounds. In fact, some deaf people who have acquired hearing complain of the "noise" of the hearing world compared with their usual "quiet."[4]

Although I would rather be able to hear, I'm not rending my clothes over being deaf or holding my breath while waiting for medical science or technology to restore my hearing. . . . I certainly don't mind taking advantage of the major benefit of being deaf: freedom from noise pollution. . . . My environment is relatively pleasant and relaxed most of the time, wherever I am.[5]

—Lew Golan

Causes of Deafness and Hearing Impairments

Here are some of the most common causes of deafness and hearing impairments:

- *Loud noises,* especially with frequent or continuous exposure, can cause hearing loss. This is a long-standing problem for factory employees who work next to loud machines. Rock musicians (and their audiences) are especially at risk. The hearing loss may be mild at first but can progress over time to total hearing loss, even when the person is no longer exposed to loud sounds. Hearing loss resulting from loud noises is a serious public health concern because it is a preventable type of deafness.

- *Aging* may result in hearing loss. Hearing impairments are far more common in people older than age 65.[6]
- *Illnesses* can cause hearing loss and hearing impairments. When a pregnant woman develops rubella (a form of measles) or cytomegalovirus, her unborn child's hearing may be affected, especially when the fetus is exposed in the first trimester. Frequent ear infections in the first few years of life can lead to hearing loss. Illnesses such as scarlet fever and meningitis can cause hearing impairment.
- *Injury* to the ears, head, or central nervous system can cause hearing loss.
- *Medication side effects* may include hearing loss. For example, the drugs streptomycin, neomycin, and gentamycin and some diuretics are known to damage the small hair cells in the inner ear that assist in hearing.[7]
- *Genetic disorders* that occur spontaneously or are inherited from parents can result in hearing impairment at birth or later in life.

Individuals with normal hearing or with any degree of hearing impairment can experience a hearing impairment called *tinnitus*. Essentially, tinnitus is a condition in which a person perceives a continuous noise coming from one or both ears or inside the head. People describe the sounds of tinnitus in a variety of ways: hissing, rushing water, whistling, radio static, buzzing, chirping, or a jet plane engine. Although the cause of tinnitus is not completely understood, loud noises and certain medications are suspected factors.

Speech Impairments

No one can estimate the number of people who speak differently, but speech disorders are quite common and often subtle. As with other disabilities, the "lines" between normal speech, unusual speech, and speech impairment are not really clear to most people. There is great variety in the way we speak. Some of us talk loudly or quickly; others have a soft and slow style. A speech disorder can be viewed as one of many speech differences, which also include differences in accent, pace, volume, and so forth. Any of these speech differences could cause some interruption in the flow of communication between two people. People's speaking styles are another example of the diversity of disability and our need to question our thinking about disabilities so that we view them primarily as differences.

To create speech sounds, a person must be able to coordinate movement of his lips, jaw, tongue, and soft palate (roof of the mouth). About 100 muscles are used to produce speech! Sometimes all of these parts don't work together just right, and pronunciation, or *articulation,* is disrupted. For example, when you listen to a person who has an articulation difference such as lisping or stuttering, the communication process can stall. An *oral-motor problem* can cause unclear articulation if the mouth muscles don't work properly. They may be too weak and loose or too tight and rigid. Sometimes the muscles don't "follow directions" from the motor center of the brain. In the case of cerebral palsy, the brain's messages aren't received clearly by the tongue, lip, and jaw muscles. Any disease or medical condition that causes movement differences, such as multiple sclerosis, stroke, Parkinson's disease, or brain injury, can also affect speech (see Chapter 6). Occasionally, a mouth injury or tooth extraction can cause a significant change in articulation.

One common articulation problem is *stuttering,* in which the person involuntarily repeats, prolongs, or blocks words or sounds. When someone tries to say "can" but instead says "c-c-c-can," you may be surprised. As with any other difference, you aren't expecting it. You can't tell by looking at a person whether she is going to stutter. Because a speech difference is not visible until the person begins communicating with you, some of the issues related to nonvisible differences (see Chapter 10) are pertinent.

Stuttering often is a normal and temporary part of a child's development as he practices all of the complex speech patterns. Stuttering at any age is *not* an emotional problem and is *not* due to nervousness. Emotions, however, can make stuttering better or worse. Anxiety, stress, and pressure to perform often increase stuttering. Situations such as speaking in public, making telephone calls to strangers, and talking to an authority figure can worsen existing stuttering problems, which partially explains why stuttering seems to come and go. It's common for a person to stutter one minute but speak fluently the next.

The worst part about being a stutterer is that I never know when I am going to stutter. I may be talking well, and then block in the beginning, the middle, or the end of the word; sometimes it is all three.[8]

—Lisa Fay

Some people never develop speech, such as some children who are born deaf. Because speech must be learned, a deaf child cannot imitate the speech of others, nor can she hear her own sounds. Some people choose not to speak because their articulation is so atypical. Occasionally, a person loses the capacity to speak but can still think linguistically and understand what others are saying. This speech impairment is one kind of *aphasia*, and it can be caused by a stroke or spinal cord injury.

[After my stroke] I started working every day with a speech therapist, and it was extremely hard. I started by learning how to pronounce letters, and then I graduated to words. I still have a problem with s's. Save. Sit. Start. Stop. . . . I was once in an Italian restaurant, and I couldn't say "spaghetti." About six months later I went back and kept saying, "Spaghetti! Spaghetti!" I was so delighted. . . . My thoughts were fine, but my tongue wasn't up to the task.[9]

—Kirk Douglas

Difficulty Understanding Communication

Sometimes, a person is able to hear and speak, but the third part of oral communication, understanding, is impaired. In this case, a person may have trouble communicating because her brain has difficulty concentrating, processing, imitating, or formulating spontaneous words. For example, someone with mental retardation may not be able to understand communication at a level that you would expect of a person of her age.

People who have had a stroke or who have brain injury or Alzheimer's disease may have difficulty understanding the meaning of spoken words, or they may not be able to recall the names of common objects or words they used to say every day. Their medical conditions have caused a loss of language ability by disrupting the brain's "command center" for oral communication. *Aphasia* is the term for an acquired impairment in the ability to use or comprehend words.

INTERVENTIONS AND SUPPORTS

We live in a world where the expected average is that everyone understands and uses oral communication. Although this is certainly the norm, this does not mean other methods are abnormal or invalid. Here's a quick overview of alternative communication methods you may encounter. You might even discover that you have used some of these methods or could benefit from trying them.

Manual Communication

Many people who have significant hearing or speech impairments use signing or other forms of manual communication. Sometimes their hearing family and friends also use signing. So, you cannot be sure a person using hand communication actually has a hearing or speech impairment unless you ask or observe other evidence such as a hearing aid.

Signing is the use of fingers, hands, arms, and other body parts in a language of gesture. Formal sign language has its own structure, grammar, and syntax. It has existed in Deaf culture since at least 1755, when a French priest closely observed the gestures of deaf people in the streets of Paris.[10] He then systematized the gestures and converted them to an established sign language, which was brought to the United

States in the early 1800s. Modern sign languages vary from country to country.

American Sign Language

Also known as Ameslan, American Sign Language (ASL) has more than 4,000 signs distinguished by the specific shapes, position, and movements made by one or both hands. People who use ASL also use facial expressions and body movements for some words. ASL is a language in its own right, and its signs represent *concepts* rather than English words. Many deaf people advocate ASL as the official language of their community.

Manually Coded English

Manually coded English systems are not distinct languages but are instead very literal translations of spoken English words and grammar. Signing Exact English (SEE) converts spoken and written English into manual signs with an emphasis on English grammar.

Fingerspelling

In fingerspelling, each letter of the written alphabet has a corresponding single hand shape. It is somewhat like "writing" in the air. It takes a lot longer to spell a word than to use a whole-word sign, but fingerspelling is useful for conveying an unconventional word or a proper noun with which the listener/viewer is not familiar.

Interpreters

At some time or another, you've probably noticed a person at a public event signing to the audience, or you may have seen an interpreter signing on television. Usually the term *interpreter* refers to a person who is fluent in both spoken and signed languages. The interpreter usually stands next to or near the person speaking and listens to what she says. Simultaneously, the interpreter signs the speaker's sentences for deaf or signing people who are present. Although friends and family members often serve as interpreters, professional interpreting involves a great deal of formal training and skill and a code of ethics.[11]

Lipreading

Lipreading (also known as speech reading) is a technique by which a deaf person can comprehend another person's speech by watching that person's lips form the words. Many people who do not read lips are misinformed about this communication method and believe that it is a straightforward, relatively easy skill to master. In fact, lipreading is quite difficult. Only about 16 of the 40 distinct sounds in the English language can be lipread clearly. So, about half of the English sounds look like some other sound on the lips. Although lipreading is easier for people who have heard spoken language at some point in their life than for people who were born deaf, it can still take years to master.

Total Communication

Total communication (TC) is an approach advocating teaching a wide variety of communication modalities ranging from lipreading to speaking to signing. Using auditory, oral, and manual communication methods, TC attempts to provide a number of different communication skills to children who have hearing loss.[12]

Assistive Devices

There are many kinds of speaking and listening devices and aids, from low-tech to high-tech, plain to fancy. People with communication impairments are working closely with speech-language pathologists, audiologists, teachers, and rehabilitation technicians to expand communication choices.

Communication Boards and Adapted Computers

Communication boards or books evolved from the basic pencil-and-paper tools that were used for many years. A variety of homemade and published materials are used by both children and adults with speech impairments. A simple version for a young child might consist of photos showing common objects and actions. The child can point to pictures as needed to communicate. Older children and adults who cannot point to pictures with their hands (because of movement disabilities) may use their feet or a pointer mounted on a headband to tap on pictures, words, or letters arranged on an alphabet board.[13]

People with communication differences also can use adapted computer keyboards that have large keys, fewer keys, or picture-based keys. Some computers are controlled by voice commands, by touching the screen, or even by gazing at a specific place on the screen. A person with a severe speech impairment can use a computer to convert typed words into a computer-synthesized voice.

For a time, the only way I could communicate was to spell out words letter by letter, by raising my eyebrows when someone pointed to the right letter on a spelling card. It is pretty difficult to carry on a conversation like that, let alone write a scientific paper. However, a computer expert in California . . . heard of my plight. He sent me a computer program he had written, called Equalizer. Using this [speech synthesizer] system, I have written a book, and dozens of scientific papers. I have also given many scientific and popular talks.

—Stephen Hawking[14]

Telephone Devices

Many telephones have a simple volume-enhancing dial in their receivers for people with mild hearing impairments. Telephone communication between deaf people or between deaf and hearing people is possible because of the telecommunications device for the deaf (TDD), also known as a teletypewriter (TTY). TDDs are machines that have keyboards, a small screen, and a place to rest the telephone receiver. When a person uses a TDD, he types words that are carried by telephone lines using specific tones that may remind you of a fax machine. TDDs come in many models, from large, sturdy table-top machines to miniature units that fit into purses or brief-cases, making them convenient to use when traveling.[15]

Telephone communication also has been enhanced by *telephone relay services*. Telephone relay services permit individuals with hearing impairments to communicate with friends, businesses, and agencies that do not yet have TDDs. Specially trained operators are available to translate TDD messages to voice messages and vice versa. For example, if you are a hearing person and you need to call your deaf father from a telephone booth not equipped with a TDD, then you may dial your state's relay service (listed in the front of the local telephone directory). The operator will place the call to your father and translate your voice message—word for word—into a typed message that your father can read on his TDD screen. Relay services are mandated under the ADA.[16]

Assistive Listening Systems

Assistive listening systems consist of environmental equipment that enhances the clarity of music, speech, and other sounds for people with hearing impairments. Many people are familiar with microphones and public address systems, but assistive listening systems help audience members with hearing impairments to hear speakers, movies, or concerts. These systems may involve hard-wiring or infrared technology and some-times, but not always, require users to wear a special headset.

Electronic Mail and Fax

You are probably familiar with electronic mail (e-mail) and fax, two communication technologies that have special bene-fits for some people with communication differences because they replace oral communication methods with written words. E-mail is superior to the telephone for conversations involving people with hearing or speech impairments. Fax communication is widely accessible to people who don't have computers; many neighborhood photocopying shops also transmit faxes. These technologies enable people with communication differences to participate more fully in daily community life, including using Internet "chat rooms," ordering catalog products, and communicating with family, friends, and colleagues in other cities.

Detection Devices and Other Supports

Many products are available to replace sound signals with visual or touch signals for people with hearing impairments.

Computer-assisted notetaking is useful in classes and meetings in which technical information is being conveyed orally to an audience. A notetaker types a summary of the presenter's remarks (and audience questions) on a computer keyboard as the presenter speaks. The person with a hearing impairment can read these notes from a projection screen or a large monitor.[17]

Closed captioning is the projection of typed words across the bottom of a television or movie screen, which provides a written translation of what the actors are saying. Captioning has been around a long time in the form of subtitles for foreign films and more recently as translations for operas. Look in your television program listings for the symbol that indicates that a show is available in captioned format, the letters CC within a box shaped like a television.[18]

Other household products that enhance daily living and safety of people with hearing impairments include doorbells and smoke detectors that trigger flashing lights instead of buzzers and alarm clocks that vibrate the bed.

Not all assistive aids are mechanical; specially trained dogs or other service animals can signal to their owner that someone is at the door, that the oven timer is buzzing, or that danger is at hand.[19] A number of programs train *hearing dogs* to assist people who are deaf or who have hearing impairments. According to the ADA, businesses, landlords, theaters, hotels, restaurants, and other public places cannot discriminate against people who use service animals.

Hearing Aids and Implants

Hearing aids have a simple purpose: to compensate for hearing loss by increasing either volume or clarity of sound. Modern aids are quite small, and newer digital models can fit completely inside the ear canal.

Cochlear implants are surgically inserted medical devices for people with profound hearing loss who have not benefited from hearing aids.[20] This is a dramatic technological innovation heralded by many people with hearing loss and their families. It is most successful in people who have already learned oral language before losing their hearing ability.

Speech-Language Therapy

Speech-language therapy is the process of learning or relearning how to form word sounds in order to be better understood when communicating with others. Professional speech-language pathologists are concerned with all three aspects of communication (hearing, speaking, and understanding), but they focus closely on the second step, a person's specific speech impairments. They recommend and provide one-to-one or small-group instruction or treatment. Speech-language pathologists can also help individuals improve their language skills, including forming sentences and initiating and maintaining conversations.

INTERACTING WITH PEOPLE
WITH HEARING OR SPEECH DIFFERENCES

Person-First Words

Remember, a person is not defined by her impairment or difference. The communication differences described in this chapter would be evident to you even if you did not have specific vocabulary to describe them. When you lack specific, respectful terms to describe a disability, however, your reactions may be more negative because the unfamiliar, unexpected, and unsettling aspects of the disability become the focus of the interaction. Understanding basic terminology can increase your comfort and enhance your actions.

Here are some preferred terms:

- A person who has lost some of his hearing ability has a hearing impairment or hearing loss. He might refer to himself as hard of hearing.
- A person who cannot hear at all might identify herself as *deaf*. Sometimes a capital *D* is used when referring to the *Deaf community* as a cultural entity, with a distinct language, history, and customs.
- A person who has any difficulty talking has a *speech impairment*. A person who does not speak at all has *mutism*—but he's never "dumb."
- People who use computerized voice synthesizers or other equipment to communicate are using *augmentative and alternative communication devices*. It's important to note that they're *using* these devices, not "depending" or "relying" on them.

Detecting Communication Differences

Everyone communicates! It's helpful to think about many communication disabilities as communication *differences*. When an alternative communication method enables a person to express and understand language, then the person's functional impairment is less pertinent. Speech is the form of communication we use most often, but it isn't the *only* way to communicate. We live in an exciting time with many alternative communication methods.

It is very helpful to know whether someone has difficulty hearing, speaking, or understanding. If he does, you can expect some communication differences and be prepared to accommodate the person's needs in social situations. When you realize that you're having difficulty communicating with someone, pause and think:

- Are you having trouble understanding *how* the person is communicating (communication *style*)? In this case, you can take your lead from him and adjust to his alternative communication method.

- Are you having trouble understanding *what* he is communicating (communication *content*)? If so, then you may need to be more directive in the interaction and create some structure. He may need help sticking to the topic, understanding your words, or finding the right words.
- Do you detect other differences as well?

A communication difference may or may not be associated with another disability difference. It's important to Detect additional disabilities because you may need to alter more of your behaviors to accommodate the other person or understand her better. Here are some examples of how communication differences *might* be related to other differences:

- An articulation difficulty might result from an appearance difference such as cleft palate (see Chapter 5) or a movement difference such as cerebral palsy (see Chapter 6).
- A rapid rate of speaking might be caused by attention difficulties or other behavior differences (see Chapter 8).
- Someone who speaks very slowly might have a nonvisible difference such as emphysema or chronic pain (see Chapter 10).

Deciding

1. What kind of communication difference is this?
2. How relevant is the communication difference to the situation?
3. What are my action options?

Understanding that someone you know has a communication difference can be very helpful. This knowledge is your signal to adapt your behavior or to accommodate the person's special needs. Remember also that there is more than one way to communicate and interact effectively. The Action Tips that follow are not prescriptions but rather possibilities for you to consider.

Action Tips

Communication Differences

When you are speaking . . .

- Don't assume that two people signing to each other are both deaf. Ask the person with whom you wish to speak whether he is deaf. Use gestures as well as words.
- Reduce competing sounds. Turn off the radio, television, noisy computer printer, and so forth. Step away from other conversing people or noisy areas.
- If you think that a person has a hearing impairment, then ask whether the person can read your lips. You can point at your lips and raise your eyebrows as though to ask a question. Also, ask whether writing would be helpful.
- When talking to anyone with a communication difference, and especially when talking to someone who reads lips, be sure to do the following:
  - Face the person and keep your hands away from your face so that your mouth is visible.
  - Stand so that the sun or light is in front of you.
  - Pronounce words clearly and speak at a moderate pace, but don't exaggerate how slowly or clearly you speak.
  - Avoid shouting—not only is it unpleasant for the hearing people around you but your words may be distorted for the listener. Some people with hearing impairments have difficulty telling sounds apart, so increased volume is not helpful.
  - Use gestures and facial expressions to help your listener.
- Be sure you have the person's attention before talking. A small wave within her range of vision or a light tap on the shoulder may work.

- If the person has a sign language interpreter, face the person, not the interpreter.
- If you have a regional accent, then realize that the listener may have greater difficulty understanding you. Is there someone else available who speaks in a style more familiar to the listener?
- Signal that you're changing topics by using a transition phrase, such as "On another topic . . ." or "There's one more thing I want to tell you . . ."
- Slow down if your talking pace is too fast. If you're not sure, ask the person whether you're talking too fast.
- Use short questions.

When you are listening . . .

- Arrange for an interpreter, if requested. If the person is your client or customer, then you may even be required to provide interpreter services.
- Listen carefully to the person's words, paying attention to his facial expressions and gestures as well.
- Show patience. Stuttering may worsen if the speaker feels that you are impatient or annoyed. Also, conversations take more time with people who have speech impairments, who use communication devices, or who use signing interpreters. Allow time for the speaker to ask you questions.
- Respond to the content of the person's message, not the communication difference. For instance, ignore the "interference" or "noise" of the stuttering.
- If you don't understand the other person's point, say so. It's not rude to admit, "I don't understand. Are you saying _____ ?" (Restate the point.) Or, try saying, "Show me." Help the person demonstrate with actions, gestures, drawing, or writing what she is unsuccessfully trying to explain with words.

When the person's communication difference seems to be caused by an impairment in understanding, try the following . . .

- Simplify your communication. Focus on the purpose of the interaction, and help the other person focus by using phrases such as "I need to ask you two more questions" or "Let's finish here before we talk about that." *Be specific:* "Do you want soda or milk?" "Who are you waiting for?"
- If the other person is nervous, frightened, or confused, provide reassurance.
- Use actions more than words. If appropriate to the roles and time frame, guide the person by touching his arm or gesturing.
- Try to Detect whether the person has a behavior difference (see Chapter 8) or a learning difference (see Chapter 9).

Doing

Whenever you interact with someone who has a communication difference, there is not just one right thing to do. Even when you aren't sure what to say or how to behave, your motivation for the interaction to succeed is the most important message you can convey. Keep in mind these general pointers:

- Focus on the other person and her abilities and competencies.
- Include the person in the social situation. Don't talk around the person—always address her, not her assistant or interpreter.
- Provide assistance if asked or if your offer was accepted.
- Get on with the task or purpose of the situation!

It's usually easy to look without staring when you encounter a person with a communication difference but no other visible differences. Try to avoid staring at people who are signing; this is similar to eavesdropping.

Debriefing

After you've interacted with someone who has a communication difference, don't skip Debriefing. Look back and reflect on the interaction, and then look forward to the next encounter with that person or a similar encounter in the future. The following Awareness Activity will help you debrief. Answer these questions privately, or talk them over with someone else who was present.

Debriefing

1. **Think about what happened this time.**
   - Did I Detect the difference accurately?
   - Did I Detect and manage my own emotional reactions?
   - Did I relax and Decide what my action options were?
   - Were my actions consistent with my Decisions? If not, why not?
   - Was the purpose of the interaction accomplished?
   - What worked well? What didn't work well?

2. **Figure out what went wrong.** If the situation went well, then congratulate yourself—and keep up the good work! If the situation did not go so well, then try to figure out why. Ask yourself whether any of these pitfalls occurred:
   - I focused on the difference too much.

- I acted as though the difference wasn't relevant at all, but actually it was.
- I got stuck in stress and forgot to relax.
- I got stuck in pity and didn't focus on abilities.
- I worried too much about "the right thing" to Do, so I Did nothing.

3. **Think about what could happen next time.** Ask yourself what you could do differently next time.
   - Detect the disability and my feelings, and relax.
   - Decide more carefully, or consider more action options.
   - Look at the person or disability by regarding, not by staring.
   - Talk to the person with person-first words, ask for information, or offer assistance.
   - Interact differently by including instead of excluding and by focusing on the person and his *abilities*.

Communication Differences

At-A-Glance

- 1 of every 10 people has a speech, language, or hearing disorder.[21]
- More than 20 million people have a hearing impairment, 550,000 of whom are deaf.[22] Only about 5% of those 20 million acquired a hearing impairment before the age of three years.[23]
- Approximately 10–20 million people could benefit from hearing aids, but only about five million people actually use them.[24]
- 50 million adults have tinnitus; 12 million have tinnitus severe enough to seek medical attention.[25]
- More than three million people stutter.[26]
- One million people have acquired aphasia.[27]

People with Hearing or Speech Differences

Ludwig von Beethoven, German composer
Joseph Biden, congressman
Lewis Carroll, author
Bill Clinton, 42nd U.S. President
Winston Churchill, former Prime Minister of Britain
Walter Cronkite, journalist
Kirk Douglas, actor
Ron Harper, athlete
Stephen Hawking, astrophysicist
Florence Henderson, actor
James Earl Jones, actor
Helen Keller, author
Bob Love, athlete
Marlee Matlin, actor
Marilyn Monroe, actor
Carly Simon, singer
Curtis Pride, athlete
Richard Thomas, actor
John Updike, author
Heather Whitestone, former Miss America
Frank Wolf, congressman

READINGS
AND RESOURCES

Books

Adaptive Technology for Special Human Needs
A. Brett & E. Provenzo (State University of New York Press, Albany, 1995)

Voices from a Culture: Deaf in America
C. Padden & T. Humphries (Harvard University Press, Cambridge, MA, 1988)

Deaf Like Me
T.S. Spradley & J.P. Spradley (Gallaudet University Press, Washington, DC, 1987)

The Diving Bell and the Butterfly
J.-D. Bauby, translated from the French by Jeremy Leggatt (Alfred A. Knopf, New York, 1997)

The Feel of Silence
B.P. Tucker (Temple University Press, Philadelphia, 1995)

Hear: Solutions, Skills, and Sources
for People with Hearing Loss
A. Pope (Dorling Kindersley, London, England, 1997)

In This Sign
J. Greenberg (Holt, Rinehart & Winston, New York, 1984)

Knotted Tongues: Stuttering in History
and the Quest for a Cure
B. Bobrick (Simon & Schuster, New York, 1995)

Look Up for Yes
J. Tavalaro & R. Tayson (Kodansha America, Inc., New York, 1997)

Mother Father Deaf: Living Between Sound and Silence
P. Preston (Harvard University Press, Cambridge, MA, 1994)

Raising and Educating a Deaf Child
M. Marschart (Oxford University Press, New York, 1997)

Seeing Voices: A Journey into the World of the Deaf
O. Sacks (HarperCollins, New York, 1990)

Train Go Sorry: Inside a Deaf World
L.H. Cohen (Houghton Mifflin, Boston, 1994)

What's that Pig Outdoors? A Memoir of Deafness
H. Kisor (Penguin Books, Ltd., London, England, 1990)

Yes, You Can, Heather!
The Story of Heather Whitestone, Miss America
D. Gray with G. Lewis (Zondervan Publishing House, Grand Rapids, MI, 1995)

Films

The Miracle Worker (1962)

Children of a Lesser God (1986)

In the Land of the Deaf (1992)

Hear No Evil (1993)

Mr. Holland's Opus (1995)

Self-Advocacy/Support Organizations

American Tinnitus Association
Post Office Box 5, Portland, OR 97207-0005
(www.ata.org)

National Aphasia Association
156 Fifth Avenue, New York, NY 10010
(800-922-4622; www.aphasia.org)

National Association of the Deaf
814 Thayer Avenue, Silver Spring, MD 20910-4500
(301-581-1788; TDD: 301-581-1789; fax: 301-581-1791;
www.nad.org/)

National Information Center on Deafness
Gallaudet University, 800 Florida Avenue, NE, Washington, DC
20002 (202-651-5051; TDD: 202-651-5052; fax: 202-651-5054;
www.gallaudet.edu; e-mail: nicd@gallux.gallaudet.edu)

Self Help for Hard of Hearing People
7910 Woodmont Avenue, Suite 1200, Bethesda, MD 20814
(301-657-2248; TDD: 301-657-2249; fax: 301-913-9413;
www.shhh.org)

Stuttering Foundation of America
Post Office Box 11749, Memphis, TN 38111-0749 (800-992-9392;
fax: 901-452-3931; www.stuttersfa.org/)

8

People Who
Behave Differently

So many people with mental illness . . . have
found themselves virtually shunned when they
disclosed their problems to others. People don't
know how to talk to them or often will deliberately avoid them.[1]

—Rosalynn Carter

This chapter focuses on behavior differences that are frequently related to mental impairments.[2] Sometimes we are
puzzled or suspicious when encountering a stranger whose
behavior is different, and we are confused by the challenges
when a co-worker or family member has a significant behavior difference.

But we *can* break through the barriers of myth, ignorance, and stereotype and become more comfortable and adept in these situations. Different behavior seems to trigger more fear in our difference detector than other disabilities. Our primitive brain makes a connection between unusual behavior and aggressive threat that is often not real (see Chapter 1).

This chapter can serve as a reference tool for you. It can help you make sense of behavior differences you have recently dealt with. It can also prepare you to detect behavior differences in the future. This chapter can help you Decide when quick action is needed and when there's little chance of immediate danger. It can also help you appreciate the diversity of behavior and the fact that most unusual behavior is simply *different*, not dangerous. Our hope is that you will move beyond your initial fear, lack of information, or uncertainty and learn new ways to react toward people with behavior differences.

MYTHS, ASSUMPTIONS, AND BELIEFS

Belief: People Should Behave in Ways that Don't Draw Attention

Most of us want to "fit in" and appear "normal" in social situations, so we generally behave in ways that do not draw attention. We maintain the appearance of "normalcy" almost all of the time. Except for clearly defined, ritualized "craziness" such as Mardi Gras parades or fraternity pranks, we try not to appear odd, bizarre, or too different from the expected average. So, when you meet someone whose behavior is different, you may feel nervous. Questions can flood your mind: Why is he acting like this? What am *I* supposed to do? What if he embarrasses me?

Myth: Different Behavior Is "Crazy" and Probably Dangerous

Not all behavior differences are caused by mental illness. Sometimes traumatic situations, illnesses, side effects of med-

tling experience of "hearing" the voice of a loved one who has recently died.

If you have visited a country with different customs, you probably felt as though you lacked the social skills to act appropriately. You may have had the sense that everyone else had "read the handbook," but *you* had to figure it out gradually and painfully from your mistakes.

BEHAVIOR DIFFERENCES YOU MAY ENCOUNTER

There are several hundred specific mental disorders,[6] and each one can have 5, 10, or more specific behavior characteristics. So, it's impossible to list here all of the ways that people behave differently. To help you better understand and relate to people who act differently, however, we highlight three general *categories* of behavior differences. These categories don't encompass every type of unfamiliar, unexpected, and unsettling behavior you may encounter, but they do address behaviors that are relatively common, usually cause discomfort or confusion in other people, and are often (but not always) caused by mental disabilities:

- *Out-of-control behavior* includes rage, wild or disorganized behavior, and repetitive behaviors.
- *Confused behavior* involves disorientation, such as forgetting who you are, where you are, or what day of the week it is. Confused behavior also includes seeing or hearing things that aren't really there *(hallucinations)* and clinging to patently absurd ideas *(delusions)*.
- *Behavior showing a lack of fundamental social skills* occurs when a person has little or no grasp of appropriate social give-and-take or basic empathy or when a person's relating style is extremely immature.

These behavior categories are worth remembering. They can guide your decision process in many situations. We've used common terminology because our purpose is not to teach you technical psychological terms but to present the behaviors as *you* would encounter them, not as a medical textbook would organize them.

Awareness Activity

The Stigma of Mental Illness

To become more sensitive to the tremendous social stigma experienced by people with behavior differences due to mental illness, try this exercise. Below, list as many negative terms for mental illness as you can think of:

_____   _____

_____   _____

_____   _____

_____   _____

_____   _____

If you can't think of more than a few negative labels, then see the Person-First Words section later in this chapter.

Now, can you think of any other disability difference that has so many pejorative names? Why is that?

REASONS WHY PEOPLE BEHAVE DIFFERENTLY

Some behavior differences are temporary and can be controlled by an individual, such as minor culture clashes. Other behavior differences last longer but are not permanent, such as the eccentricities or rebellions of adolescence. This chapter, however, focuses on behavior differences over which people have limited control and that frequently result from a mental illness.

The three types of behavior differences mentioned previously (out-of-control behavior, confused behavior, and behavior showing a lack of fundamental social skills) have *more* than three causes. Various mental illnesses can cause various behaviors, and there is *not* a direct match between a type of behavior and a mental impairment. Knowing the underlying cause of a different behavior may be helpful at times (especially in ongoing relationships), but because mental disorders lack a one-to-one correlation between illness and symptoms it is not always necessary—nor possible—to know a person's diagnosis.

Here are some of the major causes of all three categories of unusual behavior.

Alcohol and Other Drug Use

Also known as substance abuse or substance dependency, alcohol or drug use is a common cause of many kinds of out-of-control behaviors, including *rage* and *disinhibition*. A disinhibited person does things that would embarrass most of us, such as removing his clothes in public or giving a loud speech on a bus. He is unconcerned with the standard rules of behavior and what other people think and has lost all social restraint. Confusion can also result from substance use and abuse. True substance addiction (not just a single episode of intoxication) is considered to be a mental illness.

I always felt negative feedback, because I made a fool out of myself when I drank. . . . It's the only thing that I knew how to do in my life. [The only way I knew] how to be accepted, or how I thought I could be accepted by people [was by drinking]. Today I know I was not accepted by people when I drank. But it gave me an illusion of acceptance.[7]

—Seymour

Mood Disorders

Mood disorders are mental illnesses that include the extreme highs and lows of human emotions. This chapter emphasizes the highs, called *mania* or *manic periods*, that are characterized by a variety of out-of-control behaviors such as fast, pressured talking, gambling or spending sprees, disinhibition, sexual promiscuity, sleeplessness, and very high-energy behavior that persists for days at a time. During a manic episode, what we call "good judgment" is tossed aside, and recklessness takes over. Sometimes the manic behavior is channeled into a socially acceptable activity, such as extreme bursts of creativity or "workaholism."[8]

Depression is a common mood disorder, but it causes an absence of behaviors or causes behaviors that are not very noticeable in brief encounters, compared with the behavior excesses of other mental illnesses. Depression is characterized by an enduring period of sad mood, loss of interest in formerly pleasurable activities such as hobbies and other leisure interests, difficulty concentrating, social withdrawal, low energy, and, at times, the wish to die or a plan to kill oneself.

Most mood disorders involve either depression or mania, but individuals with *bipolar disorder* (sometimes called *manic-depression*) fluctuate between both states.

Depression is awful beyond words or sounds or images. . . . It bleeds relationships through suspicion, lack of confidence and self-respect, the inability to enjoy life, to walk or talk or think normally, the exhaustion, the night terrors, the day terrors. . . . When you're high, it's tremendous. The ideas and feelings are fast and frequent like shooting stars, and you follow them until you find better and brighter ones. Shyness goes, the right words and gestures are suddenly there, the power to captivate others [is] a felt certainty. . . . Feelings of ease, intensity, power, well-being, financial omnipotence, and euphoria pervade one's marrow. But, somewhere, this changes. The fast ideas are far too fast, and there are far too many; overwhelming confusion replaces clarity. Memory goes. Humor and absorption on friends' faces are replaced by fear and unconcern. . . . You are irritable, angry, frightened, uncontrollable.[9]

—Kay R. Jamison

Psychotic Disorders

Psychotic disorders can cause both out-of-control and confused behavior. *Psychosis* is an umbrella term for several specific types of unusual behavior, including disorganized speech, extremely disorganized behavior, and catatonia (no movement at all). Misperception of the world is a common element in psychosis. A misperception is an experience that *feels* real to the person having it but is obviously *unreal* to everyone else, as though one's senses were playing tricks. Misperceptions include *auditory hallucinations* (hearing things that aren't real, such as threatening or demanding voices), *visual hallucinations* (seeing things that aren't real), and *somatic (bodily) hallucinations* (having sensations such as hot coals on one's skin or insects crawling in one's stomach).

Sometimes thought distortions such as delusions cause unusual behavior. *Delusions* are beliefs that an individual is convinced are true, although others consider the beliefs to be totally absurd, impossible, or bizarre. For example, a person who believes that her thoughts can be stolen or altered by television characters is delusional. Delusions are pervasive thoughts that violate common sense, intelligence, and reason.

In my second breakdown. . . . I had been able to secure employment working as a management trainee for a large Fortune 500 conglomerate. A few months after beginning work, I started to "understand" that all decisions could be made by translating the decision-making process into numerical codes. I decoded many of the problems that I knew the corporation was having, but unfortunately in the process, I myself started turning into various animals, in an evolutionary descending manner. I spent brief periods of time as an ape, a dog, a dragon or

snake, a fish, an insect, and an amoeba; finally, I was
turned into an atom in the inside of a nuclear explosive
device that was on its way to destroy the Soviet Union and
the rest of the world as well.[10]

—Frederick J. Frese, III

Schizophrenia is characterized by psychotic behavior and
deterioration in social and school/work functioning that persists for several months. Schizophrenia may have a sudden,
dramatic onset, but usually it occurs more slowly. The person
gradually withdraws from family, friends, and work associates. She has difficulty maintaining focus in conversation,
may make irrelevant remarks, or may become unusually intense. A person with schizophrenia may lose her ability to
concentrate, organize her life, cope with daily stress, and solve
small problems. Sometimes the person is quite suspicious of
others' intentions to the point of being paranoid. A person
with schizophrenia does not have a "split personality."

It was evening and I was walking along the beach near
my college in Florida. Suddenly my perceptions shifted.
The intensifying wind became an omen of something terrible. I could feel it becoming stronger and stronger. I was
sure it was going to capture me and sweep me away with
it. Nearby trees bent threateningly toward me and tumble-
weed chased me. I became very frightened and began
to run. . . . I arrived back at my dormitory. By this time I was
hearing voices and responding to them. I was confused,
disoriented, and frightened, and remained in a different
reality.[11]

—Esso Leete

Anxiety Disorders and Tourette Syndrome

Anxiety disorders and related disorders can manifest as daily
high anxiety, with a great deal of anticipatory worrying, fret-
ting, and nervousness that disrupt sleep, work, or relationships. Or, anxiety can occur in episodic severe *panic attacks,*

precipitated by specific settings such as bridges, airplanes, or tunnels. A panicked person feels as though her heart is pounding, she can't catch her breath, and her sense of doom and peril is so great that she believes she might die.

Although all anxiety disorders can cause a person to feel out of control, *obsessive-compulsive disorder* and *Tourette syndrome* involve very visible forms of out-of-control behavior. *Obsessions* are repetitive thoughts that intrude on one's mind and cause distress. Obsessions often relate to excessive fears of impending danger, contamination, or immoral thoughts or behaviors or to a need to maintain symmetry. *Compulsions* are repetitive behaviors in which the person engages to "ward off" the obsessive thoughts, even though the person recognizes that the rituals, checking and rechecking, or counting can't realistically prevent the feared events from occurring.

Tourette syndrome is characterized by involuntary, repetitive body movements and vocalizations called *tics* (see Chapter 6). There are many kinds of tics, but facial grimacing, throat clearing, sniffing, and head or shoulder jerking are common. Tics can be barely noticeable or quite severe. They typically come and go and change over time.

He could prevent himself from giving way to outbursts in public, but the strain of controlling himself was severe and exhausting. At home, in private, he could let himself go. . . . "Tourette's comes from deep down in the nervous system and the unconscious. It taps into the oldest, strongest feelings we have. Tourette's is like an epilepsy in the subcortex; when it takes over, there's just a thin line of control . . . between you and it, between you and that raging storm. . . . You have to fight it all your life."[12]
—Oliver Sacks, referring to Carl Bennett
(a pseudonym for a surgeon with Tourette syndrome)

Dementia, Brain Injury, and Brain Tumors

Dementia, brain injury, and brain tumors all can cause unusual behavior, especially persistent confusion. *Disorientation* is a particular kind of confusion. It means not being clearly aware of one's identity, one's physical location, or the identity of others. If someone you know suddenly forgets who you are, then that person is disoriented. Uncertainty about the day of the week, the year, or well-known facts such as the name of the president of the United States can also signal disorientation. Forgetting a once-familiar driving route from work to home is a sign of serious disorientation. Temporary disorientation can be caused by drugs, a psychotic episode, mood disorders, and acute illnesses with a high fever.

Dementia is a chronic, acquired condition that involves memory impairment or loss plus impairment of one or more of these mental functions: language recognition and identification of familiar objects, movement planning and execution despite intact muscles and coordination, and cognitive function (planning, organizing, sequencing, abstracting). There are many underlying causes of dementia, but two common ones are *Alzheimer's disease* and *vascular dementia* (which is caused by a stroke and was formerly known as *multi-infarct dementia*). Prolonged alcohol and drug use can cause dementia that persists past the period of intoxication or addiction. Dementia can be a feature of other diseases, such as Huntington disease and Parkinson's disease.[13]

Glancing around, nothing was familiar. I was stopped at an intersection and the traffic light was green. Cars honked impatiently, so I pulled straight ahead, trying to get my bearings. I could not read the street sign, but there was another sign ahead; perhaps it would shed some light on my location.

A few yards ahead, there was a park ranger building. Trembling, I wiped my eyes, and breathing deeply tried to calm myself. Finally, feeling ready to speak, I started the car again and approached the ranger station. The guard smiled and inquired how he could assist me. "I appear to be lost," I began, making a great effort to keep my voice level, despite my emotional state. "Where do you need to go?" the guard asked politely. A cold chill enveloped me as I realized I could not remember the name of my street. Tears began to flow down my cheeks. I did not know where I wanted to go.[14]

—D.F. McGowin

Developmental Disabilities

Although *autism* and *mental retardation* (see Chapter 9) are not mental illnesses, the two disorders can cause a number of unexpected and unusual behaviors. Someone with a *lifelong* pattern of different social interaction may have a developmental disability called *autism*. Autism (also called *autistic disorder*) and a milder form of autism called Asperger syndrome are developmental disabilities beginning before the age of three years and characterized by a significant impairment in social interaction and communication as well as restricted, repetitive, and stereotyped patterns of behavior, interests, and activities. Does the person seem to lack a fundamental understanding of social exchange? Social aloofness or lack of social reciprocity can be obvious or subtle but are definitely present. One person may show it by avoiding social groups, by leaving the room where the party is, or by generally trying to be alone. Another person may want to be part of the group but may lack a true understanding of how to interact. She may show basic social manners but not a deeper awareness of other people's feelings. It can appear as though she does not feel or show empathy. One researcher has described this phenomenon as "their narrow and overly concrete understanding of social phenomena, and the resultant overwhelming puzzlement they experience when required to meet the demands of interpersonal life."[15]

If a person persistently behaves younger than his age or acts very immaturely or naively, then he may not understand sudden changes in social situations. He may have difficulty following a rapid, complicated conversation or understanding certain jokes or abstract concepts. Because he misses subtle social cues, he may be overly friendly with strangers or may stand too close to other people or speak too loudly. This kind of behavior can be a sign of an overall developmental delay. Someone whose social behavior, intellectual functioning, and self-care ability have been consistently delayed all his life may have *mental retardation* (see Chapter 9).

My emotions are simpler than those of most people. I don't know what complex emotion in a human relationship is. I only understand simple emotions, such as fear, anger, happiness, and sadness. I cry during sad movies, and sometimes I cry when I see something that really moves me. But complex emotional relationships are beyond my comprehension. . . . I don't understand being happy and sad at the same time.

The last couple of years, I have become more aware of a kind of electricity that goes on between people which is much subtler than overt anger, happiness, or fear. I have observed that when several people are together and having a good time, their speech and laughter follow a rhythm. They will all laugh together and then talk quietly until the next laughing cycle. I have always had a hard time fitting in with this rhythm, and I usually interrupt conversations without realizing my mistake. The problem is that I can't follow the rhythm.[16]

—Temple Grandin

All of the mental impairments mentioned previously are considered to have underlying physical causes involving brain chemistry or brain structure. Researchers are studying a variety of factors that create these brain impairments, including prenatal influences and genetic vulnerability. The environment may also be a factor in when a mental illness appears and in how severe it is. The balance between stress and trauma, and nurturing and social support in a person's life can greatly affect emotional well-being and the timing of symptoms.

INTERVENTIONS AND SUPPORTS

The variety of human behavior is awesome. You may feel that "normal" behavior is *such* a broad concept that it's hard to be certain what "abnormal" is. If you are confused about which behavior differences are actually causes for worry, and if you are concerned about a family member, friend, or co-worker, then consider these three questions:

- Has the person shown a sudden, dramatic change in behavior?
- Does the person's behavior interfere with major life activities, such as self-care, parenting responsibilities, work duties, family relationships, and enjoyment of leisure time?
- Has the problem persisted for more than a month?

If the answer to *any* of these questions is yes, then the person *may* need professional help. This section provides a brief overview of the kinds of help available for people with significant behavior differences.

Medical Evaluation

There are many medical illnesses that can cause emotional and behavior problems. The first step in helping a person with serious behavior differences is a complete physical evaluation by a pediatrician, family physician, or internist. The professional might use some of these tests:

- Blood tests to check for anemia and thyroid disorder, which can cause fatigue and loss of energy that might be mistaken for depression
- An EEG, which measures brain electrical activity, to detect seizures that may be related to aggressive outbursts[17]
- A CAT scan or MRI scan, which gives a detailed picture of brain structures, to see whether a brain tumor exists or a stroke has occurred

A doctor can also determine whether mental confusion that appears to be dementia is actually an adverse reaction to medications.

Medications

Some people with serious behavior differences can be helped by *psychoactive medications* that affect mood, disorganized thinking, misperceptions, anxiety, or specific behaviors.[18] Although any medical doctor can prescribe these medications, a psychiatrist specializes in treating emotional-behavioral conditions and the underlying mental impairments. Medication may help a person be more responsive to learning more appropriate or effective social behaviors.

Psychotherapy

Psychotherapy involves confidential discussions with a mental health professional on a regular basis to explore the person's daily life challenges. People with mental illness often benefit from counseling to manage their symptoms as well as the associated feelings of loneliness, social rejection, and self-doubt.[19] *Behavior modification techniques* may be used by the individual and/or his significant others to learn and reinforce more adaptive behaviors and reduce the frequency of maladaptive ones.

Other Supports

Self-advocacy and *support organizations* educate individuals and their families, advocate more research and services, and campaign to reduce the stigma associated with mental impairments. *Crisis intervention services* provide brief and highly focused professional mental health care following acute crises, such as after a traumatic event. Many community mental health clinics offer crisis intervention. *Hospitalization* (both inpatient and day treatment) is available for people who are experiencing severe depression, psychosis, or disorientation, or who are in immediate danger of harming themselves or others.

Other therapies can improve a person's emotional or behavioral functioning. *Occupational therapy* assists a person in regaining or learning leisure, work, or self-care skills that have been impaired by the behavior difference or mental illness. *Art, music, drama,* and *dance/movement therapies* use creative expression to release intense emotions and reduce anxiety in addition to providing another channel for professional understanding of the person's inner emotional world. *Alternative* or *complementary therapies* encompass a range of rediscovered traditional remedies such as acupuncture, herbal medicine, vitamin supplementation, massage, and folk healing. Therapeutic pets also have been used for their calming effects and companionship. Some alternative therapies are inexpensive, harmless, and often a useful adjunct to traditional treatments, but others may be dangerous or, at best, ineffective. Mental health professionals and self-advocacy organizations often have information about current research on these therapies.

INTERACTING WITH PEOPLE
WHO BEHAVE DIFFERENTLY

Person-First Words

Remember, a person is not defined by her impairment or difference. The behavior differences described in this chapter would be evident to you even if you did not have specific vocabulary to describe them. When you lack specific, respectful terms to describe a disability, however, your reactions may be more negative because the unfamiliar, unexpected, and unsettling aspects of the disability become the focus of the interaction. Understanding basic terminology can increase your comfort and enhance your actions.

Here are some preferred terms:

- *Mental illness, mental disability,* or *mental impairment*
- *Emotional disorder*
- *Psychiatric disability*
- *Disorientation*
- *Hallucination*

- *Dementia*
- *Brain disorder*

When in doubt, use words that describe the behavior specifically:

- He's forgotten my name. He doesn't recognize me.
- She claims to be Jesus' mother.
- She believes the radio announcer is stealing her thoughts.
- He said a voice told him to do it.
- She's been very depressed for the past two months.
- His enthusiasm is more like a child's.
- She has a hard time understanding your feelings. It's hard for her to see your point of view.
- He has a shoulder-jerking tic.
- She has an uncontrollable need to wash her hands many times a day.

Avoid inaccurate and negative words that perpetuate stereotypes and stigma, such as "crazy," "cuckoo," "loony," "mad," "mental case," "nervous breakdown," "nutty," "psycho," "retard," "wacko," and so forth.

Detecting Behavior Differences

Sometimes *sensing* different behavior is easier than pinning down *exactly* what is so odd or unusual. Was it her choice of words or the topic itself? Was it the expression on her face or her posture? Was the behavior wild or withdrawn? Did she move too fast or too slow? Was her stare too long and too penetrating? Or, was she unaware of your presence?

When you detect differences in someone's behavior, you're responding to a feeling in your gut, not a medical label. The important thing in detecting a behavior difference is to listen to your feelings. If behavior *seems* different, it *is* different to you—don't spend too much time figuring out the exact source of the difference or the specific mental disorder.

As you saw from the mental illnesses described previously, behavior that is out of control, confused, or that shows a serious social skill impairment can have various causes. It often takes a mental health professional to figure out which behaviors go with which specific mental disorders or disabilities, but in many situations, especially brief encounters, you don't need to differentiate causes in order to handle the situation effectively. Using the shortcut of the three behavior categories can help you manage your reactions and plan your actions. When you encounter unusual behavior, try not to get "stuck" in your surprise or nervousness. Try to get past that first-response label of "crazy" because this word is more likely to frighten you rather than calm or guide you.

Deciding

As mentioned in Chapter 4, Deciding involves relaxing and pausing to think about three questions. But when it comes to behavior differences, there is a preliminary question to ask *before* you ask the three Deciding questions.

Is This Behavior Dangerous?

Remember, just because your difference detector's first reaction is "danger," this does not mean that the behavior is *actually* dangerous. Pause and Decide whether your first impression was accurate or an overreaction. Keep in mind that most behavior differences are *not* dangerous. So, you usually have time to evaluate the situation and decide how to react. Although you may sometimes overreact to someone who is behaving differently, there also may be times when someone is acting aggressively—toward you or someone else—and you *do* have to react quickly and defensively.

Anyone can become enraged—whether or not he has a mental disability. Enraged people are not always dangerous, but they are more likely to become aggressive, so try to Detect these behaviors, which usually correspond with rage, right away:

- Eyes are narrowed, darting from side to side.
- Face is flushed.
- Posture is rigid, and the person seems "jumpy" or nervous.
- The person has a weapon in hand or nearby.
- Aggressive words (such as "I'm gonna get him. . . . Where is he?") or profanity are aimed at someone who is present or someone who the person *thinks* is present.

If your assessment is yes, this really is dangerous behavior, then proceed to the Action Tips that follow. If the behavior does not appear dangerous, then consider the three Deciding questions.

1. What kind of behavior difference is this?
2. How relevant is the behavior difference to the situation?
3. What are my action options?

Remember that there is more than one way to communicate and interact effectively. The Action Tips that follow are not prescriptions but rather possibilities for you to consider. It's better to try *some* action than to ignore the other person or leave.

Action Tips

Behavior Differences

Here are some tips for actions that might be more sensitive and helpful in response to certain people with behavior differences. Remember, these are *suggestions*, not *prescriptions*.

During an episode of out-of-control behavior . . .
These suggestions apply to a variety of behaviors, including aggressive rage and disinhibition.

- If you feel personally threatened by a person or incidental encounter, then you need to protect yourself and leave, if possible.

- Remove yourself from the person's "audience." Ignore him.
- Back away slowly.
- Avoid getting close to the person.
- Try to call for help.
- Avoid making direct eye contact or staring, which the person may interpret as a threat.
- Speak in a soft voice with a soothing tone.
- Use short sentences of five words or less.
- It's usually useless to say, "Calm down." Instead, make specific suggestions such as "Sit down here," "Rest a minute," or "Put down the stick."
- Try to get the person to agree to be escorted to a calmer, quieter place, such as his home.

Later, when the person has calmed down . . .

- Try to determine what triggered the out-of-control behavior.
- If the person is a relative, friend, or co-worker, urge him to seek professional assistance. If he refuses, then seek help for yourself.
- Contact a support organization (see the Readings and Resources at the end of this chapter).

When the out-of-control behavior is repetitive, such as a compulsion or a tic . . .

- Remember that most repetitive behaviors are harmless and best ignored.
- Refrain from interfering physically with the behavior.
- If the person is experiencing a great deal of stress, then deal with that rather than the repetitive behavior. Offer a soothing activity or escape from the stressful situation, or try deep breathing together (see Chapter 4).

For day-to-day coping with a person who has confused behavior . . .

- Provide appropriate visual cues and reminders about identity, date, or location. Use calendars, sticky notes, photos with names written on them, and so forth.

- Give the person gentle reminders, such as "Today is Sunday" or "I'm Caitlin, your daughter."
- Ignore errors that are small or inconsequential. Criticism will get you nowhere.

When a person appears to be misperceiving events . . .

- Look at the person. Make eye contact as you would with anyone else unless this seems to frighten the person.
- Reduce environmental stimulation, such as by dimming bright lights or moving to a less-crowded room.
- Use short, clear sentences.
- Focus on practical matters. What does the person need to do right now? This is not the time for abstract, deep conversation or implied meanings.
- Don't try to convince the person of her irrationality by arguing or teasing.
- Just state the facts as you see them, when it is necessary to do so. "I know you hear a voice, but I don't hear anyone shouting at you now." You can acknowledge the person's perception without saying you believe it yourself. It's usually *not* effective to explain the reason for the voices or to tell her to stop.
- Offer a pleasant distraction related to a hobby, snack, or another simple, accessible activity.
- Help the person to relax. Try deep breathing together. (See Chapter 4.)

When a person seems to lack social skills . . .

- Invite the person to join in your activity. Be specific: "Would you come and sit with us?" "Please come drink coffee with us," or "Join us for a card game, John."
- Refrain from moving too close or touching the person unless invited. Even when the person's behavior seems childlike, maintain usual adult body boundaries. For example, don't pat the person on the head, and don't act parental or condescending.

Some people who are different don't focus on the same things you do. At a movie theater, they might see something shining on a person's shirt, like a bright button, and that information might go in their eyes so strongly they don't hear the movie coming in their ears any more, even though the movie seems a lot more important to you than a bright button. They might talk about that bright button, loudly, because they're forgetting about the movie.

You might be able to process the movie and the button at the same time and quickly decide that the movie is a lot more important. But some people can't do that very well. So if someone at a movie is talking loudly about something that seems strange to you, he might be a person who processes things differently than you do.

So it might be helpful if you told the person the most important thing to focus on, kindly. You could say, "You're right about the button, but this is a movie, so you have to watch the pictures on the screen and listen to the voices from the speakers."[20]

—Brad Rand

Doing

Whenever you interact with someone who has a behavior difference, there is not just one right thing to Do. It does help, however, to remember these general pointers:

- Focus on the person and his abilities and competencies.
- Include the person in the social situation. Don't talk around the person.
- Provide assistance if asked or if your offer was accepted.
- Get on with the task or purpose of the situation!

Reacting to behavior differences in others calls for suppressing the tendency to label all unusual behavior as "crazy." It also calls for the best observation skills that you can muster to think specifically and tolerantly about the relevance of the be-havior to your interaction.

Debriefing

You've Detected behavior differences in someone, and you went ahead and Did what you planned to do. Next, you can Debrief the experience using the following Awareness Activity by yourself and in discussion with family, friends, and others. Patience, tolerance, and a willingness to be flexible with your own behavior are definite assets when the other person's be-havior is unfamiliar, unexpected, or unsettling to you. Answer these questions privately, in your thoughts, or talk them over with someone else who was present during the interaction.

Debriefing

1. **Think about what happened this time.**
   - Did I Detect the difference accurately?
   - Did I Detect and manage my own emotional reactions?
   - Did I relax and Decide what my action options were?
   - Were my actions consistent with my Decisions? If not, why not?
   - Was the purpose of the interaction accomplished?
   - What worked well? What didn't work well?
2. **Figure out what went wrong.** If the situation went well, then congratulate yourself—and keep up the good work! If the situation did not go so well, then try to figure out why. Ask yourself whether any of these pitfalls occurred:
   - I focused on the difference too much.
   - I acted as though the difference wasn't relevant at all, but actually it was.
   - I got stuck in stress and forgot to relax.
   - I got stuck in pity and didn't focus on abilities.
   - I worried too much about "the right thing" to Do, so I Did nothing.

3. **Think about what could happen next time.** Ask yourself what you could do differently next time.
   - Detect the disability and my feelings, and relax.
   - Decide more carefully, or consider more action options.
   - Look at the person or disability by regarding, not by staring.
   - Talk to the person with person-first words, ask for information, or offer assistance.
   - Interact differently by including instead of excluding and by focusing on the person and his *abilities*.

Behavior Differences

At-A-Glance

Number of Americans with Behavior Differences

- One in four families has a member with mental illness. One in five adults has a diagnosable mental disorder.[21]
- Severe mental illness affects approximately five million adults.[22]
- More than two million people are affected by schizophrenia in any given year, and only one person in five recovers completely.[23]
- Mood disorders affect nearly 18 million adults each year.[24]
- 1.8 million people have severe dementia; 1 to 5 million have mild to moderate dementia.[25]
- Panic disorders affect at least three million people.[26]
- Obsessive-compulsive disorder affects as many as five million people.[27]
- 1 out of every 2,000 people has Tourette syndrome.[28] The prevalence rate for Tourette syndrome *plus* chronic and transient tics is approximately 1 in 200 people.[29]
- More than 500,000 people have some form of autism. Autism occurs in 1 of 1,000 live births.[30]

Estimates of Substance Use in America[31]

- 18 million people have alcoholism.
- 6 million people use cocaine.
- Half a million people are addicted to heroin.

People with Mood Disorders

Patty Duke, actor
Ernest Hemingway, author
Kurt Vonnegut, author
Mike Wallace, journalist
Virginia Woolf, author

People Who Have Had Substance Addiction

Betty Ford, former First Lady
Louis Gossett, Jr., actor
John Hiatt, singer/musician
Dennis Hopper, actor
Grace Slick, singer
Stevie Ray Vaughan, musician

People with Dementia

Rita Hayworth, actor
Ronald Reagan, former U.S. president

People with Tourette Syndrome or Tic Disorder

Mahmoud Abdul-Rauf (formerly known as Chris Jackson), athlete
Jim Eisenreich, athlete
Samuel Johnson, 18th century writer
Wolfgang Amadeus Mozart, 18th century composer

READINGS
AND RESOURCES

Books

Asperger's Syndrome: A Guide for Parents and Professionals
T. Attwood (Jessica Kingsley Publishers, London, England, 1998)

A Mind of Its Own: Tourette's Syndrome, A Story and a Guide
R.D. Brun & B. Brun (Oxford University Press, New York, 1994)

Helping Someone with Mental Illness:
A Compassionate Guide for Family, Friends, and Caregivers
R. Carter (Random House, New York, 1998)

On the Edge of Darkness
K. Cronkite (Delta Books, New York, 1996)

The Gift of Fear: Survival Signals that Protect Us from Violence
Gavin de Becker (Little, Brown, Boston, 1997)

Getting Them Sober: A Guide for Those
Who Live with an Alcoholic, Volume II
T.R. Drews (Bridge Publishing, South Plainfield, NJ, 1983)

The Sky is Falling: Understanding and Coping
with Phobias, Panic, and Obsessive-Compulsive Disorder
R. Dumont (W.W. Norton, New York, 1996)

Alzheimer's: Caring for Your Loved One, Caring for Yourself
S. Fish (Harold Shaw Publishers, Wheaton, IL, 1996)

What to Do When Someone You Love Is Depressed
M. Golant & S.K. Golant (Villard Books, New York, 1996)

Alcoholism: The Facts
D.W. Goodwin (Oxford University Press, New York, 1994, 2nd ed.)

Thinking in Pictures
Temple Grandin (Vintage Books, New York, 1995)

Children with Tourette Syndrome: A Parent's Guide
T. Haerle, Ed. (Woodbine House, Rockville, MD, 1992)

Caring for the Mind:
The Comprehensive Guide to Mental Health
D. Hales & R.E. Hales (Bantam Doubleday Dell, New York, 1995)

A Parent's Guide to Autism
C.A. Hart (Pocket Books, New York, 1993)

Surviving Mental Illness: Stress, Coping, and Adaptation
A.B. Hatfield & H.P. Lefley (The Guilford Press, New York, 1993)

An Unquiet Mind
K.R. Jamison (Knopf, New York, 1995)

Hidden Victims: An Eight-Stage Healing Process
for Families and Friends of the Mentally Ill
J.T. Johnston (Doubleday, New York, 1988)

The 36-Hour Day: A Family Guide to Caring for Persons with
Alzheimer's Disease, Related Dementing Illness, and Memory
Loss in Later Life (Revised Edition)
N.L. Mace & P.V. Rabins (Warner, New York, 1991)

My Sister's Keeper: Living with a Sibling's Schizophrenia
M. Moorman (Penguin USA, New York, 1993)

Coping with Schizophrenia: A Guide for Families
K.T. Mueser & S. Gingerich (New Harbinger Publications,
Oakland, CA, 1994)

Welcome Silence: My Triumph Over Schizophrenia
C. North (Simon & Schuster, New York, 1987)

The Boy Who Couldn't Stop Washing:
The Experience of Obsessive-Compulsive Disorder
J.L. Rapoport (NAL-Dutton, New York, 1991)

A Parent's Guide to Childhood and Adolescent Depression
P.G. Shapiro (Dell Publishing, New York, 1994)

*Your Anxious Child: Raising a Healthy Child
in a Frightening World*
M.A. Shaw (Birch Lane Press, Secaucus, NJ, 1995)

Educating Yourself About Alcohol and Drugs: A People's Primer
M.A. Shuckit (Plenum, New York, 1995)

Surviving Schizophrenia: A Family Manual, Revised Edition
E.F. Torrey (HarperCollins, New York, 1988)

Films

David and Lisa (1962)

Days of Wine and Roses (1962)

King of Hearts (1967)

Ordinary People (1980)

Under the Volcano (1984)

Rain Man (1988)

The Fisher King (1991)

Benny and Joon (1993)

Mrs. Parker and the Vicious Circle (1994)

Leaving Las Vegas (1995)

Self-Advocacy/Support Organizations

Al-Anon, Alateen, and Adult Children of Alcoholics
Post Office Box 862, Midtown Station, New York, NY 10018-0862
(800-344-2666; www.Al-Anon-Alateen.org)

Alcoholics Anonymous
Box 459, Grand Central Station, New York, NY 10163
(212-686-1100; www.alcoholics-anonymous.org)

Alzheimer's Association
919 North Michigan Avenue, Suite 1000, Chicago, IL 60611
(800-272-3900; www.alz.org)

American Brain Tumor Association
2720 River Road, Des Plaines, IL 60018 (800-886-2282;
708-827-9910; www.abta.org)

Anxiety Disorders Association of America
11900 Parklawn Drive, Suite 100, Rockville, MD 20852
(301-231-9350; www.adaa.org/)

Autism Society of America
7910 Woodmont Avenue, Suite 650, Bethesda, MD 20814
(800-328-8476; fax: 301-657-0869; www.autism-society.org)

California Mental Health & Developmental Disabilities Center
(www.npi.ucla.edu/mhdd/)

Mental Health Infosource
(www.mhsource.com)
An Internet "gateway" to a large variety of mental health
information.

National Alliance for the Mentally Ill
200 North Glebe Road, Suite 1015, Arlington, VA 22203-3754
(Helpline: 800-950-6264; 703-524-7600; TDD: 703-516-7991; fax:
703-524-9094; www.nami.org; e-mail: namiofc@aol.com)

NADD (formerly National Association of the Dually Diagnosed)
132 Fair Street, Kingston, NY 12401 (800-331-5362;
fax: 914-331-4569; www.thenadd.org/)
An organization that focuses on the mental health needs of
people with mental retardation.

National Mental Health Association
1021 Prince Street, Alexandria, VA 22314 (800-969-6642;
TDD: 800-433-5959; www.nmha.org)

National Stroke Association
96 Inverness Drive E, Suite 1, Englewood, CO 80112-5112

(800-STROKES [800-787-6537]; fax: 303-649-1328; e-mail: info@stroke.org; World Wide Web site: www.stroke.org)

Narcotics Anonymous—NA World Services
Post Office Box 9999, Van Nuys, CA 913409 (818-773-9999; www.na.org)

Obsessive Compulsive Foundation
Post Office Box 70, Milford, CT 06460-0070 (24-hour information line: 203-874-3843; 203-8728-5669; www.ocfoundation.org)

Tourette Syndrome Association
42–40 Bell Boulevard, Bayside, NY 11361-2820 (800-237-7017; neuro-www2.mgh.harvard.edu/TSA/tsamain.nclk)

9

People Who
Learn Differently

I feel that retarded people are just human, just like any other normal person. They are a normal person. The only thing wrong with them, they're slow learners. Big deal.[1]

—A young woman
in a sheltered workshop

Learning is a crucial part of life. Not only do we spend most of our child and teen years in formal education, but we also continue to learn every day. Our jobs often change, steering us toward new information or skills. Household appliances, automated teller machines, telephones, and even cars appear regularly in updated versions that require us to master new procedures, vocabulary, and control switches. Lifelong learning is essential for adult functioning.

But everyone learns differently. Some of us like to watch another person perform a new task or operate a new gadget, while others prefer to read a manual. Some of us need to listen to someone instruct us, but others would rather jump right in and experiment with a "hands-on" approach. This chapter introduces you to learning differences that go beyond learning styles. Learning impairments are more than a question of style because they're caused by brain differences that can affect a person's ability to perform certain intellectual tasks, to work, and to manage daily life.

MYTHS, ASSUMPTIONS, AND BELIEFS

As with other kinds of disability differences, there are many myths about learning and intelligence differences and people who have them.

Myth: We Equate Learning Ability with Independence

When you were a child, what was the most awful taunt kids used? You probably heard "fatso," "four-eyes," "nerd," and "klutz," plus the racial and ethnic slurs common in your neighborhood and era. But for the "big guns" name calling, the words "dummy" or "retard" were no doubt at the top of the list. Why is a reference to learning differences the lowest blow in children's verbal warfare? The epithets suggest the notion of a minimum of "smarts" required for personhood. More than the words "runt," "bigfoot," or "stringbean," the word "retard" suggests that if a person doesn't learn like the rest of us, then he isn't one of us. We Americans value independence highly, so to us, a learning impairment means dependence. It is true that serious learning differences have often meant *less opportunity* to work, live independently, and lead a self-directed life. But it is also true that many people with learning impairments *do* achieve these goals in spite of environmental handicaps and others' negative attitudes. Yet many people still believe that if you have impaired learning ability, you're doomed to perpetual dependency. And dependency—to any degree—is seen as a sign of weakness and failure.

Myth: We Think of Intelligence as an Either/Or Condition

In fact, there are several kinds of intelligence. Individuals can be gifted in one type of intelligence but have less ability in another type. For example, you might have extraordinary musical or spatial intelligence, but limited interpersonal and mathematical aptitude.[2]

Myth: We Are Most Comfortable with "Average" Intelligence

We consistently devalue low intelligence and admire high intelligence, yet we tend to prefer the company of people with "just enough" intelligence. That's the expected average for most of us. Interacting with people who have much lower or higher learning ability is outside the comfort zone of most people. Adequate intelligence seems to be the ideal: If you're "too smart," then you're considered a "brain" or an "egghead" and separated into a category that seems to make many people uncomfortable.

Myth: We Assume that Intelligent People Are Good at the Three Rs

The three Rs, reading, writing, and arithmetic, are not always related to intelligence. Some people of average or higher general intelligence have specific learning disabilities that interfere with reading, number calculations, or other discrete cognitive functions.

We need to separate myth from reality when it comes to learning differences. That way, we can alter our perspective toward and interact more comfortably with people who learn in different ways or at different paces.

Mom . . . I know I'm retarded, but I'm not stupid.[3]
—Nicole Kaufman

WHAT IT FEELS LIKE

The experience of having a learning difference is not as easily imagined as the experience of having a movement or appearance difference. The impairment itself is nonvisible. But see whether you can relate to the experiences described below, in which cognitive functioning plays a key role.

Did you ever misunderstand the words on an airport loudspeaker when static alternated with recognizable words such as "delayed" or "gate change"? Try to recall your frantic behavior as you strained to get a handle on which flight and which gate were announced and your panic at the thought of missing your flight. This is similar to challenges that people with *auditory processing problems* face many times a day.

Or, imagine yourself reading some typed directions about how much medicine to give your ill child. You find that a very poor copy machine has rendered some of the letters illegible. You focus intently, squint your eyes, and still can make out only part of the message. You realize that a spoonful is involved, but you can't be sure whether it's a teaspoon or a tablespoon. This is similar to a *visual processing impairment*, even if it's only temporary.

Have you ever listened to someone at a party launch into a very detailed, very technical explanation of some topic that was clearly "over your head"? Maybe you grasped her first sentence, but the second sentence contained one or two unfamiliar terms. And by the fifth sentence, you had lost her train of thought and probably some self-confidence as well. In our society, it's considered acceptable to admit, "You've lost me!" when an expert barrels ahead on a technical, professional subject. We think it's okay to say to our doctor, "Whoa! Can you repeat that in plain English?" But a person with *mental retarda-*

tion can encounter puzzling vocabulary many times a day, and that person may not have the social skills or support from others needed to signal his confusion or to ask the speaker to explain things another way.

LEARNING DIFFERENCES YOU MAY ENCOUNTER

When you interact with someone who learns differently from you, the experience can be interesting or frustrating, largely depending on whether you're trying to teach the other person something. Learning differences are rarely apparent in fleeting or brief interactions. We are most aware of them in long-term relationships such as with family members, friends, classmates, or co-workers.

When another person writes a letter that has many spelling errors, reads you a newspaper article and stumbles over many of the words (omitting some entirely), or can't calculate the price of a 10-pound watermelon at the market, then she *may* have a *learning disability.* (On the other hand, these differences might indicate a lack of education in these areas.) If your adult cousin received special education services during his entire school career, your aunt and uncle manage his money, and he works in a sheltered day program, then he *may* have *mental retardation.*

Awareness Activity

Learning Differences

Visit a library or a bookstore, and go to a section that you consider *very technical* and *unfamiliar* to you. Try a book on quantum mechanics, an Old English text such as *Beowulf*, or a neurosurgery manual. Select a book and make a genuine effort to understand a difficult chapter. Ask yourself:

• What does it feel like to read this kind of material?

- Did I make any self-critical statements, such as *"I'm* not smart enough to understand this" or "I feel pretty stupid."
- What would help me learn this material? Would it help to watch someone demonstrate the concepts, to have the concepts presented with easier vocabulary, to learn a very small piece of information at a time, or to have a personal tutor explain it to me?

REASONS WHY PEOPLE LEARN DIFFERENTLY

There are two broad categories of learning impairments: *learning disabilities* and *mental retardation.* Learning disabilities affect one or a few intellectual functions and are most apparent in school or work situations in which reading, writing, or math skills are used. Mental retardation affects all of a person's intellectual functions as well as her skills of daily living. Let's take a closer look at these types of learning differences.

Learning Disabilities

Learning disabilities cause underachievement in reading, writing, spelling, or mathematics in relation to age or typical overall intelligence.[4] A person with a learning disability may have difficulty organizing information that her senses take in. A learning disability is usually identified in elementary school. The teacher's or the parent's first clue is the child's lower academic performance compared with her same-age peers. Psychological tests are used to identify the specific impairment(s) that underlie the performance problem. Common impairments linked with learning disabilities include the following:

- *Auditory processing*—hearing is intact, but the meaning of the heard message gets jumbled somewhere on its path between the ears and the part of the brain that interprets the message. A person with auditory processing deficits has difficulty with learning through listening.

- *Visual processing*—vision is intact, but comprehension of written words or symbols is impaired. Letters on a page can appear reversed or distorted so the person does not fully understand what she reads. A person with visual processing problems has difficulty learning through seeing.
- *Eye–hand coordination*—vision and the function of muscles are fine, but the coordination of body movements during certain activities is impaired, such as during writing.

As I write, reversals appear almost one per sentence. It is as though that part of my brain controlling letter order and spelling stalls momentarily or short-circuits, and during that instant I write "whis" instead of "wish". . . . The severity of all my symptoms can vary from day to day, from hour to hour. It feels like a tide that rises and falls, even like waves that wash in, sweep over me and then recede. Unlike the tide, however, I cannot predict the rising and subsiding of my symptoms. . . . For most of my life I had no idea why this happened to me. The experience of it has ranged from frustrating to embarrassing to devastating.[5]

— Abraham Schmitt

A person with a learning disability usually has average or above-average intelligence as measured on tests. He *can* comprehend abstract concepts, use reasoning and judgment, and think critically to solve problems. Usually this person's daily life skills, such as grooming, housekeeping, using public transportation, making friends, and holding a job, are similar to the skills of other people of the same age. When a person has a learning disability, he doesn't experience a global impairment of many life skills but rather has a *specific* difficulty in the domain of learning.

Mental Retardation

Mental retardation is another type of learning difference. Like learning disabilities, mental retardation is neither a disease nor an illness. But there are more differences than similarities between the two. Mental retardation is a condition in which *both* thinking and daily life skills are significantly impaired.[6] Deficient intellectual skills include abstract problem solving, decision making, math calculation, absorption and retention of general information about the world, and social judgment. Although learning disabilities usually don't become apparent until school age, mental retardation often is detected by family members during the preschool years because they observe a disparity between chronological age and developmental skills in the young child. Cognitive testing (also called *IQ testing*) by a professional reveals deficits in most intellectual functions. The term *mental retardation* is used when the child's test performance is lower than that of most other children of the same chronological age.

Although we strongly equate mental retardation with IQ, mental retardation is more than a problem only with "book learning." The definition of mental retardation also considers a range of specific behaviors that are needed to function as a typical adult:

- Self-care (bathing, grooming)
- Planning, preparing, and eating meals
- Housekeeping and finances
- Driving or taking public transportation
- Communicating
- Making and maintaining relationships
- Pursuing hobbies
- Working at a job
- Self-direction in all of these activities

A person with mental retardation has significant impairments in several (but not necessarily all) of these skills of daily living and community survival. She may have strengths in one or more areas, such as athletics, the arts, or making friends.

Well, when I'm in school, I write slowly and when I write fast my writing comes sloppy and people don't understand my writing. . . . Some people may be faster than I am, and some people may be slower than me. . . . I want them to stop so I can catch up. I don't want teachers to go faster than I am, too. I know I'm improving my disability, but I still have it. I may not be able to learn things and that makes me have a hard time.[7]

—Jason Kingsley

A common misconception is that people with mental retardation can't learn. But they do indeed learn. Although they learn new skills throughout their lives, the gap between *expected* overall functioning (given their chronological age) and *actual* functioning always remains. And it's possible for a person with mental retardation also to have a specific learning disability, such as a visual or auditory processing impairment or eye-hand motor incoordination.

Reasons Why People Have Learning Differences

Occasionally a child or an adult experiences a temporary learning disability resulting from an emotional trauma or a medical condition. These secondary learning problems, however, are caused by overwhelming emotions, preoccupying thoughts, or other side effects of life problems that can improve over time. The focus of this chapter, however, is on learning differences that are lifelong and caused by brain processes or structures impaired since early childhood. Using new brain imaging technology, researchers are beginning to precisely define and "match" a specific learning difference with its specific brain location. But even without a detailed "learning map" of the brain, we do know from experience that brain development can be disrupted in a variety of ways that then result in learning differences:

- Down syndrome and fragile X syndrome are two common *genetic disorders* that usually involve mental retardation. Hundreds of other genetic disorders have mental retardation as an associated feature. In many individuals with learning disabilities, there is a family history of learning problems. Researchers believe that some forms of learning disabilities are inherited.

- *Maternal illness* during pregnancy, such as rubella, diabetes, cytomegalovirus, HIV/AIDS, herpes, and many other conditions, can cause mental retardation.
- *Toxic substances* can damage a developing brain. For example, media coverage has educated the public about the dangers of prenatal exposure to alcohol, other drugs, and tobacco, as well as the negative effects of lead or mercury exposure during early childhood.
- *Lack of oxygen* can occur before birth or during a difficult delivery. A near-drowning incident also deprives a child's brain of oxygen.
- *Trauma* from auto, bicycle, or other accidents can damage specific parts of the brain or lead to more pervasive injury.
- *Severe malnutrition* before birth or in the first few years of life can damage the brain.

All of these factors can contribute to learning disabilities and mental retardation in the general population, but for a specific individual, often the cause is not known.

INTERVENTIONS AND SUPPORTS

There are no treatments or medicines that can cure learning differences. We have no interventions that address the brain impairments that underlie learning disabilities and mental retardation. Therefore, the focus of interventions and supports is to evaluate each person's specific learning needs and design the environment to maximize success at learning, working, and maintaining social relationships. With adequate supports, children with learning disabilities can reach age-level academic achievement. Children and adults with mental retardation generally need more intensive support and more kinds of support, especially with daily living skills. Their academic achievements are usually below age level, but they *are* able to enjoy friendships, work, and hobbies. Without proper accommodations, however, people with either kind of learning difference may suffer a significant loss of self-esteem, confidence, and the development of essential life skills.

Teaching Methods

Students with learning differences benefit from *individualized teaching methods* that focus on their strengths and learning styles. For example, a student with auditory processing difficulties benefits from lessons taught with many visual cues, such as pictures, and tactile experiences, such as objects to hold. When a teacher uses dry beans or small wooden blocks to demonstrate math, the child may grasp the concepts more easily than when the lesson relies exclusively on written numbers and abstract symbols.

Because a student with mental retardation may have difficulty learning the skills of daily living, she often needs specialized instruction in those areas in addition to the typical academic subjects. She may learn some things quickly but require a slower pace or different methods to learn other topics and activities. Children with learning disabilities need help in using their preferred learning modalities *instead* of the one that is impaired.

Technology

People with visual–motor learning disabilities may prefer using *computer keyboards* to writing by hand. Special computer software and hardware offer a "talk-back" feature, in which a computer-synthesized voice guides the user through an on-screen lesson, prompting and praising the person at each step of the way. *Tape recorders* can record lectures for later listening at a slower pace. An extensive array of books have been recorded on audiocassette tapes and are available to people with reading disabilities as well as visual impairments.

Personal Assistants and Job Coaches

Assistants can provide note-taking services in college classes. More intensive one-to-one services are now available for people with more severe learning differences. In the past, people with mental retardation were routinely segregated into protected programs called "workshops." Although these programs provided safety and structure, there was little opportunity to match the work activities to the unique interests and skills of each person. Today, *supported employment* is gaining popularity. This approach begins with assessment of the individual's specific interests, skills, and needs and tailors a work-training program for each person. *Job coaches* identify available jobs, coordinate on-site training, and support the person in adapting to the work situation. Similarly, *supported living* programs assist people with mental retardation who live on their own in managing daily activities such as grocery shopping, food preparation, budgeting, recreation, and transportation. Other residential options range from small group homes to apartments with specialized supports.

INTERACTING WITH PEOPLE
WHO LEARN DIFFERENTLY

Person-First Words

Remember, a person is not defined by her impairment or difference. The learning differences described in this chapter would be evident to you even if you did not have specific vocabulary to describe them. When you lack specific, respectful terms to describe a disability, however, your reactions may be more negative because the unfamiliar, unexpected, and unsettling aspects of the disability become the focus of the interaction. Understanding basic terminology can increase your comfort and enhance your actions.

Today, the words "moron," "imbecile," and "idiot" are considered disrespectful and unacceptable, even though professionals used them as medical terms in the past. Those terms, plus the obviously derogatory "MR" and "retard," should be avoided. Here are some preferred terms:

- Learning disability
- Learning difference

- Learning impairment
- Mental retardation
- Cognitive disability
- Intellectual impairment

Use the specific term if you know it, or use specific words to describe the difference:

- She has trouble remembering names and dates.
- He has a reading disability.
- She learns new information more slowly.

Detecting Learning Differences

How can you Detect another person's learning differences? Appearance does *not* usually give you a reliable clue. Most people with learning differences have no distinctive physical differences. The majority of people with learning differences have mild impairments and go to school, work, live on their own, and generally participate in community life.

Learning differences usually are detectable only during specific tasks. A person with learning disabilities may falter and struggle only in a situation requiring specific reading or math skills. Teachers and other education professionals often more readily recognize learning disabilities both because of their training and because there is less opportunity for the person to compensate for or hide his impairment in the classroom.

Many people with learning problems have techniques to compensate for and cover up their difference. You might notice that a person never volunteers to take minutes of a meeting or that she uses voice mail instead of writing memos. Sometimes these behaviors just reflect individual preferences, but many people with learning problems use these techniques to cope with or cover up their difference.

It's also difficult to Detect learning differences because some people may be reluctant to disclose their special needs. They realize that society has historically stereotyped individuals with learning differences and find it tiring to educate everyone they encounter about their learning difference. In this respect, having a learning difference is similar to having other nonvisible disabilities (see Chapter 10). The burden—or opportunity—of self-disclosure is an everpresent factor in the person's life.

> The song "Impossible Dream" expresses how I felt while fighting the academic system overcome with pervasive self-doubt. . . . No one believed that I have a learning disability. I was constantly accused by teachers, administrators, and relatives of being lazy, stupid, and too overqualified to have a learning disability.[8]
>
> —Shelley Mosley Stanzel

Deciding

1. What kind of learning difference is this?
2. How relevant is the learning difference to the situation?
3. What are my action options?

Understanding that someone you know has a learning difference can be very helpful. It alerts you to expect some differences in mastering new information, reading or writing, or daily living skills. This knowledge is your signal to adapt your behavior or to accommodate the person's special needs. Remember also that there is more than one way to communicate and interact effectively. The Action Tips that follow are not prescriptions but rather possibilities for you to consider.

Action Tips

Learning Differences

When having a conversation . . .

- Listen carefully to the person's vocabulary, and try to use words of a similar level. If the person does not seem to understand a question or remark of yours, then try to use simpler words, shorten your sentences to five to seven words or less, or focus on only one idea per sentence.

- Wait patiently for an answer; allow extra time for the person to process your comment or to respond. If you don't understand the person's point, say so. It's not rude to admit, "I don't understand. Are you saying _____ ?" (Restate the point.) Or, say "Show me what you mean." Help the person demonstrate with actions or gestures.

- If the other person still doesn't grasp your meaning, then pose the question as a choice. For example, "Are you a sports fan?" is a pretty broad, open-ended question. Try narrowing down the question: "Do you like basketball or football better?"

When you're teaching someone how to do something . . .
If you're in a situation where you need to teach the person a task or skill, then try some of these coaching ideas:

- First, ask the person about his learning needs. For example, say, "I want you to learn how to operate the new label-making machine. Do you want to watch me first? Or, do you want to take home the instruction manual before we meet?"

- Match your methods to the person's specific needs. For example, a person with auditory processing difficulties might appreciate diagrams or written procedures, but avoid giving written instructions to a person with a reading disability.

- Reduce distractions in the environment. If possible, reduce the number of people present, the noise level, and distracting objects. Move to a quiet room or corner.

- Tell the person you expect her to have questions and that she should stop you when anything is unclear. Then, periodically invite questions during the training session. Try asking, "Is any of this confusing to you? Which part?" "How am I doing? I'm not sure how well I'm getting this information across to you." "I'm sure you have some questions about that part."

- Divide the task into several smaller steps or subtasks in a specific sequence. Teach them starting from the *last step* of the sequence. For example, if you are demonstrating coffee-making, start with the *last* steps: pouring the coffee into cups and serving it. Then work backward from this step and teach one more step in the process. Keep adding steps until you've taught the entire process.

- For each step you teach, demonstrate, and then let the person try. Then give positive feedback at every step, such as "You can do it," "Try again," "Good try!" and "You've got it!" Encouragement and authentic praise are very important.
- Let the person touch the materials and tools; don't keep them in your hands.
- Adjust your pace after checking with the learner: "I talk pretty fast when I'm excited. Should I slow down?"
- At the end, ask which steps are clear and which remain confusing. Assure the person that there will be more time and opportunities for practice and questions.
- Take advantage of helpful tools and devices. Use calculators, memory-dial functions on telephones, and so forth. Tape record your directions for the person to play back several times on his own. Post signs at the task location with reminders, diagrams, or a few words of explanation.
- Ask whether the learner has ideas for doing some steps differently. Especially after trying the new task a number of times, the learner may have another way to accomplish the same task—and her methods will suit her unique learning difficulties and strengths. Try to be flexible and open to these suggestions. Remember that *most* learners deviate from "standard operating procedures" at some point. Give the person room to try another way.

Relationship Reminders

Obviously, relationships are more than conversations and task-teaching episodes. Relationships involve sharing and caring about each other. People with learning differences are no different in their needs for sharing and caring. Some people avoid getting to know their child's classmate, neighbor, or fellow church member because the other person isn't "smart enough." It may seem like too much effort.

But try challenging this belief next time the opportunity arises. Relating to a person who views the world differently from you may be a good opportunity for you to broaden your own perceptions and understanding. Intellectual exchange is just one kind of relating. Meaningful sharing and caring can occur on many other levels: working together toward a common goal, laughing, sharing a hobby, helping each other, providing emotional support, and so forth.

- **Focus on the person's strengths, skills, and talents.** The child who dismantled toys can grow up to repair electronic devices; the student who drew "cool" clothing instead of taking lecture notes can grow up to be a fashion designer; the class clown can become a stand-up comic or actor. Childhood resistance can transform into adult success. Everybody has strengths, skills, and talents. These factors are often the basis of mutual attraction and friendship. Learning differences don't have to overshadow other abilities. Ask the person with a learning difference to help you. Avoid the trap of always casting yourself as the helper and the other person as the recipient of assistance. Find a way the other person can genuinely contribute to you, to your group, or to the success of the situation.

- **Try to be sensitive** to the impact of years of frustration, misunderstanding by parents and teachers, and damaged self-esteem. Adults with learning differences may surprise you at times with "oversensitivity." Before judging their emotional reactions, gently find out whether the current situation is bringing up unsettling memories from the past.

- **Offer to coach the person when needed.** Especially in the area of social skills, it helps to let the person know what you're expecting of her. Many people with mental retardation benefit from coaching in social relationships. Subtle social signals, double meanings, and rapid conversation with complex vocabulary can slow down an interaction. When relating to someone with mental retardation, if the role situation is appropriate, and both parties agree, then you can follow the Action Tips mentioned previously and apply them to social situations. For example, it might be appropriate for you to assist a co-worker with mental retardation in understanding some of the subtle or between-the-lines assumptions about an upcoming holiday party. She might appreciate your help interpreting the invitation. The meaning of *RSVP* is *not* obvious to everyone, nor do all people understand the term *significant other*. Would a parent be an appropriate significant other to bring to the office holiday party? Maybe, but maybe not, depending on the corporate culture and customs of your office. The point is that it can be helpful and appropriate for you to offer this subtle assistance to people who seem perplexed due to cognitive impairments.

Doing

Whenever you interact with someone who has a learning difference, there is not just one right thing to Do. Even when you're not sure what to say or how to behave, your motivation for the interaction to succeed is the most important message you can convey. It does help, however, to remember these general pointers:

- Focus on the other person and his abilities and competencies.
- Include the person in the social situation. Don't talk around the person—always address him directly.
- Provide assistance if asked or if your offer was accepted.
- Get on with the task or purpose of the situation!

Debriefing

You Detected a learning difference in someone, you Decided what to Do, and you went ahead and Did what you planned to Do. Now, you can move on to the fourth step in the 4D approach, Debriefing, which means looking back and reflecting on the interaction and then looking forward to the next encounter with that specific person or a similar encounter in the future. This activity may help you Debrief. Answer these questions privately, in your thoughts, or talk them over with someone else who was present during the encounter.

Debriefing

1. **Think about what happened this time.**
   - Did I Detect the difference accurately?
   - Did I Detect and manage my own emotional reactions?
   - Did I relax and Decide what my action options were?
   - Were my actions consistent with my Decisions? If not, why not?
   - Was the purpose of the interaction accomplished?
   - What worked well? What didn't work well?
2. **Figure out what went wrong.** If the situation went well, then congratulate yourself—and keep up the good work! If the situation did not go so well, then try to figure out why. Ask yourself whether any of these pitfalls occurred:
   - I focused on the difference too much.
   - I acted as though the difference wasn't relevant at all, but actually it was.
   - I got stuck in stress and forgot to relax.
   - I got stuck in pity and didn't focus on abilities.
   - I worried too much about the right thing to Do, so I Did nothing.
3. **Think about what could happen next time.** Ask yourself what you could Do differently next time.
   - Detect the disability and my feelings, and relax.
   - Decide more carefully, or consider more action options.
   - Look at the person or disability by regarding, not by staring.
   - Talk to the person with person-first words, ask for information, or offer assistance.
   - Interact differently by including instead of excluding and by focusing on the person and his *abilities*.

Learning Differences

At~A~Glance

Number of Americans with Learning Differences

- Approximately 10 million school-age children (nearly 1 in 5) have a reading disability.[9]
- As many as 10% of school-age children have a writing disability.[10]
- As many as 6% of school-age children have a math disability.[11]
- It is estimated that between 1% and 3% of the general population have mental retardation, with the majority having mild mental retardation.[12]
- Mental retardation affects 100 times as many people as total blindness does.[13]

People Who Have Learning Disabilities

Hans Christian Andersen, author
Cher, singer and actress
Agatha Christie, author
Tom Cruise, actor
Leonardo da Vinci, artist and scientist
Thomas Edison, inventor
Earvin "Magic" Johnson, athlete
Greg Louganis, athlete
Robert Rauschenberg, painter
Nelson Rockefeller, former U.S. vice president
Woodrow Wilson, former U.S. president

People Who Have Mental Retardation

Only recently have people with mental retardation been urged and supported to achieve their potential in the world of work and the arts. Here are just a few of the many individuals with mental retardation whose achievements are worth discovering.
Chris Burke, television actor
Gretchen Josephson, poet[15]
Dwight Mackintosh, artist

READINGS
AND RESOURCES

Books

"We're People First": The Social and Emotional Lives
of Individuals with Mental Retardation
E.E. Castles (Praeger, New York, 1996)

When Your Child Has a Learning Disability:
A Survival Guide for Parents
G. Fisher & R. Cummings (Free Spirit Publishing, Minneapolis,
MN, 1995)

Retarded Isn't Stupid, Mom! Revised Edition
S.Z. Kaufman (Paul H. Brookes Publishing Co., Baltimore, 1999)

Count Us In: Growing Up with Down Syndrome
J. Kingsley & M. Levitz (Harcourt Brace & Co., Orlando, FL,
1994)

A Guide to Mental Retardation
M. McGarrity (Crossroad Publishing, New York, 1993)

Dyslexia in Adults: Taking Charge of Your Life
K. Nosek (Taylor Publishing, Dallas, TX, 1997)

Learning to Learn
C. Olivier & R.F. Bowler (Simon & Schuster, New York, 1996)

Brilliant Idiot: An Autobiography of a Dyslexic
A. Schmitt (Good Books, Intercourse, PA, 1994)

Children with Mental Retardation: A Parent's Guide
R. Smith, Ed. (Woodbine House, Bethesda, MD, 1993)

Films

Charly (1968)

Tim (1979)

A Dangerous Woman (1993)

What's Eating Gilbert Grape? (1993)

The Eighth Day (1996)

Digging to China (1998)

Self-Advocacy/Support Organizations

American Association on Mental Retardation
444 North Capitol Street, NW, Suite 846, Washington, DC
20001-1512 (800-424-3688; www.aamr.org)

The Arc
500 East Border Street, Suite 300, Arlington, TX 76010
(800-433-5255; TDD: 817-277-0553; fax: 817-277-3491;
www.thearc.org; e-mail: thearc@metronet.com)

Learning Disabilities Association of America
4156 Library Road, Pittsburgh, PA 15234-1349 (412-341-1515;
fax: 412-344-0224; www.ldanatl.org/)

Recording for the Blind and Dyslexic
20 Roszel Road, Princeton, NJ 08540 (800-221-4792;
www.rfbd.org)

Voice of the Retarded
5005 Newport Drive, Suite 108, Rolling Meadows, IL 60008
(847-253-6020; fax: 847-253-6054)

10

People with Nonvisible Disabilities

Is it a disability if it's invisible? If it's disabling enough to affect your life, it's also potentially visible. Your learning difference, your fatigue, your pain or depression could all be revealed under certain circumstances. You know you have a "real" disability when you know society will label and marginalize you once your difference shows.[1]

—Carol Gill

A disability that is visible creates immediate reactions in others if they detect it as unfamiliar, unexpected, or unsettling. A nonvisible disability may also be unfamiliar, unexpected, or unsettling to others—but only when they learn of its existence. Nonvisible disabilities, sometimes called *invisible* or *hidden disabilities,* are not usually detectable from a person's appearance, movement, behavior, or communication. Any "evidence" of the disability tends to be indirect and often surmised (or guessed at) through a person's out-of-the-ordinary patterns of behavior or subtle self-references. Some examples of nonvisible disabilities are epilepsy, allergies, heart disease, and diabetes.

MYTHS, ASSUMPTIONS, AND BELIEFS

We still have a long way to go in changing our assumptions and beliefs about people who have disabilities that are visible, and the issues become even more complex with nonvisible disabilities because of our attitudes about illness and disability. Illness implies that someone is sick with a specific condition but has the prospect of "getting well." Disability frequently implies uncertainty about the person's current state of "health" and assumptions that the disability is probably permanent.

Assumption: If You *Look* Okay, Then You Must *Be* Okay

In the absence of visible evidence otherwise, a person is expected to be "normal" or "average." Because nonvisible disabilities give no evidence of an impairment, some people think that they aren't real disabilities. For example, when you see someone transfer into a wheelchair after parking in a handicapped space, you don't question why he has parked there. But if you see someone park in that spot and *walk* away from the car, then you may feel annoyed that the person doesn't look like he has a disability. You might guess that he has a back problem or other medical condition, but the lack of information probably leaves you confused about how to evaluate what you see. Even though most of us at some point have had an impairment that wasn't visible to anyone else, we are often skeptical about someone else's disability if we can't see it.

Belief: Some People "Use" Their Disability to Their Advantage

We have mixed feelings about people with nonvisible disabilities: After all, we all have days when we don't feel well or when we want to stay home from work. We all know people who have proclaimed illness at times to avoid a dreaded task or to escape from a disappointing date. Many people with nonvisible disabilities report that friends, family, and co-workers don't understand how debilitating symptoms can be and that they are often treated as though they are "faking it," especially if symptoms come and go. For example, a woman with fibromyalgia may feel fine on some days, but on others she might not be able to get out of bed. On good days she can go to work and appear relatively "normal," so some of her co-workers wonder whether she is exaggerating the severity of her disability to avoid her work responsibilities or whether it's all "in her head."

WHAT IT FEELS LIKE

Even though you may not have a condition that you consider a disability, you have probably experienced physical or mental impairments that have interfered with your life, if only for a few hours or days or in some specific situations. If you have ever had a headache or backache so uncomfortable that it interfered with your ability to sit still and concentrate in a meeting or to make a long car or plane trip, then you have an idea of how chronic pain can influence a variety of life activities. When you have been so preoccupied with anxiety about a work or family problem that it affected your sleep, your ability to work effectively, or your appetite, you have experienced what daily life might be like for someone with a chronic anxiety disorder. If you have ever felt so tired or ill at work that you needed to go home, but no one else knew, and you didn't want to reveal any personal information, then you have had a sample of what chronic fatigue syndrome can be like.

Many of us have fleeting experiences with the kinds of disabilities that others experience on a permanent basis, such as needing to avoid people or places because of an allergy or panic reaction or attending a movie or concert where the sound was so painfully loud you had to leave (a frequent problem for people with tinnitus). Most of us have some impairments that we prefer to think of as quirks or minor inconveniences, or we joke that we're just getting old. In fact, any impairment that disables you even temporarily is a disability. The condition is the same whatever you call it, but a reluctance to use the term *disability* reflects how much stigma you still attach to the word.

NONVISIBLE DISABILITIES YOU MAY ENCOUNTER

Everybody has had some experience with illness, impairments, and disabilities, but because there is no absolute measure of pain or fatigue, everybody has a different experience, even when they have the same disability as another person. A label describes a general category of illness or disability but tells you nothing about that person's direct experience. A nonvisible disability may be

- *Chronic* (always a factor in daily life), such as diabetes, a gastrointestinal disease, or heart disease
- *Episodic but somewhat predictable,* such as seasonal allergies, tinnitus, or panic attacks in enclosed places
- *Episodic and unpredictable,* such as migraine headaches, asthma, seizures, or chronic fatigue syndrome

Some symptoms of nonvisible disabilities may be worsened by stress, weather, diet, medication side effects, or the environment.

Here are a few examples of people who *may* have nonvisible disabilities:

- One of your relatives who never drives on the freeway (He may have a phobia or a visual impairment.)

- A neighbor with a handicapped car license plate who appears to be healthy (She may have heart disease or chronic pain.)
- A co-worker who frequently walks out of staff meetings, causing others to feel resentful (He may have a chronic bladder disorder or may need to take medication.)
- A friend who likes to get together to rent videos but won't go to see a movie at a theater (He may get migraine headaches from the loud noise, or the seats may aggravate a back problem.)
- Another friend who makes plans to go places with you but often cancels with vague excuses (She may have fibromyalgia or chronic fatigue syndrome.)

Awareness Activity

Nonvisible Disabilities

1. What do you think are some issues faced by people with nonvisible disabilities that are different from those faced by people with visible disabilities?
2. Ask your friends or colleagues about their experiences with people in their lives who have had nonvisible disabilities. How did they learn about the person's disability? What were the person's attitudes and behaviors related to the disability? How did other people react?
3. Recall a time when you had a nonvisible illness or impairment that affected some aspect of your life such as work, school, physical activities, or eating and sleeping habits. Whom did you tell and not tell? How did other people react to your limitations? Did any benefits come from this experience, such as reflecting on your career goals, changing your pace of life, or gaining insight about other people with disabilities?

REASONS WHY PEOPLE
HAVE NONVISIBLE DISABILITIES

A disability may affect only one body system or function, such as when a person has a missing limb or hearing loss. Our body systems are so complex and interwoven, however, that most impairments influence multiple systems. The general categories of nonvisible disabilities include sensory impairments, body function impairments, immune system disorders, neurological impairments, mental disorders, and chronic pain related to any of the body systems. Although many disabilities could be listed in more than one category, we organize them according to the major body systems and functions that they usually affect.

Sensory Impairments

Hearing Impairments

Hearing loss may develop gradually as a person ages, affecting his ability to hear conversations and environmental sounds such as doorbells, telephones, and sirens. Tinnitus is a permanent noise in the ears that is often heard as roaring, buzzing, or ringing. It can override specific sounds, such as the whistle of a teakettle, human voices in another room, or music.

Visual Impairments

Vision loss may develop gradually with aging, or diseases of the eye. Common visual impairments include low vision, which may or may not be improved with eyeglasses; cataracts; glaucoma; color blindness; and night blindness (see Chapter 5).

Smell, Taste, and Touch Disorders

Changes in sensitivity to odors, tastes, or tactile pressure include hypersensitivity (even allergic reactions) and hyposensitivity (reduction or loss of awareness of smells, tastes, and tactile sensations). Any of these reactions may limit a person's life activities.

What really makes me sad is not being able to smell something that everyone else thinks is so nice, like "Don't these flowers smell great?" or "Doesn't that barbecue smell good?" Then there are the safety hazards. I was at my office, and there was a small fire near us. There was a flurry of activity, and I didn't even realize what was going on.[2]

—Gail Sammons

Body Function Impairments

Balance

Loss of balance often develops slowly in the early stages of conditions such as Parkinson's disease and multiple sclerosis (see Chapter 6). Dizziness (vertigo) may occur more sporadically and is sometimes linked with situations that a person is afraid of (heights, elevators) or with sudden changes in body position such as standing up too quickly. Some people must limit their daily activities in order to *prevent* balance problems.

Blood Sugar

Glucose, or *blood sugar,* produces energy for the body to function. Insulin, a hormone created in the pancreas, helps regulate glucose storage and use. Diabetes results from the body's inabilty to produce or use insulin correctly. People with diabetes need to plan their days around specific food requirements and insulin injections. Complications from diabetes are the leading cause of blindness.

Breathing

Asthma restricts air flow through muscle constriction, tissue swelling, and mucous production in the bronchial tubes. Asthma episodes can be triggered by airborne particles such as smoke, pollens, and food. Stress can exacerbate episodes.

Asthma is chronic, and far from developing an immunity, we develop a lifelong susceptibility. The first line of treatment in asthma is avoidance. But avoidance of what? The asthmatic is doomed to gnaw on the event until he finds a clue, a cause. What did he do? What did he eat? What did he breathe? Were there feathers in the pillows? Peanuts in the sauce?[3]

—Tim Brookes

Allergic reactions to certain toxins such as perfumes, pesticides, solvents, or foods can affect any number of body systems, with respiratory problems being a major symptom. Other reactions can include chronic respiratory or digestive problems; difficulty concentrating; skin problems; and increased sensitivity to other environmental irritants such as dust, mold, pets, and foods. The major treatment is to remove known and potential irritants from the person's living environments.

You can't go where you want to go, you can't work at what you want to do or even at what you were trained to do. You can't wear the kind of clothing you want to wear. Friends are affected. Your whole life is affected.[4]

—Stephen Edelson

Digestive System

Disorders of the digestive system include gastroesophageal reflux, nausea, stomach ulcers, intestinal disorders such as irritable bowel syndrome (IBS), incontinence (lack of bladder or bowel control), and chronic bladder and kidney infections or disease. Diet and reduction of stress and fatigue can ease some symptoms. Medications may cause drowsiness and may require food restrictions. Kidney disease may require daily dialysis treatments in home or medical settings.

Bladder diseases, like many other serious diseases, have a way of insinuating themselves into almost every aspect of life. They can disrupt school or work, make a disaster out of social occasions, inhibit your ability to travel, make sports and recreational activities almost impossible.[5]

—Rebecca Chalker and Kristine Whitmore

Irritable bowel syndrome (IBS) is one of those disorders employees are unlikely to report, simply because they are embarrassed to blame absenteeism or tardiness on their bowels.[6]

—Gerard Guillory

Heart Disease

Heart disease results from thickening and loss of function in the arteries supplying blood to the heart. Symptoms can be mild, such as long-term chest and arm pain, acute, or even fatal. There often is chronic but unpredictable shortness of breath. Physical activities and lifestyle are almost always affected, and diet restrictions and medications may be needed.

Immune System Disorders

AIDS

Acquired immunodeficiency syndrome (AIDS) is a progressive illness caused by the human immunodeficiency virus (HIV), which enters the body through a transfer of body fluids, such as through contaminated blood transfusions or sexual contact with a person who is already infected. The virus causes the body's immune system to shut down and lose the ability to protect itself from other illnesses. A person who is HIV-positive may have no visible symptoms until she develops AIDS.

Cancer

Cancer is a disease in which some body cells multiply without normal immune regulation. Cancer can occur in any part of the body and is fatal unless faulty cell growth is stopped before critical bodily functions are affected.

Persons with cancer may confide their illness to their employers, who slap them on the back and say, "We're with you all the way". . . . But when the hair falls off and the wig goes on and their work schedules must be adjusted for chemotherapy, suddenly the support may disappear.

Fortunately for every workplace horror story there exists a tale of compassion and kindness: A nurse's co-workers take turns driving her to chemotherapy treatments, a Fortune 500 company sets up a home office for a worker too weak to commute to work, colleagues of a newly hired secretary donate their own sick leave to allow her to take 12 days to recover from surgery.[7]

—Susan Vaughn

Chronic Fatigue Syndrome

Chronic fatigue syndrome, also known as chronic fatigue and immune deficiency syndrome (CFIDS), is characterized by fatigue, poor concentration, and occasional physical symptoms such as fever. There is no known cause or cure. Symptoms come and go at unpredictable intervals and may last for years.

Lupus

Lupus is an autoimmune disorder of unknown cause in which the body's immune system literally attacks itself. Because of the high risk for contracting illnesses, a person's daily life may become increasingly self-protective and isolated, as she avoids public places, crowds, and even small social gatherings.

Learning Disabilities

There are many kinds of specific impairments that cause or increase learning difficulties. Chapter 9 describes specific learning disabilities. People with learning impairments often conceal their difference by avoiding activities that might expose their disability.

Attention Deficit Disorder and
Attention-Deficit/Hyperactivity Disorder

A person with attention deficit disorder (ADD) deals with issues of short attention span, distractibility, and impulsivity. He often has difficulty completing tasks and following through with work, school, or household responsibilities. When hyperactivity also accompanies this disorder (ADHD), he may experience a greater degree of restlessness, impulsivity, irritability, and a general "on-the-go" quality. ADD and ADHD may contribute to or coexist with specific learning disabilities.

Mental Illnesses

Mental disorders are not easily or always visible, although they can manifest in behavior or communication. Chapter 8 describes specific mental disorders. When a mental disorder is being successfully treated or is in remission, the person may still have many concerns in his day-to-day life. For instance, a mild anxiety about giving a speech may cause him to wonder, "Is this a panic attack? Is my illness coming back? Will I lose control of my behavior in public?"

Neurological Impairments

Seizure Disorder/Epilepsy

Seizure disorder (also called *epilepsy*) is a condition in which electrical impulses are discharged in the brain, causing sudden, unexpected changes in behavior, movement, or sensation (see Chapters 6 and 8) that can range from brief staring episodes or rapid blinking to shallow or interrupted breathing, muscle jerks, falls, or loss of consciousness.[8] Onlookers may mistake seizures for heart attacks, strokes, mental illness, unruliness or disobedience, or intoxication.

There are more than 30 different types of seizures that vary in severity and length. Many seizure disorders are effectively controlled with medication, but there is such a long tradition of fear and superstition associated with epilepsy that many people feel unsettled when they meet someone with this condition, even if the seizures are under control. A seizure disorder may restrict some life activities such as driving or traveling because of the unpredictable nature of seizures.

There is often a stigma and fear attached to people with epilepsy. This can be attributed in part to the historical myth about epilepsy which linked seizures with the super-natural or insanity. More often it is ignorance or misunderstanding which creates fear and uncertainty.[9]

—Lindsay Gething

Pain

Chronic pain (pain lasting more than three months) is associated with such nonvisible disabilities as neurofibromatosis (nerve damage), fibromyalgia (widespread, deep muscle pain of unknown cause), digestive disorders, back injuries, and other physical conditions. People with chronic pain struggle with issues of poor concentration, fatigue, and discomfort in many daily activities. Many people avoid *optional* activities because of the amount of energy they need to perform their daily *required* activities, such as working, going to school, or parenting.

People who suffer nausea or chronic pain engage in a constant process of shuttling their attention between body demands and social and environmental constraints. Are the chairs firm? Can I lie down if I need to? Will there be time or space to move around or stretch? Can I get out? Deciding whether to accept an apparently simple invitation to travel can turn into a fretful dilemma packed with ambivalence and apprehension.[10]

—Robert Shuman

Episodic pain may be present with a wide variety of disabilities. Migraine headaches are one of the most common and debilitating causes of episodic pain. They can have a number of causes, ranging from environmental factors, to food sensitivities, to medication side effects, and each person often has multiple or unknown triggers. People who experience migraine headaches often have many of their planned activities prevented or interrupted by the unpredictable onset and severe pain of a migraine.

The tolerance commanded by less disabling conditions like a sore throat or a stomachache is typically lacking if you miss work and use a headache as an excuse.[11]
—Joel Saper and Kenneth Magee

Substance Abuse

Substance abuse or *addiction* refers to chronic or episodic abuse of or dependence on alcohol, illegal drugs, or prescription medications. Problems with substance abuse are a major cause of absenteeism at work as well as domestic violence and automobile accidents. Someone who is under the influence of a substance may show dramatic behavioral changes (see Chapter 8), but during intervals of nonuse, the disability itself is nonvisible.

INTERVENTIONS AND SUPPORTS

Medications and Therapies

Many nonvisible disabilities are at times considered psychological or emotional problems because of the lack of visible differences or biological "proof." Some of the better known examples of this include asthma, some allergies, migraine headaches, and most mental disorders. We now know that these differences have a biological basis that often can be modified with medications.

Therapeutic interventions for individuals and groups include cognitive and behavior therapies, psychotherapy, and supportive counseling. Alternative and complementary therapies are gaining in popularity and in reported (if often controversial) effectiveness for some individuals. Some of the better-known interventions include acupuncture, aromatherapy, chiropractic treatment, herbal supplements, homeopathy, hypnotherapy, massage and touch therapies, meditation, yoga, and spiritual healing. A number of established medical centers are incorporating alternative therapies into traditional medical care for many illnesses and disabilities.

Personal Supports

People who have observable disabilities that affect their appearance, movement, communication, or behavior often benefit from assistance and support from others. For example, some children with cerebral palsy may need extra help with eating, dressing, and communicating; people with behavior changes due to Alzheimer's disease may need supervision for their day-to-day routines and on outings. Some people with nonvisible disabilities have to rely on others if they need medication, are especially tired, or need to get to a bathroom immediately.

Personal supports usually occur in the context of a relationship: a family member, a hired assistant, a co-worker, a spouse, a relative, a partner, or a friend who offers support or care. With a chronic nonvisible disability, communication must evolve in a way that respects the needs and integrity of both the giver and the receiver of support and care.

Most people with common chronic conditions show no outward signs of being ill. For children, this aspect of chronic illness can be both positive and negative. While it often allows the child to fit into his or her peer group more easily, it also makes it more difficult for the child—and often his or her parents—to explain any limitations the disease may impose on diet or exercise habits . . . or changes in his or her behavior. . . . "A piece of cake won't hurt you" was a well-meaning statement recently made to four-year-old Amy by a friend's mother who was unaware that the little girl had diabetes and could in fact be hurt by a piece of cake if it had not been planned for in her daily food plan.[12]

—Susanne Levert

Support Groups

Support groups enable people with common concerns to share their experiences, receive mutual understanding and caring from others who have "been there," obtain valuable information about resources, and join together for advocacy and political action. Many communities have support groups that meet on daily, weekly, or monthly schedules; they are often advertised in newspapers or can be found through religious organizations or professional organizations pertaining to a particular disability or illness. There also are many support groups for family members of people with chronic conditions.

Some groups are led by health professionals; many are organized and led by people who have had the particular condition. In addition to face-to-face meetings (which some people find difficult to attend), there are newsletters and many support opportunities on the Internet through World Wide Web sites, chat groups, and mailings. There are also many formal organizations (see the Readings and Resources section at the end of this chapter) that can provide information and referrals.

INTERACTING WITH PEOPLE WHO HAVE NONVISIBLE DISABILITIES

Person-First Words

Remember, a person is not defined by her impairment or difference. The nonvisible differences described in this chapter would be evident to you even if you did not have specific vocabulary to describe them. When you lack specific, respectful terms to describe a disability, however, your reactions may be more negative because the unfamiliar, unexpected, and unsettling aspects of the disability become the focus of the interation. Understanding basic terminology can increase your comfort and enhance your actions.

Avoid terms such as *suffers from, is afflicted with,* or *is a victim of.* It may be true that someone suffers with a disability, but only that individual can make such an evaluative statement. It's easier, more correct, and less stigmatizing to say, "She has fibromyalgia," "He has migraine headaches," and so forth. For example, you might say

- "She has diabetes" instead of "She's a diabetic"
- "He has epilepsy" or "He has a seizure disorder" instead of "He's an epileptic"
- "She has mental illness" instead of "She's mentally ill"

Detecting Nonvisible Disabilities

When an impairment is visible in a person's appearance, movement, behavior, communication, or learning, you and the other person both know that the disability exists. It may never be mentioned, but it is a piece of information that *is* perceived and *can* be openly acknowledged whenever it is relevant or important. With a nonvisible disability, however, interactions can be more complex, and much will depend on what you know and what the other person knows you know.

The Dilemma of Telling Other People

A person who has a nonvisible disability lives with a complex dilemma. More often than not, she has a choice about whether to tell others, whom to tell, and how much to tell. By not telling anyone, she protects herself from the possibility of real or imagined stigma or discrimination. But *not* telling others presents challenges and issues in ongoing relationships.

When a person has a nonvisible disability, she has to deal with some of the following issues:

- Feeling reluctant to prove her needs, even if she could benefit from supports and is entitled to them under the Americans with Disabilities Act
- Fearing rejection by friends or co-workers, but wanting to tell others and be believed and supported
- Anticipating a lack of understanding from others who may think she is exaggerating but also wanting to explain disruptions of normal routines
- Not wanting to answer other people's questions or hear about their own experiences but also wanting advice and information
- Pretending to feel fine when she isn't to avoid being viewed as "disabled"
- Wanting *some* family members or co-workers to know but realizing that if she tells some people, they will probably tell others
- Disliking deception but also being afraid that telling others may jeopardize work assignments or promotions or decrease social invitations

People with chronic illness engage in a difficult struggle to act "as if" they are "all there." Such performances can be quite exhausting. Often told, "But you look so good," by others just learning of their illness, they fight to keep the facts of their life—fatigue, colostomy, pain, for example—from intruding on their many roles. Those with chronic illness become quite skilled at impression management and learn, sometimes cruelly, with whom they can be themselves.[13]

—Robert Shuman

Deciding

1. What kind of nonvisible difference is this?
2. How relevant is the nonvisible difference to the situation?
3. What are my action options?

Knowing when someone has a nonvisible disability can be very helpful. It alerts you to be sensitive to potential triggers or stressors for the other person and also to help accommodate the person's special needs in social situations. Remember also that there is more than one way to communicate and interact effectively. The Action Tips that follow are not prescriptions but rather possibilities for you to consider. It's better to try *some* action than to ignore or avoid the other person.

Action Tips

Nonvisible Disabilities

Here are some action tips for you to consider when interacting with people who have nonvisible disabilities.

If the person has told you about her disability . . .

- "How are you?" takes on new meaning. We want to know how other people are and often ask, "How are you?" but if the answer is anything but "Fine," we aren't sure where to go from there. We may want to know how a person is doing, but we may not be sure how much we want to know, and she may not be sure how much we want to know either.
- Ask about the disability. Shared knowledge often implies permission to talk about the disability. You may feel comfortable and close enough to ask the other person the status of her condition, or you may leave the initiative up to her. If you feel uncertain whether to ask on a regular basis or never bring it up, gently raise the topic but respect the person's wishes about information sharing.
- Ask before offering advice. If someone tells you about an impairment or illness, then you may find yourself offering a solution without having been *asked* for one. Many people who tell someone about a nonvisible disability find themselves flooded with suggestions and stories of amazing cures or doomsday

scenarios. Ask whether the person is interested in knowing about the experiences of some other people you know.

- Ask about offering assistance. Depending on the nature of your relationship, you might want to ask the person how you can be helpful in specific situations. If you work together, are neighbors, or belong to the same church, for example, then there may be overlapping needs or activities in which you would like to be of assistance. The person may be pleased with your interest or may feel that your unsolicited attempt to help is intrusive.

- Withhold judgment. We live in a "fix-it" society, and many of us believe that we have control over a lot more things in life than we actually do. There are an endless number of "how-to" and "self-help" books and articles today that imply that there are specific treatments to receive, products to buy, and new ways to think and feel that will bring us greater health, happiness, self-esteem, and control. This carries over into our personal relationships. You may think you know exactly what the other person "should" do to feel better—or even to "get well"—but each person's experience with pain, disability, and help-seeking is unique. A person may want your support but not necessarily your opinion.

If the person hasn't told you anything, but you sense that something is different . . .

It's awkward to confirm a speculation about a disability if you don't know why a person hasn't mentioned anything. Consider the following:

- The person may have a disabling condition that she is minimizing or is not ready to talk about.
- She may want to tell you but may feel shame or embarrassment about the impairment.
- She may be unsure whether you would support or reject her.
- She may be unsure whether you would keep it confidential.
- She may be concerned that telling anyone might hurt her chances for a promotion or a special project at work.

If a third person has told you about the person's disability . . .
You may know that someone has a nonvisible disability even though he doesn't know that you know. You may have learned about a co-worker's diabetes from another employee. A friend may have mentioned a mutual friend's inability to take vacations because of her flying phobia. You may wonder if this has been told to your friend in confidence and what you should do now. Discussing this with the person who told you can help you decide what to do with that information.

- Is this information in any way relevant to your relationship with your friend?
- Is this information going to influence how you interact with the person?
- Do you have the same nonvisible difference and want to offer support? Do you have information about resources or know someone who has a similar problem that you would like to talk about? Tell the third person who gave you the initial information, and decide whether and how to reach out to your mutual friend.
- Have you sensed that the person with the disability is stressed? Would you like to offer support? The stress may or may not be related to a disability. If you want to offer friendship and support, then do.

Doing

Despite your possible surprise or shock at learning about another person's nonvisible disability, you'll probably find that at many times the disability has very little, if any, relevance to your interactions. Even if you aren't sure what to say or how to behave, your motivation for your interactions to succeed is the most important communication you can convey. Remember these general pointers:

- Focus on the other person and his abilities and competencies.

- Include the person in the social situation. Don't talk around the person—always address him directly.
- Provide assistance if asked or if your offer was accepted.
- Get on with the task or purpose of the situation!

Debriefing

You learned about a nonvisible difference, you Decided what to Do, and you went ahead and Did what you planned to Do. Now you can move on to the fourth step in the 4D approach, Debriefing, which means looking back and reflecting on the interaction and then looking forward to the next encounter with that specific person or a similar encounter in the future. This Awareness Activity may help you debrief. You may answer these questions privately, in your thoughts, or talk them over with someone else who was present during the encounter.

Debriefing

1. **Think about what happened this time.**
   - Did I Detect the difference accurately?
   - Did I Detect and manage my own emotional reactions?
   - Did I relax and Decide what my action options were?
   - Were my actions consistent with my Decisions? If not, why not?
   - Was the purpose of the interaction accomplished?
   - What worked well? What didn't work well?
2. **Figure out what went wrong.** If the situation went well, then congratulate yourself—and keep up the good work! If the situation did not go so well, then try to figure out why. Ask yourself whether any of these pitfalls occurred:
   - I focused on the difference too much.
   - I acted as though the difference wasn't relevant at all, but actually it was.
   - I got stuck in stress and forgot to relax.
   - I got stuck in pity and didn't focus on abilities.

- I worried too much about "the right thing" to do, so I did nothing.
3. **Think about what could happen next time.** Ask yourself what you could do differently next time.
   - Detect the disability and my feelings, and relax.
   - Decide more carefully, or consider more action options.
   - Look at the person or disability by regarding, not by staring.
   - Talk to the person with person-first words, ask for information, or offer assistance.
   - Interact differently by including instead of excluding and by focusing on the person and his *abilities*.

Nonvisible Differences

At-A-Glance

Number of Americans with Nonvisible Differences

- Approximately 1 million people have HIV, with 40,000 new infections each year.[14]
- An estimated 12 million people have asthma. It is the leading cause of absenteeism from school and work and the most frequent reason people seek medical care.[15]
- 15.7 million people—nearly 6% of the U.S. population—have diabetes. An average of 800,000 new cases are diagnosed yearly.[16] Diabetes is the fourth leading cause of death by disease and the leading cause of blindness in people ages 20–74. Each year 12,000–24,000 people lose sight from diabetes, and 54,000 people lose a foot or a leg from complications.[17]
- At least 15 million people have some form of urinary incontinence.[18]
- Irritable bowel syndrome is the most common gastrointestinal problem seen in hospital clinics, where it accounts for 40%–50% of outpatient referrals. At least one third of the population is affected by IBS at some time in their life.[19]

- 14 million people have heart disease. 1.5 million people have heart attacks every year; 500,000 are fatal. 50 million people have high blood pressure.[20]
- More people have lupus than AIDS, cerebral palsy, multiple sclerosis, sickle cell anemia, and cystic fibrosis combined. Between 1.4 and 2 million people have been diagnosed with lupus.[21]
- More than 30 million people experience recurring migraine headaches.[22]
- Fibromyalgia, the most common cause of widespread musculoskeletal pain, affects more than 10 milion people, 90% of whom are women.[23]
- Three million people experience panic disorder.[24]
- Two million people have epilepsy; 100,000 new cases are diagnosed each year, three quarters of who are children and adolescents.[25]
- 50 million adults have tinnitus, 12 million experience tinnitus so severe they become incapacitated.[26]

READINGS
AND RESOURCES

Books

American Diabetes Association Complete Guide to Diabetes
American Diabetes Association (Bantam Doubleday Dell,
New York, 1996)

Catching My Breath: An Asthmatic Explores His Illness
T. Brookes (Times Books, New York, 1994)

Overcoming Bladder Disorders
R. Chalker & K. Whitmore (HarperCollins, New York, 1990)

Living with Environmental Illness:
A Practical Guide to Multiple Chemical Sensitivity
S. Edelson (Taylor Publishing, Dallas, TX, 1998)

Irritable Bowel Syndrome:
A Doctor's Plan for Chronic Digestive Troubles
G. Guillory (Hartley and Marks, Point Roberts, WA, 1996)

Living with Asthma
A. Rooklin & S. Masline (Penguin USA, New York, 1995)

Crohn's Disease and Ulcerative Colitis
F. Saibil (Firefly Books, New York, 1997)

Freedom from Headaches
J. Saper & K. Magee (Simon & Schuster, New York, 1995)

Heart Family Handbook
J. Schoenberg & J. Stichman (Hanley and Belfus, Philadelphia,
1990)

The Psychology of Chronic Illness:
The Healing Work of Patients, Therapists, and Families
R. Shuman (HarperCollins, New York, 1996)

AIDS Update 1998
G. Stine (Prentice Hall, Upper Saddle River, NJ, 1998)

Lupus: Living with It
S. Szasz (Prometheus Books, Amherst, NY, 1995)

Films

Beaches (1988)

And the Band Played On (1993)

Philadelphia (1993)

Safe (1995)

One True Thing (1998)

Self-Advocacy/Support Organizations

AIDS/HIV National AIDS Clearinghouse
Post Office Box 6003, Rockville, MD 20849-6003 (800-458-5231;
fax: 301-738-6616; e-mail: aidsinfo@cdchac.aspensys.com)

American Association of Kidney Patients
100 South Ashley Drive, Suite 280, Tampa, FL 33260
(800-749-2257; e-mail: aakpaz@enet.net)

American Cancer Society
(800-227-2345; www.cancer.org)

American Diabetes Association
1660 Duke Street, Alexandria, VA 22314 (800-342-23837;
www.diabetes.org)

American Heart Association
7272 Greenville Avenue, Dallas, TX 75231-4596 (800-553-6321;
www.amhrt.org; e-mail: chuck@amhrt.org)

American Liver Foundation
75 Maiden Lane, Suite 603, New York, NY 10038 (800-465-4837)

Asthma and Allergy Foundation of America
1125 15th Street, NW, Suite 502,Washington, DC 20005
(800-624-0044)

CFIDS Association of America
(www.cfids.org; e-mail: info@cfids.org)

Children and Adults with Attention Deficit Disorder
8181 Professional Place, Suite 201, Landover, MD 20785
(800-233-4050; www.chadd.org)

Crohn's Disease and Colitis Foundation of America
38 Park Avenue South, Floor 17, New York, NY 10016-7374
(800-932-2423)

Epilepsy Foundation of America
4351 Garden City Drive, Landover, MD 20785 (800-332-1000;
www.efa.org; e-mail: postmaster@efa.org)

Help for Incontinent People, Inc.
Post Office Box 544, Union, SC 29379 (800-252-3337)

Lupus Foundation of America
1300 Pickard Drive, #200, Rockville, MD 20850-4303
(800-558-0121; e-mail: lupus@piper.hamline.edu)

National Chronic Pain Outreach Association
(540-997-5004)

National Organization for Rare Disorders
Post Office Box 8923, New Fairfield, CT 06812-1783 (800-999-6673)

Project Inform (HIV/AIDS treatment information)
205 13th Street, #2001, San Francisco, CA 94103 (800-822-7422;
www.projinf.org)

United Ostomy Association, Inc.
36 Executive Park, Suite 120, Irvine, CA 92714-6744 (800-826-0826)

11

Understanding and Guiding Children's Reactions to Differences

Before a parent can scold or silence an inquisitive child, I will approach and ask the child if she is wondering about my eye patch. I keep a smile on my face to let her know that it is okay for her to be curious. Speaking to her directly, I answer her unasked questions. Depending on the age, I offer appropriate language and simply tell her that I had an operation, the doctor fixed my eye, and it doesn't hurt. That is usually all that is needed to satisfy a child's concerns.[1]

—Linda Shafritz

UNDERSTANDING CHILDREN'S REACTIONS

As we discuss in Chapter 3, beliefs and attitudes are formed early in life. So, if we can guide our children in their early life experiences with people who have differences, they can grow up with more accepting attitudes and more comfortable reactions. Because children today are exposed to more people with differences in neighborhoods and schools, this goal is more attainable than ever. But how exactly can we help children reject stereotypes and improve their interaction skills? How can we expand their personal comfort zones? This chapter explores children's reactions and provides specific suggestions for parents, teachers, and children's group leaders.

HOW CHILDREN DETECT DIFFERENCES

Sometimes children barely notice a disability difference that you find unexpected. For example, meeting a preschool teacher who uses a wheelchair might surprise you more than your three-year-old daughter because your lifetime of experience has caused your difference detector to orient to this teacher as unexpected; your daughter, however, has never met another preschool teacher so she does not know that most preschool teachers don't use wheelchairs. At other times, children are *more* distressed by unfamiliar disability differences than you are; they have less understanding of the causes of disabilities and may feel more vulnerable. For example, a child may fear that a disability is contagious and can "spread" from the other person to the child. But whether children Detect and react faster or slower than adults, children still have the same types of discomfort when a disability is unfamiliar, unexpected, or unsettling.

Children tend to fixate on one fascinating part of a situation instead of the whole picture, and they miss relevant details and the larger meaning. When this happens, the *person* with the difference ceases to exist, the *reason* for the interaction gets ignored, and the *difference* becomes the object of total fascination. A teacher once observed her class on a field trip at a complicated factory assembly line. At the end of the tour, the guide looked earnestly at the children and asked, "Are there any questions?" The first question was, "Yeah, what are those brown spots on your hands?" This fixation might also happen, for example, when a child and adult both see a post office clerk with a facial difference. The adult might recognize the difference as a cleft lip because his former roommate had the same difference. The adult would know it's unrelated to the man's ability to sell stamps. The child, however, would perceive the same difference but would not have the adult's information and experience. The child may stare directly at the man in a state of uncertainty and curiosity.

HOW CHILDREN DECIDE
ABOUT DISABILITY DIFFERENCES

Children have a smaller world view than adults. They haven't seen as many people or as wide a range of differences. A child's comfort zone is still evolving. In the absence of specific knowledge about a difference, a child tends to make certain assumptions.

It's Broken

A child tends to see a disability as the result of a body being "broken." He assumes that the person "started out okay but later got damaged." When interacting with a person who is blind, deaf, or unable to walk, he'll assume that those impairments represent a *recent loss of ability* for the person, rather than a *lifelong characteristic*. Occasionally, a child's explanation is accurate, such as when a five-year-old encountering a woman without arms speculated, "When she was getting born, something went wrong, and her hands just growed out of her shoulders."

It Hurts

Children older than two years of age may assume that a physical difference is painful. Their response is often empathic because they can remember their own pain from an injury and may feel unsettled by this memory. Sometimes a child's assumption that the difference is painful is accurate, such as when a person has a leg cast or a wired jaw. At other times, her worry about nonexistent pain can interfere with the interaction, such as when the other person has leg braces.

It Can Be Fixed

Because children often conclude that something's broken or hurting, they may insist on talking about how the difference could and/or should be fixed, why it hasn't already been fixed, and who could fix it. Children expect differences to be fixed because they're used to adults fixing things for them. Dad puts Band-Aids on skinned knees, Mom gives cough syrup for a pesky cough, and the doctors at the hospital put casts on broken arms.

I Can Catch It

Children have an emerging sense of "germs" and contagion from age four, but they can overgeneralize this concept. Especially in the case of appearance differences, children may shrink away from a person with a disability, fearing that close proximity or touching could cause the difference to spread.

CHILDREN'S REACTIONS
TO DISABILITY DIFFERENCES

Your child's natural curiosity or fascination causes him to fixate on certain parts of interactions. His assumptions that the difference is something broken, hurting, in need of fixing, or contagious may cause him to do the following:

- Notice the difference even before you do
- Mention the difference even when it's not relevant to the situation
- React before thinking

- Get more involved with the person than appropriate *or* withdraw completely from the person
- Ignore the typical or positive aspects of the person

These tendencies are normal, because a child's difference detector is operating on its own, with little input from the reasoning brain. Instead of challenging your child's perceptions, use her experiences to broaden her comfort zone. Guide her in using her Detecting, Deciding, Doing, and Debriefing skills. Rather than ignore your child's reactions, accept your responsibility to be the "4D coach."

CHILDREN'S REACTIONS REFLECT THEIR CULTURE

We've talked about children's difference detectors and lack of information accounting for their initial reactions to disability differences, but children also are building their base of information about disabilities and differences. This information does not always come from personal experience or their parents' or teachers' instruction—it's just as likely to come from television, stories, and movies.

Television, Stories, and Movies

From a very young age, children absorb many of the beliefs and biases of their culture. The power of television cannot be underestimated—its influence is a common cultural thread woven through all income levels, communities, and ethnicities. It is estimated that children in the United States watch 28 hours of television per week.[2] As the number of television portrayals of people with disabilities grows, children will have more exposure to people with disabilities.

In the late 1970s *Sesame Street* introduced a major shift in the media portrayal of disability differences when it included people with disabilities as cast members. Nickelodeon's documentary piece, *What Are You Staring At?* brought together children with and without disabilities for a candid discussion hosted by Linda Ellerbee, with guests John Hockenberry and

Christopher Reeve. For the most part, however, when a child with a disability appears on television, the disability is usually the *focus* of the story, instead of being incidental to it. A well-known television series, *Life Goes On*, had some episodes in which the son's learning differences were the central focus and others in which they were in the background.

Some stories send negative messages about differences. There is a long tradition of children's fairy tales that feature characters with physical differences. Many of these stories have moral themes about family love, good winning over evil, and following parents' directions that are certainly pertinent today. These lessons, however, are often taught at the expense of characters with a physical impairment. One troubling theme is that virtue is rewarded with physical beauty, so that the Ugly Duckling turns into a swan, the frog becomes a prince, and Cinderella becomes a princess. Or, a character who looks different, such as Rumpelstiltskin, may have magical powers that are scary to children. Whether in book or movie form, the stories send children certain messages about people who are different: the Ugly Duckling and Rumpelstiltskin experience rejection and fear from others, and good people have nicer appearances. Pinocchio becomes increasingly "deformed" as his dishonesty grows. The title character of *The Hunchback of Notre Dame* hides in shame due to his different body. The seven dwarfs in *Snow White* are portrayed as childlike and one-dimensional, with their simple names defining their character. For children, it's not difficult to conclude that body differences reflect inner character traits of goodness and evil.

Occasionally movies foster tolerance by treating disability differences in a matter-of-fact way. They don't spotlight the person with a disability to portray him as a hero, a cute mascot, or an object of pity. *The Baby-Sitters Club* (movie and book series) incorporated a deaf child who signs and another character with diabetes.

GUIDING CHILDREN'S INTERACTIONS

We tend to avoid the topic of disability differences, rather than embrace it. The social cost of turning away from this issue is too great, however, both for us and our children. The challenge of understanding differences is far greater for children than for adults because children have so much to learn, and they depend on us to help them interpret the world in a helpful, reassuring, consistent manner. It's better to talk about differences—if children learn that everybody's different, then they won't have to "unlearn" so many stereotypes as adults.

Our challenge and our responsibility is to interpret the social world for our children. We need to give them essential information about disabilities, challenge stereotypes whenever we see them, and encourage their innate compassion. These tasks are difficult, especially when we ourselves have not been well-informed about differences, still cling to stereotypes, and at times find it hard to relax and behave authentically and appropriately. As parents, teachers, friends, mentors, child care providers, and health care professionals, each of us needs to recognize the importance of this process to the quality of society for future generations.

Children are understandably curious about disabled people and often stare at them, only to have their parents yank their arms and say, "Don't look." Nothing could better communicate to a child a sense of horror for disability.[3]
—Robert F. Murphy

Children can use the 4D approach, but they do need a little help from you. Let's turn to the 4D approach for guidance in coaching.

DETECTING

As we explained in Chapter 4, detecting a difference means noticing it, something children are remarkably adept at doing. Often, a child's difference detector will be working at full speed when you're in public, usually at some inopportune time such as when you're rushing through the supermarket or at an automated teller machine. "Look at that man with no legs!" your four-year-old will announce loudly. Although the comment may startle you, it is actually an accurate description of the difference.

You may be caught off-guard by your child's reaction if the difference is unexpected or unsettling for her. There might be some specific disability differences you encounter frequently and have habituated to, so they don't grab your attention anymore. At other times, your child may be fascinated because she has detected a *familiar* difference. For instance, after seeing someone using a hearing aid, your child may exclaim, "Hey, Dad, that man has a hearing aid just like Uncle Jorge!"

Recall that one goal in an inclusive society is to view disabilities as nothing more and nothing less than what they are. Children have a natural tendency to notice differences rather than deny them, no matter how irrelevant the differences are, so children most often challenge us by Detecting differences before we do or by pointing out differences that we would prefer to ignore. So, the challenge is guiding the child in the detection process and laying the groundwork for Deciding, Doing, and Debriefing. Here is how you can help your child.

Acknowledge Your Child's Observations

No matter how untimely, loud, or awkward a child's observation is, always acknowledge what he sees, hears, touches, or otherwise perceives. A child's world is full of many things that he doesn't understand. Although you don't have time or knowledge to explain everything—and a child doesn't have the ability to grasp it all—you do have an obligation to confirm what he sees.

Echo

You might just reflect your child's statement back to her, "Yes, Judy, he doesn't have legs." Use the child's own words in this first step. If she says, "That man is acting funny," then it's okay to say, "You noticed his funny behavior. He acts differently."

Ask

Check out what the child knows. Try not to assume! Handing over the facts too quickly could make you feel better, but it might not help a child cope with the next situation of differences. For example, ask your child, "What do *you* think that woman's machine is for?" Your child may answer, "It's so she can breathe on the moon." Children's answers can amuse or startle us, but they are helpful reminders of how they interpret the world—usually based on their own fears, insecurities, and needs.

Elaborate

You could add one more fact to help your child focus on the person's *abilities*, rather than just the disability. "See how he makes that wheelchair go back and forth; it takes him places like your feet take you!" "She does speak very slowly, but she has a cheerful personality."

Here's an example of an adult elaborating on the observations of a ten-year-old child:

Child: He's walking funny, like he's drunk.
Adult: Do both of his legs walk funny?
Child: No.
Adult: Which one does?
Child: The right one.
Adult: Now look at how his right arm is swinging around more. So, it looks like his left arm and leg are pretty coordinated, but his right arm and leg are not. The muscles on the right probably aren't getting clear messages from his brain, so they're not moving the way he wants. What else do you see?
Child: He's really watching the stoplight. He's crossing the street now.
Adult: If he were drunk, both legs would be stumbling, and he wouldn't be concentrating so well. It looks like his muscles work differently than ours.
Child: Why?

Adult: I'm not sure, but it could be something like cerebral palsy or multiple sclerosis, or he might have had a stroke a while ago, like Grandma did.

Of course, your explanation has to be geared to the child's age and language skill. It should be brief, grounded in observable facts—share what you *do* know. When you do not have all the details to explain a difference, create questions together with your child.

Adult: She's having a hard time reading the menu. Why do you think that might be?
Child: Maybe she has a learning disability, like Mariko in my class. Mariko has a hard time reading, too.
Adult: Or, maybe she just moved to our country and doesn't know how to read English?
Child: Maybe she's blind.
Adult: Probably not blind because she's looking at the clock and the paintings. It could be another kind of visual impairment.

The important point about elaboration is that it creates a pattern for thinking and talking about differences without judgment. Elaboration sets the tone for approaching differences with tolerant interest and acceptance rather than fear, shame, or disgust. The outcome of the discussion is not as important as calm exploration of the child's ideas and feelings.

Acknowledge Your Child's Feelings

Although children can be remarkably neutral at times when adults are flustered or embarrassed, they also can have strong emotional reactions to differences.

Observe Your Child's Emotions

You can usually discern your child's emotions by voice tone, facial expression, and body posture—as well as by his words.

Pay attention to these signals as you acknowledge your child's feelings.

Label the Feelings

If the child says how she is feeling, then your task is easy. Simply affirm the feeling: "I see that you're afraid." If your child doesn't use her own words first, then provide words to help label her feelings: "You look shocked," "Does that make you sad?" "Are you surprised to see a grown-up who can't talk?"

Talk About It

Explore the facts and feelings in some detail. When the situation allows, talk about it right then. For example, if a person with a tic shared an elevator with you and your child and the two of you have just exited, then that might be a good time to talk about the difference.

If the timing is just not good, then tell your child exactly when you'll talk about it. One example of bad timing is when a bank teller with a facial difference is handling a complicated transaction while your six-year-old is yanking on your jacket and asking a dozen questions. A child can handle a brief delay, and the extra time can help you plan what to say. "You know, Vahik, I can't explain it right now, but as soon as I finish here we'll talk about it."

Later, you can ask questions to get the discussion going: "Tell me what you noticed about the man in the bank," "I saw you staring earlier. What were you thinking?" "How did you feel?"

Acknowledge Your Own Reactions

Share Your Feelings

Sharing your feelings with the child is especially useful when you express a range of feelings. For example, "I was scared but also a little curious about how that voice machine works." Sharing your feelings is also effective when you share a progression of feelings: "At first I was shocked when I realized that short person was a grown-up and not a child. Then I noticed what a nice smile she had, and then I got used to her height and didn't pay much attention to it." Or, "I felt sorry for my friend who has a tic. I worried about him getting in trouble at school. I wondered about why his tic would come and go. Finally, I talked to him about it, and then I understood what was happening. I got used to his tics."

Help Your Child to Relax When Needed

As mentioned in Chapter 4, occasionally people feel some pretty strong negative emotions, such as shock or fear, when meeting a person with a disability difference. Sometimes a child has negative reactions or gets tense like we do. If her first feeling is a big dose of fear, panic, disgust, or shock, then she probably needs help relaxing. Explain to the child that she doesn't need to act on a negative first impression and that it helps to relax. Talk about how relaxing lets people think about other feelings and also helps people decide what to do next.

Of course, the moment the child is distressed about a difference is *not* the best time to teach relaxation skills! If your child does not already know how to relax, pick a calmer time and teach him (see the Debriefing section of this chapter).

Model Relaxation

Demonstrate to your child how you calm down when you're upset. Make sure your child understands that this is just a temporary setting aside of the distress, not a denial of the reason behind it.

Remind Your Child to Relax

If your child *does* know some relaxation strategies, then cue her to use them. "You can quiet down now. Remember how you breathe in and out three times, deeply and slowly. Blow out the nervousness. We can talk about it when you're a little calmer and more relaxed."

Key Points

Helping Children with Detecting

1. Acknowledge your child's observations.
2. Acknowledge your child's feelings.
3. Acknowledge your own reactions.
4. Relax when necessary.

DECIDING

Children also need guidance with Deciding about differences. After all, they know so little about differences and disabilities and have only basic notions about social roles. You can adapt the three Deciding questions from Chapter 4.

1. What kind of difference is this?
2. What are you and the other person supposed to be doing?
3. What are your action choices?

1. What Kind of Difference Is This?

If you have acknowledged the child's observations about the disability difference by echoing, asking, and elaborating, then she can learn to categorize the difference much as an adult would. Help your child decide

- Does the person *look* different?
- Does the person *move* differently?
- Does the person *talk* or gesture differently?
- Does the person *act* differently?
- Does the person seem to *learn* differently?

Keep in mind that the goal is not making a medical diagnosis but finding a working category that describes the
difference in terms of daily life functioning. Categorizing
helps the child look more closely at the difference and the
person, thus offsetting stereotyping tendencies. It also dissi-
pates discomfort by converting it to respectful curiosity.
And last, categorizing paves the way for choosing meaningful actions.

2. What Are You and the Other Person Supposed to Be Doing?

Children are far less clear about what is expected of them in
interactions and what they can expect of others. They are just
beginning to learn about the social roles that guide behavior
in social situations. Because children aren't yet able to focus
on roles during an interaction, they may direct their attention
to the disability instead. So, you need to remind your child of
the roles in a situation by giving simple, direct prompts. For
example, remind your child how *friends* behave toward each
other, how we react to *strangers* in the supermarket, how *Girl
Scouts* speak to *visitors,* or what kinds of questions you can ask
a *relative* but not a stranger. If your child is staring at the ice
cream shop clerk's atypically shaped hand, then you can say
gently, "She's waiting for the money, Ming. Give her your
dollar."

Sometimes your child needs to be reminded of social limits such as respecting others' body boundaries. "You need to
move over to the right side of the sidewalk, Teresa. We don't
follow a stranger so closely. That's getting into their personal
space." Occasionally a young child feels threatened by the
other person. For example, a five-year-old said this about a
woman without arms: "No arms! She can't hug anybody. . . .
She can't hurt me or anything, *can* she?" After addressing
your child's feelings, remind her of the purpose of the social
situation. Help your child figure out whether the person with
a difference is a passerby whom you'll never see again, a

neighbor to get to know better, the parent of a child at the park, and so forth.

A common theme of adult–child coaching and guidance—and the basic idea behind Deciding—is "think before you act." Encountering people with differences is no exception to this rule. When feeling and thinking come first, a child is likely to have a more satisfying and successful interaction.

3. What Are Your Action Choices?

Brainstorm Choices

Help your child see that there are choices about what to do. Avoid the trap of teaching "right" and "wrong" behavior. There are always *at least* two ways to act, and helping your child brainstorm the possibilities will teach him much more than when you simply deliver a "correct" answer.

Brainstorming choices on the spot is challenging because there's no time to come up with a long list of choices: "Do you want to sit next to the lady [with an oxygen mask], or do you want me to?" It's much easier to come up with choices in situations that allow for more time. For example, if there's a new student in your child's class who has leg braces, then you can come up with a variety of options. "Let's think of what your choices are here. What could you do?"

- Not talk to her ever
- Ask her to play Four Square at recess
- Ask her questions (why does she have leg braces, does she ever take them off, do they hurt)
- Call her to see whether she has the spelling list
- Join in teasing
- Be quiet when others tease her
- Speak up when they tease her
- Invite her to our house to play
- Go tell a teacher when they tease her

"Good. We've thought of so many things you could do!" Try writing down all of the options on the worksheet on page 281. (You can reproduce it to use it again.) For a four- to seven-year-old, you can write in the words she dictates. Encourage an older child to record her own words.

You'll notice that not all the alternatives in the previous list are great ideas! But helping your child list all possibilities is a good approach because

- It makes him feel in control and competent enough to think through a challenging situation.
- It reveals to him that situations are rarely black or white—there are gray areas in between.
- It helps him to consider the merits and weaknesses of various actions.

Evaluate Choices

Anticipating the likely outcomes or results—good and bad—of various options is an essential life skill. When the situation does *not* require a split-second choice, look at each item on the list with the child. Make two blank columns to the right of your list. At the top of one column, write *Good Outcomes,* or draw a plus sign or a smiley face, depending on the child's age. At the top of the other column, write *Problem Outcomes,* or draw a minus sign or a frowning face. Then help your child anticipate the possible outcomes of each item on your list (see the example on p. 282).

Choose the Actions to Try Next Time

Encourage your child to choose her actions. Remember that her age and personality will shape her choices about what feels comfortable and authentic at the time. Although it's helpful to brainstorm all kinds of actions, your child needs to choose actions that feel both comfortable and doable.

| Action Ideas for _____ Date_____ |||
| Situation _____ |||
Action	Good Outcomes	Problem Outcomes

Action Ideas for _Jamal_ Date _March, 1999_

Situation _Marina is a new girl in my class who wears leg braces._
She sits at my table.

Action	Good Outcomes	Problem Outcomes
Not talk to her ever.	I wouldn't have to get used to her.	Her feelings might be hurt. Maybe she's nice, and I'd never know it.
Ask her to play Four Square at recess.	She can play that game because she doesn't need to run.	None?
Ask her questions about her disability.	I wouldn't have to wonder and guess about it. She might be glad to tell me the facts.	She might think I'm nosy.

Key Points

Helping Children with Deciding

1. What kind of difference is this? Does the person *look* different? *move* differently? *talk* differently? *act* differently? *learn* differently?
2. What are you and the other person supposed to be doing?
3. What are your action choices?
   - Brainstorm action choices.
   - Evaluate the choices.
   - Choose one or more actions.
4. Help your child choose one or more actions to try next time.

DOING

Obviously, Doing means carrying out the action. Doing is the process of the child's *trying* an action to test his predictions about outcomes. Urge your child to take action and observe carefully what happens. If you are going to be present, then you can offer to give your child a signal or a prompt to go ahead and start the action as planned. Other adults, such as the Boy Scout den leader, a teacher, or a camp counselor, also can help support your child as he takes action. You should think about the three following factors to help your child succeed.

A Child Must Be Able to Do the Action

A planned action may sound great, but if the child has never behaved in that specific way before, it's unlikely that she will try such a brand-new behavior in this situation. To prepare her, you can practice the new behavior using role play or make-believe. Or, you could make sure that your child picks a behavior that she is already able to do.

Your Child Must Have the Opportunity to Do the Action

A child who is able to do or say something must also have the opportunity to put this ability to use. For example, if the child decides to say something to the person with the disability difference, then he must be close enough to the person to have a conversation.

A Child Needs Support While Doing the Action

As the child carries out the chosen actions, she'll need your support or assistance from others. If your daughter wants to invite a peer with a disability to join her YMCA day camp, then help her approach the director ahead of time. Also, for new actions to become comfortable habits, children need encouragement. You and other adults who observe the new action should provide positive feedback. Often it's enough to just smile, or say, "Thank you," or "Great idea!"

A Note on Personality

Keep in mind that despite your best efforts, encouraging new behaviors can be challenging, depending on the child's personality. As with adults, a child's personality is a factor that shapes his reactions and actions regarding people with disability differences. *Personality* is your child's enduring emotional and behavioral tendencies that reoccur in a variety of new situations. You may notice these patterns when your child meets someone new who has a disability difference.

Shy and Cautious

If your child tends to be shy and cautious, then she may cling to you, try to ignore the person with a difference, or stare quietly. Your child may resist saying even the simplest greeting. She may keep a great physical distance between herself and the other person. Your most successful approach might be to suggest words for her to say or to demonstrate something appropriate to say. Even though your child is quiet, she is watching you carefully and noting your feelings and behavior. She is more likely to relax when you relax. If your child benefits from preparation, and you can anticipate the encounter (even by a few moments), then you may ease some of your child's hesitancy.

Impulsive and Outgoing

If your child tends to be impulsive and outgoing, then he may blurt out something inappropriate or may touch the person without realizing he's invading that person's body boundaries. He may be flighty and not pay attention to your explanations. Or, he may have an extreme emotional outburst and exhibit a fear that seems to other people to be really out of proportion to the situation. If your child is easily overwhelmed in new situations, then he may need help to focus his attention, control urges, and contain emotions. Your child may benefit from calm, firm directions, such as "Come hold my hand." Redirect him from intrusive behavior without criticizing, by stating what you would like him to do at the moment. Be serious but not threatening or angry.

Key Points

Helping Children with Doing

1. Be sure the child is able to carry out the action.
2. Be sure the child has the opportunity to try the action.
3. Be sure to support the child's attempts to carry out the action.

DEBRIEFING

Remember that for your child (and you), learning how to list and evaluate choices takes place over time, not just within a single interaction. So, it's very important to debrief with your child, because each Debriefing experience sets the stage for making interactions better next time.

What Happened?

Most of the time when dealing with differences, Detecting and Deciding take the bulk of the time, whereas Doing occurs very quickly. Debriefing is the process of thinking and talking afterward about what happened. To debrief a situation, ask the child,

- "What did you do?"
- "What did she do then?"
- "And then what happened?"
- "How did you feel?"
- "How do you think she was feeling?"
- "What happened next?"
- "Did you expect that to happen or not?"
- "How did it turn out for you?…for her?
- "Did you stay relaxed? Or were you nervous or scared?"
- "Did you 'take care of business' in the situation?" ("Did you do what you were supposed to do?")
- "What would you do differently next time?"

Refer back to your list of options. Support your child's efforts, not just the apparent successes. Remember, you're trying to teach skills to serve him for a lifetime, not just a strategy for a single uncomfortable situation.

Key Points

Helping Children with Debriefing

1. Review what happened: who said what and who did what.
2. Describe feelings: how your child felt and how the other people seemed to feel.
3. Talk about what to try next time.

VIGNETTE: AN ADULT COACHING A CHILD

A seven-year-old boy talks over a situation with his mother:

1. Boy: Mom, today we had to read with the third graders. We each had a partner who we took turns reading with, and my partner had this really yucky thing on her finger, like a blob hanging on it. . . .
2. Mom: How did you feel, looking at her finger?
3. Boy: I was really scared!
4. Mom: What were you thinking to yourself? What were you saying in your mind?
5. Boy: It was saying to me to get away quick!
6. Mom: What would happen if you *couldn't* get away, what do you think might happen to you?
7. Boy: I don't know! She might *touch* me!
8. Mom: And *then* what might happen?
9. Boy: It's *yucky!*
10. Mom: It was kind of a shock for you. Well, what did you *say* to her? . . . What's her name?
11. Boy: Nothing! Her name is Danesha.
12. Mom: What do you want to know about Danesha's finger that looks different?
13. Boy: What it's called. . . . how she got it.
14. Mom: Good questions! Next time, what could you say to her to find out?

15. Boy:	I'd just walk away and try not to look. . . . Her hair was pointy back and really weird, and she really had a lisp. . . .
16. Mom:	So, Danesha looks different from you. But *you* have a lisp, too. You both have that in common!
17. Boy:	I guess. . . .
18. Mom:	How would *you* feel if all the kids "walked away quick" when they saw *you*?
19. Boy:	Sad . . . except her friend who already knows she has that finger wouldn't walk away . . .
20. Mom:	But now *you* already know about Danesha's finger. So when you see her again, you'll be more used to it. Could you try something new next time you see her?
21. Boy:	Maybe.
22. Mom:	What could you try?
23. Boy:	Close my eyes?
24. Mom:	Well, that would make it kind of hard for you to read! Why don't you try two things: Ask her a question to help you not be afraid, and then notice something *good* about her. What was good about her. . . . her smile, how well she read, her friendliness . . .
25. Boy:	There wasn't *anything* good!
26. Mom:	Come on, think hard.
27. Boy:	I can't think of anything!
28. Mom:	Will you try again tomorrow, and I'll be waiting to hear about something good.
29. Boy:	Okay.
30. Mom:	Thanks for telling me about Danesha. I can see that was a hard situation for you.

This dialogue illustrates several of the points about helping children interact with people with disability differences. The mother helped her child by:

- Helping him label and express his feelings, including fears (lines two, four, six, eight)

- Helping him problem-solve ways to get more information about the disability (lines 12, 14)
- Pointing out a commonality between him and Danesha (line 16)
- Drawing out his empathy (line 18)
- Pointing out that the disability difference is only one of Danesha's attributes (lines 24, 26, 28)
- Praising her son's openness and sharing, not just his successes (line 30)

Awareness Activity

Five Principles to Teach Children

It's okay to teach children by correction and coping during an interaction. But it's also important to look for opportunities (and create them) to *proactively* instill values and beliefs, such as the following:

1. *Disability* is a word that means many different things. It has specific meanings for each person, ranging from a small nuisance to a constant, major challenge.
2. A disability is always just one dimension of a person.
3. The physical environment can be more handicapping than the disability.
4. A difference is not always a good indicator of ability, and neither a difference nor ability are indicators of personal worth.
5. Our goal is to make an inclusive community, free of stereotypes, where differences are treated as no more or less important than they are for the specific people in a specific situation.

Help children learn these principles by drawing pictures, making puppets, arranging dolls, and dictating or writing stories with themes. You can try some of the following activities with one child or a group.

- Think of a less intrusive disability, and compare it with a more serious one.
- List as many disabilities as you can possibly think of.
- Look at a magazine photograph, or think about a television or book character, and describe five things about that person that are the *same* as you (or that are typical).
- If you needed to use a wheelchair, could you easily enter your house and all of its rooms? What would need to be changed?
- Think of someone who has a visible disability but other abilities; now think of someone who has a typical appearance but is not able to do certain things (nonvisible disability).
- What is the meaning of the saying "You can't judge a book by its cover"?
- Has anyone ever unfairly judged you based on your appearance? your abilities?

Key Points

Using the 4D Approach with Children

1. Observe how the child Detects the disability difference.
2. Explain how relevant the disability difference is in *this* situation. Help the child Decide which actions to try.
3. Support and encourage the child in Doing what seems appropriate. Try saying and Doing things in a new way.
4. Debrief the action. Talk with the child about how well his actions worked, and what to try next time.

SKILLS FOR EFFECTIVE INTERACTION: EXPANDING A CHILD'S COMFORT ZONE

It's easier to deal with most challenges in life by *preparing* for them instead of simply reacting to them. You can motivate a child to accept other people's differences every day in a variety of ways. The following sections suggest several ways of equipping a child with social interaction skills that will help increase her comfort with many kinds of differences. These are useful strategies for daily life, not just for situations involving people with disability differences.

Identify and Express Feelings

In the Detecting section of this chapter, labeling feelings is identified as a step in the detection process. Detecting feelings about disability differences will be relatively easy for the child who is used to labeling feelings in many daily situations. One of the best gifts you can give your child is an awareness of feelings and a vocabulary for expressing them. It's never too soon to talk about feelings with children. When we frequently and comfortably use words to narrate our range of emotions, our children are more likely to do the same. Parents' earliest techniques involve modeling (or demonstrating) how they label their own feelings. Later, parents and preschool teachers can interpret a child's feelings from his behavior and body language and express that feeling for the child, such as, "Chase, are you feeling sad that Daddy went to work?"

To help your child get used to thinking and talking about feelings in general, ask her questions such as "How did you feel when you got lost at the park?" "How did you feel when you won that game?" "How are you feeling now?" or "Are you angry [sad/upset/disappointed]?" Teach your child feeling words. Acknowledge that it's okay to have more than one feeling at a time and for feelings to change rapidly.

When talking about feelings with your child, don't judge them as good or bad. There is no right or wrong in this area! All feelings are real and valid. Some feelings are comfortable, such as joy, curiosity, and love. Other feelings such as fear, envy, or confusion cause discomfort. Before you try to get rid of your child's uncomfortable feelings, help him ask, "What is this feeling telling me?" Hurt feelings might be telling your child that he would prefer to be treated kindly. Angry feelings could be telling him that another person doesn't understand. Explain to your child that feelings teach us about ourselves when we pay attention to them instead of bottling them up or hastily getting rid of them.

Uncomfortable feelings sometimes are a part of life. Protecting children from uncomfortable feelings is not only unrealistic but also deprives them of a necessary learning experience. Angry feelings go away if they are "vented" or expressed through actions—some of which are safer and more appropriate than others. For example, hitting people and breaking toys are dangerous behaviors that will hurt people and possessions and cause sad feelings in others. But slapping a pillow or wet clay, drawing an angry picture, or shouting outdoors are behaviors that might help a child get rid of anger.

Develop Empathy

Empathy is the ability to feel what another person is feeling. It is "walking in another person's shoes." That means taking in her whole experience in its complexity, both positive and negative features. It also means not jumping to conclusions based on stereotypes or expecting your own similar experience with a specific disability to be the same as someone else's. *Sympathy*, however, is an *I* experience: Your illness, loss, disappointment makes *me* feel sad. Often there's a fine line between sympathy and *pity*, the state of feeling very sorry for the other person. When children are encouraged to pity a person with a disability difference, it's demeaning and creates an unequal relationship. The other person becomes an *object of pity*. Also, pity is so strong it can overshadow the other person's abilities and strengths.

Empathy can be taught and learned. Most children exhibit basic empathy by the time they are three years old. But young children are also so naturally self-centered that they need to be reminded that others have feelings, too. As children grow up, sometimes peer pressure competes with their empathic feelings. For example, preteens have a strong need to blend in with and be liked by their peers, so they may be inhibited from expressing empathy in group situations.

When you are reading a book with a young child, discuss the character's feelings. When an older child writes a book report, ask him questions about feelings. Here are some feeling questions to try:

- How did that character feel when _____?
- How did the main character's feelings change from the beginning to the end of the story?
- Was there a time when that character had several feelings at once?
- Can you picture yourself in this same situation? How would you feel?

It's important to note that empathy is a starting point, not an end. Imagining *yourself* in another person's situation might open the door to better interaction, but understanding *the other person's* true and unique experience of her own situation is the ultimate goal.

Relax Under Stress

Previously, we advised you to remind your child to relax if he became uncomfortable in the Detecting process. But that relaxation skill is something that must be taught at other times and practiced regularly so that when a tense situation arises, the child can remember a familiar activity. Relating to people with disability differences is not always stressful for a child, but sometimes it can be. To help improve interactions, you can teach your child to relax, which is helpful in many other situations, such as taking a test, giving a speech, going to the dentist, performing in a music recital, or learning a new skill such as riding a bike. A child can move through the 4D approach with greater self-assurance and success when she knows how to relax.[4]

One of the easiest relaxation techniques for most children is relaxed breathing. When people get worried, their breathing becomes fast and shallow. Slowing down our breathing helps us to physically calm down. Children can learn the same breathing techniques that help adults. Slow and deep breathing eases panicky short, fast breathing. It is simple to teach, quick to do, and easy to remember.

Awareness Activity

Teaching Relaxed Breathing

Relaxed breathing can be practiced anytime, anywhere—but to teach it the first time, choose a quiet room, ideally one with low lighting. Sit comfortably on a chair or couch, with both feet on the floor. Rest your arms on your lap or at your sides. Have the child do the same. When you are both in position, use a calm, soft voice to give these instructions:

1. Watch me as I breathe in *slowly and deeply* through my nose, and exhale *slowly* through my mouth. [Demonstrate a long, slow inhale through your nose and exhale through your mouth; exaggerate the length of your exhale.]
2. Now watch me breathe in and out again using my *slow and deep* breathing. Count on your fingers how long my exhale lasts. [Repeat the demonstration, closing your eyes and raising one finger up for each count of the exhale.]
3. How long was my exhale? Good.
4. Now you try it with me. [Repeat the demonstration, talking the child through it as both of you count on your fingers.]
5. Great job. Now try it with your eyes closed, and make that exhale longer.
6. Whenever you're nervous or scared, you can take *three slow breaths* to feel more relaxed. Then, you can Decide what to say and Do in the situation.

Act More Assertively

Children can learn to become more assertive during interactions with people who have differences. As with empathy and relaxation, you can demonstrate assertiveness. You can show the child how you speak up for yourself in social situations. You can remind him to speak up for himself. Then, encourage his efforts, whether they are successful or not.

Acting assertively means knowing what you want or think and saying it clearly to other people. It does *not* mean pushing people around with words or actions, which is aggression. Speaking up assertively is helpful when someone needs to step up and set a good example. For example, your child might be the first one in her class to say something positive to a new student with a disability. Giving a compliment or inviting the new student to join in a game are examples of positive assertion. Being assertive is helpful in protesting negative situations as well. Responding to teasing, declaring a different opinion from the group, or reporting a problem to an adult are examples of assertiveness that can help resolve problem situations or prevent them from getting worse.

An assertive child is more likely to think of lots of action choices when handling a disability difference situation. Plus, the assertive child is more likely to actually carry out the actions. He will have the confidence and the belief that he is entitled to speak up or take action. An assertive child can also manage his difficult feelings by sharing them and getting his emotional needs met.

Become More Informed About and Aware of Disabilities

Read Books About Disabilities and Books Featuring Characters with Disabilities

Books about disabilities are a great source of information for children, exposing them to a variety of disabilities and prosenting positive role models. Depending on the child's age, you can read to her, listen to her read aloud, take turns reading, or give your child something to read on her own. The important thing is that you talk about the reading at some time. Here are some discussion questions:

- What was the story about?
- How did you like the story? What were your favorite parts?
- What didn't you like? Did any part scare or confuse you?
- What kind of difference was described in this book?
- What questions do you have about that disability?
- What abilities did that person have?
- What barriers did that person face? Does that happen in real life? What could or should be done about those?
- In what ways was that character the same as you? Different than you?
- Could you imagine this person being your friend? Why or why not?

Watch Television and Movies Together

Ask the child questions similar to the ones for reading. Remember that even though television and movies are very influential in children's lives, they do not have to be controlling or major forces. Television and movies do offer exposure to people with disabilities that many children otherwise would never have. Any reactions to and interactions with people with disability differences that a child and adult see on the television or in movies provide terrific opportunities for discussion about values and for answering the child's questions.

Get to Know Children with Differences in Your School and Neighborhood

Sometimes children with disabilities are not included in social activities or asked to come over and play as often as typical children. Frequently this is because parents of typical children are hesitant and unsure whether the child is fragile or has special needs. If you have these concerns, then you could approach the parents of the child with a disability. You could ask directly whether it is possible for your children to spend time together. Because of general lack of information or fear, some people might be reluctant to encourage a child with a disability to join your scout troop, church youth group, or car pool. If your child is four years of age or older, he or she will have opinions about potential friends, so be sure to talk about your plans *before* you make them.

Highlight the Times When a Family Member Experiences a Disability

You can help your child become used to differences by talking about the times that someone in your family has a disability. If a sprained ankle causes Dad to use crutches, talk about how your home is designed for people who can walk, not people who use crutches or wheelchairs. Talk about how you could adapt your home to be more accessible to people who move differently. If you're taking pain or allergy medication that makes your brain feel cloudy, and helping your eighth grader with algebra becomes a huge challenge, then talk about how a parent with learning disabilities might feel. If your daughter needs to wear an eye patch for a few days, then use this opportunity to enhance her empathy and awareness. Instead of focusing on the temporary aspect ("Don't even think about it; it'll come off in no time"), ask her to notice how other people are reacting. Talk about how her different appearance triggers feelings and reactions in others.

Learn About Adaptive Equipment and Technology

You can prepare your child to interact with people who have disabilities by showing him various adaptive devices that he might see someone using. Take advantage of your excursions into the community to show him telephones that have telecommunications devices for the deaf (TDDs). If possible, switch your television to closed captioning, or point out television shows that have closed captioning. Try out an audio description service at a movie theater near you. Point out wheelchairs, walkers, and crutches with the same interest you might have in sports cars or fashion. Learn about the innovations in computers, vans, and new sports equipment that is available to people with disabilities for activities such as skiing, tennis, basketball, rock climbing, scuba diving, and countless others. Attend a Disabilities Expo or Special Olympics in your area.

Key Points

Skills for Effective Interaction

1. Identify and express feelings.
2. Develop empathy, not pity.
3. Relax in stressful situations.
4. Act more assertively.
5. Become more aware of and informed about disabilities.

   - Read books about disabilities and books featuring characters with disabilities.
   - Watch television and movies together.
   - Get to know children with differences in your school and neighborhood.
   - Highlight the times when a family member experiences a disability.
   - Learn about adaptive equipment and technology.

MAKING A DIFFERENCE IN YOUR COMMUNITY

When disability awareness is second nature in your family, you may feel inspired to spread this awareness to groups of children. The activities suggested previously in the Skills for

Effective Interaction section can all be adapted to groups of children—some possibilities follow.

Your Child's Classroom

Because inclusive education is being practiced in more school districts, interacting with peers with disabilities occurs quite often and sometimes presents very real, immediate challenges. You can help overcome these challenges in several ways.

Raise Awareness

Many books and curricula have been published to help teachers and school staff. Your local college library is likely to have dozens of books in its special education section. You could urge the school, your PTA, or a booster group to purchase one of the newer educators' guides. (See the Readings and Resources at the end of this chapter for a brief listing of books for teachers and school staff.)

Share a Book, and Lead a Discussion

If you and your child have read about a specific difference, then you can share this new knowledge with your child's classmates. Many children's books about disabilities are listed in the Readings and Resources at the end of this chapter. You can also look for "Special Needs" or "Growing Up" sections in large bookstores.

Survey the School for Accessibility

Enlist students in an accessibility committee to measure doorways, bathroom stalls, and sink heights. Have them compare the actual measurements with the accessibility specifications in the local building code. Don't forget to check the playground, cafeteria, nurse's office, auditorium, library, and gym. Have the committee consider how students using wheelchairs and those with visual or hearing impairments move around the campus. Don't forget to include students with disabilities on the committee.

Invite a Guest Speaker

In nearly every class, there is someone who has a parent or sibling with a disability difference. Try inviting this person to lead a class discussion. Or, look for a teacher with a disability at your own school or a nearby one.

I rolled into my first classroom. I told each class about my disability (osteogenesis imperfecta) and then opened up to their questions. No stone was left unturned. If a student was too embarrassed to talk to me openly, he or she was welcome to talk to me privately. Within two weeks, I heard no more questions about my wheelchair's top speed or whether there was a cure for my disability.[5]

—Kathy D. Collins

Youth Organizations

You can also help increase awareness of disabilities in youth organizations or clubs. For example, the Girl Scouts of the United States of America has a nationally distributed booklet for leaders focusing on including girls with special needs.[6] The Brownie Scout and Junior Girl Scout handbooks have sections that deal with human diversity and explore prejudice, discrimination, and stereotypes.

Religious or Ethnic Heritage Classes

The value of full community inclusion for people of all abilities taps into many fundamental religious principles. Consider how inclusion of people with disability differences is consistent with specific tenets of your religious faith. You may find that the two are intertwined and reinforcing. Weave disability themes into religious class lessons. Also, advocate for including children with disabilities in religious classes.

Sports Teams

Children with disabilities have a history of having separate sports groups. Organizations such as the Special Olympics have provided a safe and supportive environment for children with disabilities to enhance their athletic talents and experience teamwork, competition, and the discipline of practice. Many children's sports organizations, however, could expand their boundaries to include children with special needs. A child with a disability could participate in soccer, tee-ball, or basketball not only as a player but also as an assistant coach, referee, or equipment manager.

PUTTING IT ALL TOGETHER

I had just begun to use a wheelchair. I was at a very busy mall waiting for the elevator. A little girl was not only staring at me, she was walking around the chair while staring. . . . After circling twice, the little girl came up to me and looked me directly in the eye and stated: "You have on the same 'Mickey Mouse' earrings that I have. I went around you twice to check to make sure they were the same."[7]

—Linda Lee Sheffer

In this chapter, we have explored some ways adults can guide children when they see and interact with people with disability differences. Human diversity is a fact of life, but disability diversity has been an unsettling and often taboo topic for adult–child dialogue at home, in classrooms, in churches, and at play. Direct, supportive, and age-appropriate guidance is the responsibility of *every* adult, not just teachers and people with disabilities. Childhood and adolescence are the best time to begin learning about disabilities and interacting with people different from oneself. It's also a time for developing values of respect for all human differences, advocacy for social equality and environmental accessibility, and commitment to community inclusion for people of all ages and abilities. If children today receive *education* about disabilities, *exposure* to people with disability differences, and guidance in developing *empathy*, then their personal comfort zones will expand, and they will reap the benefits of an inclusive society that is enriched by its diversity.

READINGS
AND RESOURCES

Books About Disability Differences (General)

Health, Illness, and Disability:
A Guide to Books for Children and Young Adults
P. Azarnoff (R.R. Bowker, New York, 1983)

Understanding Abilities, Disabilities, and Capabilities:
A Guide to Children's Literature
M.F. Carlin, J.L. Laughlin, & R.D. Saniga (Libraries Unlimited,
Englewood, CO, 1991)

We Are All Alike. . . . We Are All Different (Ages 4–7)
Cheltenham Elementary School Kindergartners (Scholastic,
New York, 1991)

What It's Like to Be Me, Second Edition
Helen Exley (Ed.) (Friendship Press, New York, 1984)

Accept Me as I Am: Best Books
of Juvenile Nonfiction on Impairments and Disabilities
J.B. Friedberg, J.B. Mullins, & A.W. Sukiennik
(R.R. Bowker, New York, 1985)

A Guide to Children's Literature and Disability
National Information Center for Children and Youth with
Disabilities (Washington, DC, 1990–1994)
To order, call 800-999-5599 or 800-695-0285.

Why Does that Man Have Such a Big Nose? (Ages 3–8)
M.B. Quinsey (Parenting Press, Seattle, 1996)

Kids Explore the Gifts of Children with Special Needs
S. Vaughn (Addison Wesley Longman, Reading, MA, 1994)

Read It Again: Books to Prepare Children for Inclusion
Westridge Young Writers Workshop (John Muir Publications, Santa Fe, NM, 1994)

Books About Appearance Differences

A Picture Book of Louis Braille
D.A. Adler (Holiday House, New York, 1997)

David's Story: A Book about Surgery (Ages 8–11)
B. Brink (Lerner Publications, Minneapolis, MN, 1996)

Two Very Little Sisters
C. Carrick (Clarion Books, New York, 1993)

Books About Movement Differences

Cerebral Palsy (Ages 11–15)
N. Aaseng (Franklin Watts, New York, 1991)

My Buddy (Ages 4–8)
A. Osofsky (Henry Holt, New York, 1992)

Follow Your Dreams
C. Panzarino (National Spinal Cord Injury Association, Silver Spring, MD, 1995)

Books and Videos
About Communication Differences

On Being Sarah (Ages 11–13)
E. Helfman (Albert Whitman & Co., Morton Grove, IL, 1992)

Silent Dancer (Ages 6–12)
B. Hlibok (Messner, New York, 1981)

When I Grow Up
C. Hodges (Jason & Nordic Publishers, Hollidaysburg, PA, 1995)

Mary Marony and the Snake (Ages 5–8)
S. Kline (Putnam Berkley, New York, 1992)

Jessi's Secret Language
(The Baby-Sitters Club, #16) (Ages 9–12)
A.M. Martin (Scholastic, Inc., New York, 1988)

Listen for the Bus: David's Story (Ages 4–10)
P. McMahon (Boyds Mill Press, Honesdale, PA, 1995)

A Place for Grace (Ages 3–7)
J.D. Okimoto (Sasquatch Books, Seattle, WA, 1996)

Do You Stutter? Straight Talk for Teens
Stuttering Foundation of America (Memphis, TN, 1996)
To order this videotape, call 800-992-9392.

Books About Learning Differences

Charlsie's Chuckle (Ages 5–11)
C.W. Berkus (Woodbine House, Bethesda, MD, 1992)

The Summer of the Swans (Ages 10–14)
B. Byars (Viking, New York, 1970)

Big Brother Dustin (Ages 3–7)
A.R. Carter (Albert Whitman & Co., Morton Grove, IL, 1983)

Sixth Grade Can Really Kill You (Ages 9–12)
B. DeClements (Scholastic, New York, 1995)

The Don't-Give-Up-Kid and Learning Differences,
Third Edition (Ages 5–10)
J. Gehret (Verbal Images Press, Fairport, NY, 1996)

Books About Behavior Differences

Russell Is Extra Special:
A Book About Autism for Children (Ages 4–8)
C.A. Armenta (Magination Press, New York, 1992)

Hi, I'm Adam: A Child's Story
of Tourette Syndrome (Ages 7–12)
A. Buehrens (Hope Press, Duarte, CA, 1993)

Coping with Depression, Third Edition (Ages 12–17)
L. Clayton & Sharon Carter (Rosen, New York, 1995)

What Do You Mean, I Have ADD? (Ages 5–12)
K.M. Dwyer (Walker & Co., New York, 1996)

Polly's Magic Games:
A Child's View of Obsessive-Compulsive Disorder
C.H. Foster (Dilligaf Publishing, Ellsworth, ME, 1994)

My Sister, Then and Now:
A Book About Mental Illness (Ages 10–15)
V.L. Kroll (Carolrhoda Books, Minneapolis, MN, 1992)

Kristy and the Secret of Susan
(The Baby-Sitters Club, #32) (Ages 9–12)
A.M. Martin (Scholastic, Inc., New York, 1990)

Books About Nonvisible Differences

Someone Special, Just Like You (Ages 3–7)
T. Brown (H. Holt & Co., New York, 1984)

When Someone Has a Very Serious Illness (Ages 4–11)
M. Heegaard (Woodland Press, Minneapolis, MN, 1991)

Nanny's Special Gift
R. Potaracke (Paulist Press, New York, 1993)

My Friend Emily:
A Story about Epilepsy and Friendship (Ages 5–11)
S.M. Swanson (Writer's Press Service, Boise, ID, 1994)

"I Remember!" Cried Grandma Pinky
J. Wahl (Troll Communications, LLC, Mahwah, NJ, 1994)

Books to Help Children Express Feelings

Dealing with Feelings (series) (Ages 4–8)
E. Crary (Parenting Press, Seattle, 1996)

How I Feel (series; includes stickers) (Ages 2–6)
M. Leonard (Smart Kids Publishing, San Diego, 1997)

Sachiko Means Happiness
K. Sakai (Children's Book Press, San Francisco, 1991)

Inside Out: My Book
About Who I Am and How I Feel (Ages 9–12)
G. Van Kleef Douthit (Hazelden Publishing & Education,
Center City, MN, 1991)

Materials for School Staff and Students

Friends at School (Ages 4–8)
R. Bunnell (Star Bright Books, Andover, England, 1996)

Learning to Care: Classroom Activities
for Social and Affective Development
N.D. Feshbach & S. Feshbach (Addison Wesley Longman,
Reading, MA, 1983)

Kids with Special Needs: Information and Activities
to Promote Awareness and Understanding (Ages 6–11)
V. Getskow & D. Konczal (The Learning Works, Santa Barbara,
CA, 1996)

Quick-Guides to Inclusion and Quick-Guides to Inclusion 2
M.F. Giangreco (Paul H. Brookes Publishing Co., Baltimore, 1997,
1998)

Include Us!
To order this videotape, education guide, and sing-along cas
sette, call TiffHill Productions (888-462-5833).

12

Expanding Our Vision

Viewing people with disabilities as social units in need of repair or rehabilitation before being ele vated to the status of "real" persons or citizens seems now to be outmoded, both legally and socially. Fitting in with the social structure has become much less important than changing the system to fit the individual.[1]

—Marsha Rioux

This book was written to help you understand and change uncomfortable reactions to and interactions with someone who has a disability difference. You've learned how to Detect disability differences, Decide what to Do more thoughtfully and calmly, and Debrief your reactions and interactions in order to handle future situations more effectively.

Our hope is that after reading this book and trying the activities, you have gained

A new awareness . . .

- By questioning old assumptions and beliefs
- By recognizing that disabilities are a part of everybody's life experience
- By learning about changing social attitudes and policies
- By learning about specific disability differences
- By expanding your personal comfort zone for diversity

A deeper understanding . . .

- Of typical reactions you've had
- Of uncomfortable interactions you've had
- Of influences on your beliefs and behaviors

A few more skills . . .

- Detecting differences more accurately and comfortably
- Deciding how you want to act
- Doing what feels the most positive and appropriate
- Debriefing your interactions so they get easier and better over time

As you build on your new level of confidence, you may be inspired to look beyond individual interactions and consider your potential impact on your community. In this chapter, we suggest ways you can influence the groups in your life.

DISABILITY DIFFERENCES
ARE A PART OF EVERYBODY'S LIFE

Disability diversity is a permanent feature of our world. Everybody has had or will have a personal experience with disability at some time in his life. Despite great strides in science and medical technology and our personal efforts to maintain our health and prevent injuries, disabilities are part of the diversity of human life. Genetic variation will always be present. Accidents will always be a source of injury and disability. Toxic substances will continue to affect developing fetuses, children, and adults. As people live longer, many will experience the disabilities that frequently occur with aging.

The more we recognize our shared vulnerability, the more we can begin to accept disabilities as an ever-present—and natural—part of the human condition. Moving beyond judgmental comparisons of people with and without disabilities ("us" versus "them") is a necessary step toward comfortably acknowledging our deeper human bond.

EXPANDING OUR PERSONAL COMFORT ZONE

This book was written to help you look inside yourself at your feelings, life experiences, and cultural assumptions so you can expand your personal comfort zone by learning new ways to relate to others who have disability differences. Imagine: If *your* personal change process is repeated by many other people, then there could be significant community change.

CIRCLES OF CHANGE FOR NEW COMMUNITIES

In the ideal world, my differences, though noted, would not be devalued. Nor would I. Society would accept my experience as "disability culture," which would in turn be accepted as part of "human diversity." There would be respectful curiosity about what I have learned from my differences that I could teach society. In such a world, no one would mind being called Disabled. Being unable to do something the way most people do it would not be seen as something bad that needed curing. It would be seen as just a difference. Differences might make you proficient in some contexts, deficient in others, or not matter at all.[2]

—Carol Gill

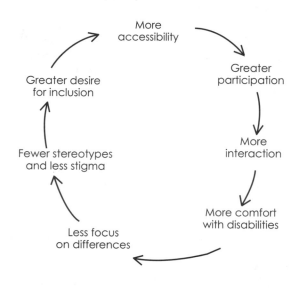

Person-to-Person Change

A new community begins with *you,* and change spreads one
person at a time. As others watch you interact with people
with disabilities and applying the skills presented in this
book, you can serve as a role model for others who may feel
uncomfortable relating to people different from themselves.
You can demonstrate comfort, confidence, and positive approaches. Your words and actions will be observed by others:
your use of person-first language and your relaxed and authentic interactions with people who have disability differences. By interacting differently, you can spark changes in others and in the environment. For example,

- In conversations, people will notice when you use person-
  first words as you talk about children with disabilities or a
  man with Down syndrome.
- When a friend drops his fork from the dinner table and
  comments, "I'm such a spaz," you may point out that that
  isn't funny.

- If you notice a new boy in your daughter's class who has a facial difference, then you can greet him warmly and welcome him to the school.
- When you stand in line next to a woman using a wheelchair, you can make eye contact and greet her comfortably.
- When you see a sign in a store that says "No Morons Allowed," you might tell the owner you find that offensive.

When other people notice how you've handled the situation, they may handle a similar situation more comfortably the next time. You will be part of an ever-expanding circle of appreciation and accommodation of human differences.

Person-to-Group Change

Person-to-person change is a great way to begin larger community change. But as you increase your awareness of social attitudes about people with disability differences, you will be able to go to the next level: reaching out to groups of people.

Think about how you can facilitate change in your workplace, place of worship, and social or hobby groups. As you interact with these groups, consider ways you could help them become more aware of disabilities and more accommodating. Take advantage of your enhanced skills and "insider" status to suggest ways the groups could change:

- **Look at the members and leaders.** You might want to bring up the topic of disabilities at a formal or informal meeting. Do any members or leaders have disabilities? Are there ways in which people with disabilities have been discouraged from joining or assuming leadership roles? Encourage members and leaders to embark on an outreach effort together.
- **Look at the settings where activities take place.** Enlist others in the group to help assess how physically accessible the meeting environment is. Are doorways wide enough for wheelchairs? Is there handicapped parking? Are there

ramps or elevators in addition to stairs? Does the group own assistive listening and visual devices?

- **Look at the group's public information.** Does disability information appear in printed materials such as news articles or recruitment pamphlets? Is person-first language used? Does the group state that meeting places are accessible to people with disabilities? Are written materials also available in large print, audiocassette, and braille?

- **Listen to discussions in meetings.** In discussions and meetings, what messages are conveyed about people with disabilities? Are stereotypes perpetuated (emphasizing pity, charity, or heroics)? Or, are people with disabilities seen as valued equal participants in the group?

- **Look at orientation materials for new staff.** Are disability awareness issues addressed in new-employee handbooks or training sessions?[3]

- **Suggest and support activities that promote disability awareness,** such as the following:
  - If you are an active group member, then you can help organize a *diversity awareness committee* to advocate for issues.
  - Consider making a presentation about the *4D approach.* A proactive, positive approach is more likely to succeed than a focus on deficiencies and criticism.
  - *Survey members* to discover how many have disabilities. A confidential questionnaire could ask people what accommodations they need to participate in the group more often or actively. If your group is a church or other neighborhood organization, then you could contact potential members in the area to discover how many people with disabilities could become involved.
  - *Invite speakers* from disability self-advocacy and support groups. Have group members with disabilities educate members who don't have those disabilities. If you have a disability, then you could talk about your own experiences, including obstacles and resources you have encountered in this group or other settings. A disabilities

workshop, booth, or fair are other effective and fun ways to raise awareness.

- Conduct *disability simulation activities* using some of the Awareness Activities in this book.

Group-to-Group Change

When you serve as an agent of change within a group, you and the rest of your group will quickly realize the power in numbers. For example, if you are making progress at your own religious or professional group, then you could join with other local groups and move on together to your regional organization. When several groups work on disability issues, they can share ideas and materials.

The limited scope of small groups is another reason that a higher level of change is often needed. You can only reach so many people in a small, face-to-face group setting. To change the larger community, many disability advocates have turned to the political system. Several disability laws were ahead of their time in the sense of promoting values and policies that were not common practice. For example, the Rehabilitation Act of 1973, the Americans with Disabilities Act, and the Individuals with Disabilities Education Act promoted new awareness, attitudes, and behavior before many individuals and communities thought they were ready or willing to adopt the concepts (see Chapter 2). Sometimes individuals and groups change so slowly that they need a nudge from public policy and laws.

To effect larger community change, you'll benefit by collaborating with disability self-advocacy groups that have an explicit agenda of social change. Many such groups exist at the local, state, and national level. (See the Readings and Resources at the end of this chapter as well as Chapters 5–10.) These groups interpret and implement federal legislation to change important aspects of people's daily lives. They are committed to promoting the independence, self-determination, and full community participation of people with disabilities.

FROM DISABILITY AWARENESS
TO DIVERSITY AWARENESS

As you approach groups to talk and teach about disability differences, you will soon see that this topic is part of a larger issue: human diversity. Disability differences are just one piece
of the wide array of human differences. Awareness of disability differences is very closely related to awareness of other
kinds of diversity, such as ethnicity, race, age, culture, and religion. Recognizing the rich and varied human experience and
approaching it with openness and curiosity expands your personal comfort zone for diversity and is the foundation of
awareness and community change.

In our world, people were either deaf or hearing. We regis-
tered both with equal lack of concern: the designation
was relevant but unremarkable. We were already accustomed to cultural differences, even within our own family—our father was Jewish, our mother Protestant; our pa-
ternal grandparents were deaf, the rest of us hearing;
Andy (who was adopted) was black, the rest of us white.[4]
—Leah Hager Cohen

The logical next step is to celebrate human diversity of
other sorts. Here are some suggestions for enhancing diversity
awareness in your home and community:

- **Explore your own ethnic heritage.** Learn more about your
  racial, ethnic, geographic, and cultural roots. Consider
  how your heritage has shaped your behavior, beliefs about
  differences, and child-rearing practices.
- **Get to know people who are different from you.** Expand
  your social network to include people with different ethnic
  origins, first languages, and so forth. Encourage your children to do the same. Talk to your children about how these
  differences enrich daily life. Much of the advice in this
  book about interacting with people who have disability

differences can be applied to interactions with people who have other differences.

- **Attend ethnic and religious festivals.** National and ethnic celebrations are a good way to experience the ambience of another culture or group without actually traveling to the group's country of origin. Attending a variety of religious festivals enables you to see both the shared and unique aspects of spiritual pursuits.
- **Discover other languages.** If you're lucky enough to have another language as your first one, then preserve it in your family. It links you to your past. Learn a few words, such as "Hello" and "Thank you," in several languages. Learn some phrases and words in sign language. Marvel at the variety of the spoken word and hand signs and how phrases in certain languages seem so expressive, even when heard by people who do not speak the language. When you are in crowded public places, watch and listen to conversations in other languages, noting the people's pace, rhythm, and use of gestures. Can you detect the theme of the conversation?
- **Broaden your family's foods.** Consider the range of foods you grew up with and how many of those you continue to cook or eat. Do your children eat from a wider—or narrower—range of cuisines than you did as a child? Rediscover and introduce your family to your childhood favorites. Search the grocery store or farmers' market for "exotic" fruits and vegetables. When sampling foods of other ethnic groups and countries, offer some to your child (without forcing). Although children will sometimes respond with an emphatic "Yuck!" at other times they will be marvelously open to the new item. Organize an ethnic potluck luncheon at your office. And remember, "ethnic food" is not a single thing. *Every* food has an ethnic origin!
- **Be attentive to differences in nature.** Examples of variations, patterns and exceptions, and sameness and difference are everywhere. Observe your pet's offspring. Explore with your children or grandchildren how trees are similar and how they are different, how the songs of birds

differ, how different insects move, and how fish of all different species and sizes live together.

- **Visit galleries and museums.** Art galleries and museums provide rich glimpses into history and other cultures. Many museums offer programs that are designed for children and use hands-on activities to bring alive the cultural context of contemporary and traditional folk art and artifacts. Natural history museums can add to your children's growing appreciation of differences whether it be dinosaurs, living customs of different cultures, or amazing gems and minerals.
- **Explore books and movies that celebrate differences.** Differences are everywhere. As we describe in Chapter 1, we tend to compare and evaluate differences and then devalue those we don't like. When you read books and watch movies with your children, find opportunities to talk about differences and to teach the value of variety in learning and entertainment. Instead of just reading or watching and moving on, take time to compare each family member's opinions about stories and characters, and watch your children become more sensitized to—and appreciate—details in differences.

Celebrate diversity instead of color-blindness. Many baby boomers grew up with the idea of a color-blind, "melting-pot" society—a popular post–World War II liberal notion in America. While it may seem noble to tell a child not to notice the differences in others—"It doesn't matter if a person is black, brown, or green" — it does, in fact, matter. Color-blindness is not a solution to racism. Diversity does not happen by neglect or default, it comes about by actively embracing difference.[5]

—Clyde W. Ford

WHAT WE CAN LEARN FROM OTHER PEOPLE'S DISABILITY EXPERIENCES

Most pivotal life experiences have both rewards and challenges. Typical life changes such as getting married, becoming a parent, and being promoted at work always have some negative aspects. Life crises, such as the death of a loved one or the loss of a job, involve loss and grief but often lead us in surprisingly positive directions as well.

Most people imagine that acquiring a disability would be a totally negative life experience for them. The negatives loom large, especially when an impairment is first diagnosed or if there is a deteriorating course. The prospect of medical problems involving pain, financial burden, and employment disruption can seem overwhelming. Fears about the future, concern about relationships and acceptance in the community, and doubts about self-worth may all feel insurmountable. Imagining yourself with limitations can be very unsettling, and you may assume that this is how people with disabilities always feel.

Everybody's personal experience with having a disability is unique. For some, it is a personal tragedy, and adjustment is difficult. For others, the experience evolves into a highly positive personal transformation. People who grow up with a disability difference have different experiences from people who acquire disabilities through injury or illness. Disabilities differ in severity, in the discomfort they cause, and in the degree to which they interfere with daily living. People differ in their personality styles, their personal supports, and their access to adaptive equipment and adequate medical care. There is no "right" way to adapt to disability. Limitations can set people apart because of their differences, or they can present a challenge for the community to find ways to include everyone.

We all use adapted equipment. Take, for example, the pencil I'm holding. It allows ideas in my brain to be recorded on paper. But millions and millions of people cannot use this pencil; generally they're in the first grade. So what do we do? We make larger pencils for them that they can hold. We give them a piece of adapted equipment. If there's enough people who can't use something, it will be adapted.[6]

—J. Scherer

The traditional view—that disabilities are all "bad"—is being challenged by many people in the disability community who give their disability the attention it demands but do not define themselves by their limitations.

The experience of disability can only be evaluated by the person who has the disability. An outsider cannot draw conclusions about another person's self-perception without knowing that person's thoughts, feelings, and beliefs. A disability is a *potential* nuisance, gift, annoyance, wake-up call, burden, self-esteem threat, challenge, disaster. Although having a disability does indeed often involve disastrous and sad personal experiences, it also encompasses many other feelings and experiences. There is no single "disability experience" that can be described. Such a diverse, complex, and evolving human experience cannot be reduced to a single evaluative statement.

Having a disability is a profound, often life-changing experience, and everybody can learn from the challenges people with disabilities experience. People who have lived with disabilities are the most qualified to describe the complexity of their experience. Here are some examples of the unexpected potential of disabilities, expressed by the people who have made these discoveries for themselves.

There is no question that my life has taken a hit, but I can look back on it all and see the positives. Most important, it has saved my marriage . . . I had this idea that a person's accomplishments were what defined him. Today I'm a lot more at peace with myself.[7]

—Beck Weathers

I parked myself on a ramp. It was a beautiful, cool afternoon, and I just looked up at the mountains for about two hours and felt very, very peaceful. . . . These are things that I thought I would learn to do when I was 75, not 43.[8]

—Christopher Reeve

I honestly believe . . . that as a result of it [bipolar disorder]
I have felt more things, more deeply; had more experiences, more intensely; loved more, and been more loved;
laughed more often for having cried more often; appreciated more the springs, for all the winters; worn death "as
close as dungarees," appreciated it—and life—more; seen
the finest and the most terrible in people, and slowly
learned the values of caring, loyalty, seeing things through.[9]

—Kay R. Jamison

I certainly don't like the stage [of multiple sclerosis] that
I've got to, because it means now I've got to ask for help.
I'm fiercely independent . . . [but] I've gained in friends—
real friends. They seem to have the attitude that my needs
are their needs as well. In a way it's been a better life. . . .
I've grown a lot . . . but I have moments of great anguish
too, that no one ever sees.[10]

—Ellen

In a fundamental sense, disability demonstrates the super-
ficiality of physical standards in modern society.[11]

Harlan Hahn

A couple of months ago I realized that my body was re-
sponsible for giving me my politics. . . . If I didn't have cerebral palsy I wouldn't have the politics I've developed. . . . I
don't dress to project myself as a good looking person. . . .
I dress how I want to dress and that means being an individual and not wanting to buy into "the way women
should dress."[12]

—A woman in Boston

Disability is a great teacher, and if one listens, she teaches
with conviction about pride and vanity and limitations. . . .
There is something liberating about not seeing an unkempt
beard, a stained shirt, the color of skin, and the shapes of

noses. Some of the props for prejudice are simply knocked out, and I would like to believe that the result is beneficial. There must be a reason for the portrayal of justice as blind.[13]

—Robert Hine
on blindness

People with disabilities have experiences which are sources of knowledge that are not directly accessible to non-disabled people. . . . Much of it would enrich and expand our culture and some of it has the potential to change our thinking and our ways of life profoundly. People with disabilities are in better positions to notice and criticize cultural myths about the body and mind, as well as such matters as self-worth, intimacy, sexuality, dependency, and independence. [14]

—Susan Wendell

Even if the physical environment in which I live posed no physical barriers, I would still rather walk than not be able to walk. This is, however, quite definitely *not* to say that my life is not worth living, nor is it to deny that very positive things have happened in my life *because* I became disabled. I can therefore value my disability, while not denying the difficulties associated with it.[15]

—Jenny Morris

LOOKING TO THE FUTURE

There are rewards for making the world physically and emotionally accessible to all people, including benefits that accrue to society as a whole. The more perspectives that can be brought to bear on human experience, even from the slant of a wheelchair or a hospital bed, or through the ears of a blind person or the fingers of someone who is deaf, the richer that experience becomes. If it is both possible and pleasant for me and my kind to enter, the world will become a livelier place. You'll see.[16]

—Nancy Mairs

Understanding and changing our reactions to disabilities can only occur when we acknowledge our discomfort with our beliefs and behavior and challenge ourselves to try new ways of thinking and interacting. Our hope is that *Everybody's Different* has helped you in this process of expanding your personal comfort zone and breaking down stereotypes. By gaining a new awareness of disability differences, a better understanding of your emotional reactions, and improved interaction skills, you have also promoted the circle of change in your community.

READINGS
AND RESOURCES

Books

Mixed Matches: How to Create Successful
Interracial, Interethnic, and Interfaith Relationships
J. Crohn (Fawcett Columbine, New York, 1995)

Many Peoples, Many Faiths:
An Introduction to the Religious Life of Humankind
R.S. Ellwood (Prentice Hall, Upper Saddle River, NJ, 1987)

We Can All Get Along: 50 Steps You Can Take
to Help End Racism at Home, at Work, in Your Community
C.W. Ford (Bantam Doubleday Dell, New York, 1994)

Valuing Diversity: New Tools for a New Reality
L.B. Griggs & L. Louw (McGraw-Hill, New York, 1995)

Venture into Cultures:
A Resource Book of Multicultural Materials and Programs
C.D. Hayden (Ed.) (American Library Association, Chicago,
1992)

Making Friends: The Influences of Culture and Development
L.H. Meyer, H.-S. Park, M. Grenot-Scheyer, I.S. Schwartz, &
B. Harry (Eds.) (Paul H. Brookes Publishing Co., Baltimore, 1998)

Video

Responding to the Handicapped
Produced by Films for the Humanities and Sciences,
Post Office Box 2053, Princeton, NJ 08543 (800-257-5126;
www.films.com)

Organizations that Promote Disability Awareness, Full Community Inclusion, and Social Change

ABLEDATA
8455 Colesville Road, Suite 935, Silver Spring, MD 20910
(800-227-0216; fax: 301-608-8958; www.abledata.com)

A database of assistive technology, rehabilitation equipment, and resources, maintained by the National Institute on Disability and Rehabilitation Research, U.S. Department of Education.

Americans with Disabilities Act
Civil Rights Division, U.S. Department of Justice, Box 66118, Washington, DC 20035-6118 (800-514-0301; TDD: 800-514-0383; www.usdoj.gov/crt/ada/adahom1.htm)

Association on Higher Education and Disabilities (AHEAD)
Post Office Box 21192, Columbus, OH 43221 (614-488-4972; fax: 614-488-1174; www.AHEAD.org/)

An international organization of professionals committed to the full participation in higher education of people with disabilities.

Disabilities, Opportunities, Internetworking & Technology
(www.weber.u.washington.edu/~doit/)

Promotes education and careers, particularly in math, science, and technology.

Disability Rights Education and Defense Fund, Inc.
2212 Sixth Street, Berkeley, CA 94710
(voice/ TDD: 510-644-2555; fax: 510-841-8645)

A nonprofit public benefit corporation dedicated to the independent living movement and the civil rights of people with disabilities.

Mobility International USA
Post Office Box 10767, Eugene, OR 97440

A nonprofit organization promoting international exchange, community service, and leadership opportunities for people with disabilities.

National Arts and Disabilities Center
University of California at Los Angeles, University Affiliated Program, 300 UCLA Medical Plaza, Suite 3330, Los Angeles, CA 90095-6967 (310-825-5054; fax: 310-794-1143; www.dcp.ucla.edu/nadc/)

Promotes the inclusion of artists and consumers with disabilities in every aspect of the arts community.

National Association of Protection and Advocacy Systems
900 2nd Street, NE, Suite 211, Washington, DC 20002 (202-408-9514; TDD: 202-408-9521; fax: 202-408-9520; protection and advocacy.com)

Each state's protection and advocacy agency has a legal "watchdog" function to monitor the compliance of public and private organizations and promote state legislation to ensure individual rights and community inclusion for people with disabilities.

National Council on Independent Living
1916 Wilson Boulevard, Suite 209, Arlington, VA 22201 (703-525-3406; e-mail: ncil@tsbbs08.tnet.com)

National Information Center for Children and Youth with Disabilities (NICHCY)
Post Office Box 1493, Washington, DC 20013 (800-695-0285; www.nichcy.org/)

PEAK Parent Center, Inc.
6055 Lehman Drive, Colorado Springs, CO 80918 (800-284-0251; TDD: 719-531-9403; fax: 719-531-9452; www.peakparent.org)

A parent-training, information, and advocacy center devoted to inclusive education.

President's Committee
on Employment of People with Disabilities
1331 F Street, NW, Washington, DC 20004-1107
(202-376-6200; TDD: 202-376-6205)

A small federal agency whose mission is to communicate, coordinate, and promote public and private efforts to enhance the employment of people with disabilities. The agency provides consultation about employment-related accommodations through the Job Accommodation Network.

Web Accessibility Initiative (WAI)
W3C, The Massachusetts Institute of Technology, Laboratory for Computer Science, 545 Technology Square, Cambridge, MA 02139 (617-253-2613; www.w3.org/WAI/)

The World Wide Web offers the promise of transforming many traditional barriers to information and interaction among different people. WAI is a program of the international group known as the World Wide Web Consortium (W3C), which is committed to promoting a high degree of usability on World Wide Web sites for people with disabilities through five primary areas: technology, guidelines, tools, education and outreach, and research and development.

World Institute on Disability
510 16th Street, Oakland, CA 94612-1502
(510-763-4100; www.wid.org)

A research and training institute working toward independence and quality of life for people with disabilities. The World Institute on Disability collaborates with an international network of people with disabilities, policy makers, corporations, nonprofit organizations, government agencies, and individuals to achieve its mission.

ENDNOTES

CHAPTER 1

1. Minow, 1991, p. 54.
2. Groce, 1985, p. 54.
3. Schumann, 1993, p. 327. For further nontechnical reading on evolution and the brain's detection of differences in the environment, see the Chapter 1 Readings and Resources.
4. Ackerman, 1990, p. 129. The items in this list are categorized by the five senses with which we are most familiar. Your brain, however, also reacts to mismatches caused by changes in temperature, pain, position, and gravity. For more detailed descriptions of these other senses, see Ackerman (1990).
5. Goleman, 1997, p. 5.
6. Sylwester, 1995, p. 84.
7. Murphy, 1987, p. 118.

CHAPTER 2

1. Some people with disabilities prefer to call themselves "disabled," "handicapped," or "crippled." Personal preferences should always be honored.
2. This is a restatement of the definition in the Americans with Disabilities Act (ADA) of 1990, PL 101-336. Under the ADA, people who have a *record* of such an impairment and those *regarded* as having an impairment are also considered as having a disability.
3. Gill, 1996, p. 9.
4. Shapiro, 1994, p. 7.
5. Shapiro, 1994.
6. Bureau of the Census, 1997.
7. Ibid.
8. Brett & Provenzo, 1995.
9. Wright, 1997.
10. National Stroke Association, 1997.
11. McIlwain & Bruce, 1996, p. 15
12. Rooklin & Masline, 1995, p. 8.
13. Johnson, 1992, p. 29.
14. "Paul Longmore," 1996, p. 27.
15. Emphasis (not without controversy) has also been placed on the identification and possible prevention of disabling conditions through genetic counseling, prenatal testing procedures, and selective abortion.

16. Schneider, 1990, p. 260.
17. Pfizer Foundation, 1997.
18. Morris, 1991, p. 29.
19. Hockenberry, 1995, p. 132.
20. Blotzer & Ruth, 1995, p. 3.
21. Mairs, 1996, p. 32.
22. Miller, 1994, p. 236 (Burmester, Callahan, & Dieterle speaking).
23. Dr. Mary Cerreto, personal communication, 1998.
24. Van der Klift & Kunc, 1994, p. 391.
25. Shapiro, 1994. Judy Heumann, also a polio survivor with quadriplegia, finished college and applied for and was denied a teaching position in New York. She sued the board of education for discrimination, got a great deal of support and press coverage, and in 1970 cofounded a political action group, Disabled in Action, with Ed Roberts. She has been Assistant Secretary of Education during the Clinton administration.
26. Shapiro, 1994, p. 51. This material is excerpted from a detailed history of the disability culture movement and is highly recommended reading for a full picture of its evolution and participants.
27. Brown, 1996, p. 32. Some people argue that a disability culture is not needed because the goal is for people with disabilities to be fully included in the mainstream culture and argue that the idea of a separate culture is divisive. Others say that the two cultures are not mutually exclusive: Inclusion is the goal, but there are similarities and differences among people with disabilities and they can best find support and expression in their self-identification as a distinct culture. The lively debates and opinions are themselves a reflection of the diversity within the disability population.
28. PL 93-112.
29. PL 105-17, PL 94-142. PL 94-142 guaranteed that every school-age child, regardless of disability, would receive an evaluation of his or her educational needs and an IEP that could include additional related services essential for academic progress, such as speech-language or occupational therapy, adaptive physical education, or mental health counseling. An LRE clause similar to the one in the Rehabilitation Act of 1973 further protected the child from having to move away from his or her home or be segregated on separate special education campuses.
30. PL 88-352.
31. Orlin, 1995. The ADA would protect, for example,
    • A person with a disabled spouse from being denied employment because of an employer's unfounded assumption that the applicant would use excessive leave to care for the spouse

- An individual who does volunteer work for people with acquired immune deficiency syndrome from a discriminatory employment action because of that relationship
- A child whose sibling has HIV disease from being refused admission to a day care center
- An employee from having health insurance benefits reduced because the employee has a dependent with a disability (p. 38)

32. PL 103-3.
33. Cohen, 1998, p. 22.

CHAPTER 4

1. Charkins, 1996, p. 160.
2. An effective and humorous videotape that does attempt to convey some universal rules is *The 10 Commandments of Communicating with People with Disabilities* by Irene M. Ward and Associates (1994), available from Program Development Associates, 5620 Business Avenue, Suite B, Cicero, New York 13039 (800-543-2119). The video has closed captioning and audio description.
3. Relaxed breathing can be practiced anytime, anywhere. But learning it the first time is easier if you choose a quiet room, ideally with low lighting. Position yourself comfortably, with both feet on the floor if possible. Rest your arms on your lap or at your sides. Close your eyes. When you are in position, imagine a calm, slow, soft voice giving these instructions:
   - Breathe in slowly and deeply through your nose, and exhale slowly and quietly through your mouth.
   - Now breathe in and out again using slow, deep breathing. Notice how long your inhalation and exhalation are by tapping the counts: 1...2...3...4...5...6.
   - On the third breath, try making your inhalation and exhalation longer.
   - Whenever you're nervous or scared, take three slow, deep breaths in and out, and you will feel more relaxed. Then you can Decide what to say and Do in the situation.
4. Davis, 1995, p. xvi.
5. Macgregor, 1990, p. 253.

CHAPTER 5

1. Ablon, 1988, p. 148.
2. Macgregor, 1990, p. 250.
3. Bernstein, 1990, p. 131.
4. Charkins, 1996, p. 81.
5. Macgregor, 1990, p. 253.

6. Phillips, 1990, p. 852.
7. The article on conjoined twins was a milestone in the media's role in both reflecting stereotypes and shaping social change. Not too many years ago, people with such unusual body forms were displayed as "freaks" in traveling carnivals. Several television programs have also featured stories emphasizing the twins' similarities to other children rather than their differences.
8. Ablon, 1988, p. 139.
9. Updike, 1989, p. 45.
10. Some of these Awareness Activities were adapted from *Unwrapping the Package: Dispelling Myths about Unusual Appearances*, by AboutFace International (no date).
11. National Organization for Albinism and Hypopigmentation, 1997.
12. National Psoriasis Foundation, 1996.
13. National Rosacea Society, 1997.

CHAPTER 6

1. Gill, 1994, p. 45.
2. Wendell, 1996, p. 90.
3. Bussard, 1997, p. 31.
4. McCrum, 1996, p. 116.
5. Saraceno, 1996, p. A1.
6. Hawking, 1995.
7. Engle, 1997, p. 239.
8. Beisser, 1990, p. 24.
9. Rosenblatt, 1996, p. 51.
10. Shapiro, 1994, p. 219.
11. Hockenberry, 1995, p. 207.
12. McIlwain & Bruce, 1996, p. 15.
13. National Information Center for Children and Youth with Disabilities, 1991.
14. Cline, 1997.
15. Bureau of the Census, 1995, Report 97-5.
16. American Parkinson's Disease Association, 1998.
17. Spinal Cord Injury Information Network, 1998.
18. National Stroke Association, 1997.
19. Bureau of the Census, 1995, Report 97-5.

CHAPTER 7

1. Mavor, 1998, p. 89.
2. Sacks, 1990, pp. 8–9.
3. Adapted from Getskow & Konczal, 1996, p. 104.

4. The terms *hearing loss, hearing disorder,* and *hearing impairment* are used interchangeably in this book. The term *deaf* refers to an audiological condition. It's important to remember that a deaf person may have very good hearing when using an effective hearing aid. Other deaf people cannot hear human speech to a functional level either with or without hearing aids.

5. Golan, 1995, pp. 144–145. Prolonged exposure to sounds of 85–90 decibels (dB) or higher can cause hearing loss. Here are some examples from everyday life of noises and corresponding decibel levels (at close range):

Firecracker	140 dB
Jet plane	120 dB
Rock music	110 dB
Lawnmower	90 dB
Traffic	80 dB
Conversation	60 dB
Rustling leaves	40 dB

6. U.S. Department of Health and Human Services, National Center for Health Statistics, 1994, Table 13.

7. Suss, 1993.

8. Fay, 1993, p. 107.

9. Douglas, 1997, p. 59.

10. Sacks, 1990.

11. The primary professional organization for interpreters is Registry of Interpreters for the Deaf, 8719 Colesville Road, Suite 310, Silver Spring, MD 20910 (301-608-0050). For a discussion of mandated use of interpreters, see McEntee, 1995.

12. The selection of a particular signing method for a child who is deaf is a major decision parents have to make. Some parents focus on their child's ability to read and write standard English in hearing classrooms and to communicate with hearing family members using a sign language based on English structure (such as SEE). Other parents want their child to master ASL and be included in the Deaf community. This decision process underscores the fact that language conveys a sense of identity, heritage, and community membership.

    Some people in the Deaf community believe that reliance on manual English systems and lipreading deprives deaf children of critically important Deaf history and culture; others disagree. For two views of this controversy, see Cohen, 1994, and Padden & Humphries, 1988.

13. Parette, Dunn, & Hoge, 1995, offer an excellent overview of communication aids.

14. Hawking, 1995.

15. Here are some TDD tips and etiquette:

- Identify yourself at the beginning of your call by typing, [YOUR NAME] HERE. The other person has no other way of knowing who is on the line.
- Using a TDD is similar to using a walkie-talkie: Only one party can talk at a time. TDD users give clear signals when they finish a statement and are ready for the other person to respond. GA means "go ahead," similar to the "Over" that walkie-talkie users say to indicate, "It's your turn to talk." End every statement with GA, and wait for the other person to use GA before you begin typing your response.
- Many TDD users omit punctuation and adopt abbreviations to expedite their conversations, such as ASAP (as soon as possible), OK (okay), and THX (thanks). Other abbreviations include HD (hold), OIC (oh, I see), TMW (tomorrow), U (you), R (are), and WUD (would).
- Type SK after your final closing statement. SK (stop keying) means "I'm hanging up now" or "I'm signing off now." When the second person types SK, the conversation has ended.

16. The ADA mandated that all states have a 24-hour relay system in place by July 26, 1993 (Strauss, 1993).
17. Virvan, 1991.
18. Closed captioning is often available on commercially recorded videotapes, and since 1980, increasing numbers of television movies and pre-recorded shows have provided closed captioning. To see the captions, your television must have a telecaption decoder, which is a feature of most televisions produced since 1993.
19. The ADA uses the term *service animals* to refer to such animals as dogs or monkeys who perform tasks for owners with disabilities. Various other terms for dogs are also in use, such as *assistance dogs, service dogs, hearing dogs,* and *Seeing Eye dogs.* For a referral to a service dog program near you, contact Delta Society, National Service Dog Center, 289 Perimeter Road E, Renton, WA, 98055-1329 (800-869-6898; TDD: 800-809-2714).
20. The cochlear implant is a medical device, not a hearing aid, so its cost is often covered by medical insurance.
21. National Information Center for Children and Youth with Disabilities, 1991.
22. U.S. Department of Health and Human Services, National Center for Health Statistics, 1994, Table 1. Other estimates of the number of people with speech, language, or hearing disorders are higher: the Better Hearing Institute estimates 25 million people; the National Institute on Deafness and Other Communication Disorders estimates 28 million people.
23. U.S. Department of Health and Human Services, National Center for Health Statistics, 1994, Table 13.

24. *The Washington Post*, 1997.
25. Better Hearing Institute, 1997.
26. Stuttering Foundation of America, 1989.
27. National Aphasia Organization, 1998.

CHAPTER 8

1. Carter, 1998, p. 20.
2. This is a time of great change regarding behavior terminology. Many terms are used to refer to the disorders or impairments that sometimes underlie behavior differences. Although there is no consensus, there *is* a trend toward terms that are both informative and respectful. Current terms include: *mental impairment, mental disability, psychiatric disability, brain disorder,* and *mental illness.* A discussion of the subtleties, distinctions, and overlaps among these terms is beyond the scope of this book.
3. Rosalynn Carter works to dispel this myth in her book, *Helping Someone with Mental Illness* (Random House, New York, 1998):

    It is a myth that mental illness makes people violent and evil monsters. It is true that a very small percentage of those with the serious illnesses who do not receive proper treatment are dangerous, especially when also using alcohol or drugs. But the stereotype of the mentally ill person as violent is erroneous. . . . While less than 3% of mentally ill patients have the potential for violence, 77% of those depicted on prime-time TV are presented as dangerous. (pp. 18, 229)
4. The Greater Long Beach and San Gabriel Valley chapter of the Autism Society of America performed a public service when they printed this message on the back of their business cards for parents to carry on public outings:

    Dear Onlooker,
    My child has the disability of *Autism.* He/she has problems with language and behavior. I am teaching him/her to behave appropriately in the community. I apologize for any inconvenience or disturbance it may cause you. If you would like to know more about *Autism,* please call your local chapter of the Autism Society.
    Thank you for your interest.
5. Shuman, 1996, p. 36. See also Lyons & Hayes, 1993, and Doe's "Thoughts on Thinking Differently," in Shaw, 1994.
6. American Psychiatric Association, 1994.
7. Singer, 1997, p. 269.

8. For a fascinating discussion of the relationship between mood disorders and creativity, see Jamison's *Touched with Fire: Manic-Depressive Illness and the Artistic Temperament* (1993).
9. Jamison, 1995, pp. 67, 218.
10. Frese, 1993, pp. 68–69.
11. Leete, 1993, pp. 114–128.
12. Sacks, 1990.
13. Cummings & Benson, 1983.
14. McGowin, 1993, pp. 7–8.
15. Klin & Volkmar, 1996.
16. Grandin, 1995, pp. 89, 91–92.
17. In rare cases, violent outbursts may be due to a brain disorder called *complex partial epilepsy* (also called *temporal lobe epilepsy*). Although most seizures involve specific body movements such as a jerking arm or leg or loss of consciousness (see Chapter 7), complex partial epilepsy can cause angry or odd behavior that is really "out of character" for the person. The person may feel detached from the behavior and social situation, may describe it as a daydream, or may not remember it at all.
18. Go to Mental Health Net and CMHC System's web site (http://www.cmhc.com/guide/pro22.htm) for information regarding medications for mental disorders (called *psychoactive, psychotropic,* or *psychopharmacological treatment*).
19. The following mental health professionals can provide psychotherapy:
    * *Psychiatrists* (M.D.) are medical doctors who have completed a specialized residency; they may provide psychotherapy as well as psychiatric diagnoses and medication management. Psychiatrists rely primarily upon interviewing to make diagnoses and decide which medications might help.
    * *Clinical psychologists* (Ph.D.) have been trained to provide psychotherapy as well as *psychometric evaluation,* standardized tests of many psychological attributes, including intelligence, personality, and various emotional states.
    * *Neuropsychologists* (Ph.D.) have similar training but focus on the connection between brain impairments and specific mental skills such as memory, judgment, problem solving, and so forth.
    * *Clinical social workers* (M.S.W.) have training in psychotherapy as well as in locating and coordinating a variety of community services to support the person with mental disabilities and his or her family.
    * *Psychiatric nurses* (R.N.) may practice psychotherapy.
    * *Family counselors* (M.F.C.) have training in counseling families.

- *Certified counselors* have completed training programs in specific behavior problems, such as substance abuse, sexual dysfunction, or posttraumatic stress disorder, or treatment methods, such as hypnosis; professional psychotherapists often obtain specialized certification.

20. Rand, 1995.
21. National Mental Health Association, 1997.
22. National Institute of Mental Health, 1998.
23. Ibid.
24. Ibid.
25. U.S. Congress, Office of Technology Assessment, 1990.
26. World Almanac and Book of Facts, 1998.
27. OC & Spectrum Disorders Association, 1998.
28. Weinberger in Long, 1998a.
29. Long, 1998b.
30. Autism Society of America, 1998.
31. American Psychiatric Association, 1998.

CHAPTER 9

1. Castles, 1996, p. 107.
2. Gardner (1983) identified seven types of intelligence: linguistic, logical-mathematical, spatial, bodily-kinesthetic, musical, interpersonal, and intrapersonal. Armstrong (1987) also discussed multiple intelligences.
3. Kaufman, 1999.
4. Hammill, Leigh, McNutt, & Larsen define *learning disabilities* as

    A heterogeneous group of disorders manifested by significant difficulty in the acquisition and use of listening, speaking, reading, writing, reasoning, or mathematical abilities. These disorders are intrinsic to the individual, presumed to be due to central nervous system dysfunction, and may occur across the life span. (1981, p. 10)

5. Schmitt, 1994.
6. The American Association on Mental Retardation (AAMR) definition is presented in detail in *Mental Retardation: Definition, Classification, and Systems of Supports, Ninth Edition*:

    Mental retardation refers to substantial limitations in present functioning. It is characterized by significantly subaverage intellectual functioning, existing concurrently with related limitations in two or more of the following applicable adaptive skill areas: communication, self-care, home living, social skills, community use, self-direction, health and safety, functional academics, leisure, and work. Mental retardation manifests before age 18." (Luckasson et al., 1992, p. 5)

Levels of retardation are specified in the American Psychiatric Association's (1994) *Diagnostic and Statistical Manual of Mental Disorders, Fourth Edition*:

- Low normal intelligence—IQ score of 70 to 80
- Mild mental retardation—IQ score of 50–55 to 70
- Moderate mental retardation—IQ score of 35–40 to 50–55
- Severe mental retardation—IQ score of 20–25 to 35–40
- Profound mental retardation—IQ score below 20–25

It is important to note that most people with mental retardation have a mild level of impairment.

The AAMR describes levels of mental retardation in terms of the support needed by an individual. Instead of using the terms *mild, moderate, severe,* and *profound mental retardation,* the AAMR uses *mental retardation requiring intermittent, limited, extensive, or pervasive support* (Luckasson et al., 1992).

7. Kingsley & Levitz, 1994.
8. Stanzel, 1996, p. 96.
9. Shaywitz, Escobar, Shaywitz, Fletcher, & Makuch, 1992.
10. Lyon, 1996.
11. Badian & Ghublikian, 1983; Norman & Zigmond, 1980.
12. Hodapp & Dykens, 1996.
13. Batshaw, 1997.
14. American Psychiatric Association, 1994.
15. Gretchen Josephson has mental retardation resulting from Down syndrome. A book of her poems, edited by L.O. Lubchenco, was published in 1997.

CHAPTER 10

1. Gill, 1994, p. 46.
2. Gail Sammons, personal communication, 1998.
3. Brookes, 1994, p. 19
4. Edelson, 1998, p. 29.
5. Chalker & Whitmore, 1990, p. 256.
6. Guillory, 1998, p. 101.
7. Vaughn, 1997, p. D5.
8. A person having a seizure may need assistance and/or medical attention and may need reassurance after the seizure is over. For more information on what to do when a person has a seizure, contact a health care professional or the Epilepsy Foundation of America, 4351 Garden City Drive, Landover, MD 20875 (800-332-1000; www.efa.org; e-mail:postmaster@ efa.org).

9. Gething, 1992, p. 122.
10. Shuman, 1996, p. 15.
11. Saper & Magee, 1995, p. 16.
12. Levert, 1996, p. 16.
13. Shuman, 1996, p. 16.
14. Stine, 1998.
15. Rooklin & Masline, 1995, p. 7.
16. Centers for Disease Control and Prevention, 1997.
17. *World Almanac and Book of Facts*, 1998, p. 616.
18. Chalker & Whitmore, 1990, p. 3.
19. Brewer, 1997, p. 5.
20. American Heart Association, 1996.
21. Lupus Foundation of America.
22. Saper & Magee, 1995, p. 15.
23. McIlwain & Bruce, 1996, p. 8.
24. *World Almanac and Book of Facts*, 1998.
25. National Information Center for Children and Youth with Disabilities, 1991.
26. Petrou, 1998.

CHAPTER 11

1. Shafritz, 1994, p. 39.
2. Comstock, 1991.
3. Murphy, 1987, p. 130.
4. A book for 3- to 12-year-olds is *Relax*, by C. O'Neill, 1993.
5. Collins, 1997, p. 12.
6. Girl Scouts of the USA, 1990
7. Sheffer, 1997, p. 9.

CHAPTER 12

1. Rioux, 1992, p. 60.
2. Gill, 1994, p. 45.
3. See, for example, *Part of Your General Public Is Disabled: A Handbook for Guides to Museums, Zoos, and Historic Houses*, by Jan Majewski (1987), available from the Smithsonian Accessibility Program, 900 Jefferson Drive, SW, Room 1239, Washington, DC 20560-0426 (202-786-2932; TDD: 202-786-2414; fax: 202-786-2210).
4. Cohen, 1994, p. 4.
5. Ford, 1994, p. 78–79.
6. Scherer, 1993, p. 20
7. Weathers, 1997, p. 92.
8. Rosenblatt, 1996, p. 51.
9. Jamison, 1995, pp. 179–180.
10. Gething, 1992, pp. 146–147.

11. Hahn, 1993, pp. 223–224.
12. An unnamed woman in Willmuth & Holcomb, 1993, p. 203.
13. Hine, 1993, p. 187–188. Robert Hine became blind at age 50; his vision was restored 15 years later.
14. Wendell, 1996, p. 68.
15. Morris, 1991, p. 71.
16. Mairs, 1996, p. 106.

REFERENCES

Ablon, J. (1988). *Living with difference: Families with dwarf children.* New York: Praeger.

AboutFace International. (no date). *Unwrapping the package: Dispelling myths about unusual appearances.* Toronto, Ontario, Canada: Author.

Ackerman, D. (1990). *A natural history of the senses.* New York: Random House.

American Psychiatric Association. (1994). *Diagnostic and statistical manual of mental disorders* (4th ed.). Washington, DC: Author.

American Psychiatric Association. (1998). *Let's talk about facts: Substance abuse* [On-line]. Available: http://www.psych.org/public-info

Americans with Disabilities Act (ADA) of 1990, PL 101-336, 42 U.S.C. §§ 12101 *et seq.*

Armstrong, T. (1987). *In their own way.* Los Angeles: Jeremy P. Tarcher.

Autism Society of America. (1998). *What is autism?* [On-line]. Available: http://www.autism-society.org

Badian, N.A., & Ghublikian, M. (1983). The personal-social characteristics of children with poor mathematical computation skills. *Journal of Learning Disabilities, 116,* 154–157.

Batshaw, M.L. (Ed.). (1997). *Children with disabilities* (4th ed.). Baltimore: Paul H. Brookes Publishing Co.

Beisser, A. (1990). *Flying without wings: Personal reflections on loss, disability, and healing.* New York: Bantam Doubleday Dell.

Bernstein, N. (1990). Objective bodily damage: Disfigurement and dignity. In T.F. Cash & T. Pruzinsky (Eds.), *Body images: Development, deviance, and change* (pp. 131–148). New York: The Guilford Press.

Better Hearing Institute. (1997). *Hearing stats and key facts* [On-line]. Available: http://www.betterhearing.org

Blotzer, M.A., & Ruth, R. (1995). *Sometimes you just want to feel like a human being: Case studies of empowering psychotherapy with people with disabilities.* Baltimore: Paul H. Brookes Publishing Co.

Brett, A., & Provenzo, E. (1995). *Adaptive technology for special human needs.* Albany: State University of New York Press.

Brewer, S. (1997). *Irritable bowel syndrome.* New York: HarperCollins.

Brookes, T. (1994). *Catching my breath: An asthmatic explores his illness.* New York: Times Books.

Brown, S.E. (1996, August). We are who we are...so who are we? *Mainstream, 20*(10), 28–33.

Bureau of the Census. (1995). *Current population reports: Americans with disabilities, 1994–95.* Washington, DC: Author.

Bureau of the Census. (1997). *Bureau of the Census Brief 97-5: Disabilities affect one-fifth of all Americans.* Washington, DC: Author.

Bussard, L. (1997). *More alike than different: An inspiring message for anyone coping with life's difficulties.* Bellevue, WA: More Alike Than Different Publishing.

Carter, R. (1998). *Helping someone with mental illness: A compassionate guide for family, friends, and caregivers.* New York: Random House.

Castles, E.E. (1996). *"We're people first." The social and emotional lives of individuals with mental retardation.* New York: Praeger.

Chalker, R., & Whitmore, K. (1990). *Overcoming bladder disorders.* New York: HarperCollins.

Charkins, H. (1996). *Children with facial difference: A parents' guide.* Bethesda, MD: Woodbine House.

Civil Rights Act of 1964, PL 88-352, 20 U.S.C. §§ 241 *et seq.*

Cline, C. (Ed.). (1997). *FAQs of life.* New York: Cader Books.

Cohen, G. (1998, June). Enabling the disabled: An interview with Dr. Henry B. Betts. *Hemispheres*, pp. 20–24.

Cohen, L.H. (1994). *Train go sorry: Inside a deaf world.* Boston: Houghton Mifflin.

Collins, K.D. (1997, May). I teach. *New Mobility*, p. 12.

Comstock, G. (1991). *Television in America* (2nd ed.). Thousand Oaks, CA: Sage Publications.

Costello, E.J. (1996). State of the science in autism: Report to the National Institutes of Health, Epidemiology. *Journal of Autism and Developmental Disorders, 26,* 126–129.

Cowley, G. (1996, June 3). The biology of beauty. *Newsweek*, pp. 61–66.

Cummings, J.L., & Benson, D.R. (1983). *Dementia: A clinical approach.* Boston: Butterworth Publishers.

Davis, L.J. (1995). *Enforcing normalcy: Disability, deafness, and the body.* New York: Verso.

Doe, T. (1994). Thoughts on thinking differently. In B. Shaw (Ed.), *The ragged edge: The disability experience from the pages of the first fifteen years of the* Disability Rag (pp. 22–24). Louisville, KY: The Advocado Press.

Edelson, S. (1998). *Living with environmental illness: A practical guide to multiple chemical sensitivity.* Dallas, TX: Taylor Publishing.

Education for All Handicapped Children Act of 1975, PL 94-142, 20 U.S.C. §§ 1400 *et seq.*

Engle, S. (Ed.). (1997). *Silver linings: Triumphs of the chronically ill and physically challenged.* Amherst, NY: Prometheus Books.

Family and Medical Leave Act (FMLA) of 1993, PL 103-3, 5 U.S.C. §§ 6381 *et seq.*, 29 U.S.C. §§ 2601 *et seq.*

Fay, L. (1993). An account of the search of a woman who is verbally impaired for augmentative devices to end her silence. In M.E. Willmuth & L. Holcomb (Eds.), *Women with disabilities: Found voices* (pp. 105–115). Binghamton, NY: Haworth Press.

Ford, C.W. (1994). *We can all get along: 50 steps you can take to help end racism at home, at work, in your community.* New York: Bantam Doubleday Dell.

Frese, F.J., III. (1993). Cruising the cosmos, part 3: Psychosis and hospitalization: Consumer's personal recollection. In A.B. Hatfield & H.P. Lefley (Eds.), *Surviving mental illness: Stress, coping, and adaptation* (pp. 68–69). New York: The Guilford Press.

Gardner, H.H. (1983). *Frames of mind: The theory of multiple intelligences.* New York: Basic Books.

Gething, L. (1992). *Person to person: A guide for professionals working with people with disabilities* (2nd ed.). Baltimore: Paul H. Brookes Publishing Co.

Getskow, V., & Konczal, D. (1996). *Kids with special needs: Information and activities to promote awareness and understanding.* Santa Barbara, CA: The Learning Works.

Gill, C. (1994). Questioning continuum. In B. Shaw (Ed.), *The ragged edge: The disability experience from the pages of the first fifteen years of the* Disability Rag (pp. 42–49). Louisville, KY: The Advocado Press.

Gill, C.J. (1996). Becoming visible: Personal health experiences of women with physical disabilities. In D.M. Krotoski, M.A. Nosek, & M.A. Turk (Eds.), *Women with physical disabilities: Achieving and maintaining health and well-being* (pp. 5–15). Baltimore: Paul H. Brookes Publishing Co.

Girl Scouts of the USA. (1990). *Focus on ability: Serving girls with special needs.* New York: Author.

Golan, L. (1995). *Reading between the lips: A totally deaf man makes it in the mainstream.* Chicago: Bonus Books.

Goleman, D. (1997). *Emotional intelligence.* New York: Bantam.

Grandin, T. (1995). *Thinking in pictures.* New York: Vintage Books.

Groce, N. (1985). *Everyone here spoke sign language: Hereditary deafness on Martha's Vineyard.* Cambridge, MA: Harvard University Press.

Guillory, G. (1998). *Irritable bowel syndrome: A doctor's plan for chronic digestive troubles.* Point Roberts, WA: Hartley and Marks.

Hahn, H. (1993). Can disability be beautiful? In M. Nagler (Ed.), *Perspectives on disability: Text and readings on disability* (2nd ed., pp. 223–224). Palo Alto, CA: Health Markets Research.

Hammill, D.D., Leigh, J., McNutt, G., & Larsen, S. (1981). A new definition of learning disabilities. *Journal of Learning Disabilities, 4,* 336–342.

Hawking, S. (1995). *Disability advice: My experience with ALS* [amyotrophic lateral sclerosis]. Available: http://www.damtp.cam.ac.uk/user/hawking/home.html

Hine, R. (1993). *Second sight.* Berkeley: University of California Press.

Hockenberry, J. (1995). *Moving violations: War zones, wheelchairs, and declarations of independence.* New York: Hyperion.

Hodapp, R.M., & Dykens, E.M. (1996). Mental retardation. In E.J. Marsh & R.A. Barkley (Eds.), *Child psychopathology.* New York: The Guilford Press.

Individuals with Disabilities Education Act Amendments of 1997, PL 105-17, 20 U.S.C. §§ 1400 *et seq.*

Individuals with Disabilities Education Act (IDEA) of 1990, PL 101-476, 20 U.S.C. §§ 1400 *et seq.*

Jamison, K.R. (1993). *Touched with fire: Manic-depressive illness and the artistic temperament.* New York: Free Press.

Jamison, K.R. (1995). *An unquiet mind.* New York: Alfred A. Knopf.

Johnson, M. (Ed.). (1992). *People with disabilities explain it all for you.* Louisville, KY: The Advocado Press.

Kaufman, S.Z. (1999). *Retarded isn't stupid, Mom!* (Rev. ed.). Baltimore: Paul H. Brookes Publishing Co.

Kingsley, J., & Levitz, M. (1994). *Count us in: Growing up with Down syndrome.* Orlando, FL: Harcourt Brace & Co.

Klin, A., & Volkmar, F.R. (1996). *Asperger's syndrome: Guidelines for treatment and intervention* [On-line]. Available: http://www.info. med.yale.edu/chldstdy/autism/page51.html

Leete, E. (1993). The interpersonal environment: A consumer's personal recollection. In A.B. Hatfield & H.P. Lefley (Eds.), *Surviving mental illness: Stress, coping, and adaptation* (pp. 114–128). New York: The Guilford Press.

Levert, M. (1996). *AIDS: A handbook for the future.* Brookfield, CT: Millbrook Press.

Long, P.W. (1998a). Ask the experts. *Internet Mental Health* [On-line]. Available: http://www.mentalhealth.com/fr20.html

Long, P.W. (1998b). *Questions and answers about Tourette syndrome (TSA).* Internet Mental Health [On-line]. Available: http://www. mentalhealth.com/fr20.html

Lubchenco, L.O. (Ed.). (1997). *Bus girl: Poems by Gretchen Josephson.* Cambridge, MA: Brookline Books.

Luckasson, R., Schalock, R.L., Coulter, D.L., Snell, M.E., Polloway, E.A., Spitalnik, D.M., Reiss, S., & Stark, J.A. (1992). *Mental retardation: Definition, classification, and systems of supports* (9th ed.). Washington, DC: American Association on Mental Retardation.

Lyon, G.R. (1996). The state of research. In S.C. Cramer & W. Ellis (Eds.), *Learning disabilities: Lifelong issues* (pp. 3–61). Baltimore: Paul H. Brookes Publishing Co.

Lyons, M., & Hayes, R. (1993). Student perceptions of persons with psychiatric and other disorders. *American Journal of Occupational Therapy, 7*(6), 541–548.

Macgregor, F. (1990). Facial disfigurement: Problems and management of social interaction and implications for mental health. *Aesthetic Plastic Surgery, 14,* 249–257.

Mairs, N. (1996). *Waist high in the world: A life among the nondisabled.* Boston: Beacon Press.

Majewski, J. (1987). *Part of your general public is disabled: A handbook for guides to museums, zoos, and historic houses.* (Available from the Smithsonian Accessibility Program, 900 Jefferson Drive, SW, Room 1239, Washington, DC 20560-0426)

Mavor, A.H. (1998, March). Mouth piece. *Hemispheres,* p. 89.

McCrum, R. (1996, May 27). My old and new lives. *The New Yorker,* pp. 112–118.

McEntee, M.K. (1995). Deaf and hard-of-hearing clients: Some legal implications. *Social Work, 40,* 183–187.

McFarquhar, L. (1997, July 21). The face age. *The New Yorker,* pp. 68–70.

McGowin, D.F. (1993). *Living in the labyrinth: A personal journey through the maze of Alzheimer's.* New York: Delacorte Press.

McIlwain, H., & Bruce, D. (1996). *Stop osteoarthritis now!: Halting the baby boomers' disease.* New York: Fireside Books.

Mental Health Net and CMHC Systems. (1998). *Psychopharmacological and drug references* [On-line]. Available: http://www.cmhc.com/guide/pro22.htm

Miller, N.B., with "The Moms": Burmester, S., Callahan, D.G., Dieterle, J., & Niedermeyer, S. (1994). *Nobody's perfect: Living and growing with children who have special needs.* Baltimore: Paul H. Brookes Publishing Co.

Minow, M. (1991). *Making all the difference: Inclusion, exclusion, and American law.* Ithaca, NY: Cornell University Press.

Morris, J. (1991). *Pride against prejudice: Transforming attitudes to disability.* Philadelphia: New Society Publishers.

Murphy, R.F. (1987). *The body silent.* New York: Henry Holt.

National Aphasia Organization. (1998). *Aphasia fact sheet* [On-line]. Available: http://www.aphasia.org/NAAfactsheet.html

National Information Center for Children and Youth with Disabilities. (1991). *General information about speech and language disorders* (Fact Sheet No. 11). Washington, DC: Author.

National Institute of Mental Health. (1998). *Mental illness in America* [On-line]. Available: http://www.nimh.nih.org

National Mental Health Association. (1997). *Did you know?* [On-line]. Available: http://www.nmha.org/infoctr/didyou.cfm

Norman, C.A., & Zigmond, N. (1980). Characteristics of children labeled and served as learning disabled in school systems affiliated with Child Service Demonstration Center. *Journal of Learning Disabilities, 13,* 542–547.

OC & Spectrum Disorders Association. (1998). *Most frequently questions about OCD* [On-line]. Available: http://www.ocdhelp.org/faq2.html#common

O'Neill, C. (1993). *Relax.* Swindon, England: Child's Play International.

Orlin, M. (1995, March). The Americans with Disabilities Act: Implications for social services. *Social Work, 40*(2), 233–238.

Padden, C., & Humphries, T. (1988). *Deaf in America: Voices from a culture.* Cambridge, MA: Harvard University Press.

Parette, H.P., Dunn, N.S., & Hoge, D.R. (1995, September). Low-cost communication devices for children with disabilities and their family members. *Young Children,* 75–81.

Paul Longmore: "Disability isn't just a set of obstacles to be overcome." (1996, October). *Exceptional Parent, 26*(10), 24–27.

Petrou, C.M. (1998). *Tinnitus information & support center* [On-line]. Available: http://members.aol.com/MyTinnitus/index.html

Pfizer Foundation. (1997). Status of caregiving in America. *Pfizer Journal, 1*(3).

Phillips, M. (1990). Damaged goods: Oral narratives of the experience of disability in American culture. *Social Science and Medicine, 30*(8), 849–857.

Rand, B. (1995). *How to understand people who are different* [On-line]. Available: http://www.students.uiuc.edu/bordner~ani/brad_rand.html

Rehabilitation Act Amendments of 1986, PL 99-506, 29 U.S.C. §§ 701 *et seq.*

Rehabilitation Act Amendments of 1992, PL 102-569, 29 U.S.C. §§ 701 *et seq.*

Rehabilitation Act of 1973, PL 93-112, 29 U.S.C. §§ 701 *et seq.*

Rioux, M. (1992, Spring). Rights, justice, power: An agenda for change. *Ability,* 60–61.

Rooklin, A., & Masline, S. (1995). *Living with asthma.* New York: Penguin USA.

Rosenblatt, R. (1996, August 26). New hopes, new dreams. *Time,* 51.

Sacks, O. (1990). *Seeing voices: A journey into the world of the deaf* (pp. 8–9). New York: HarperCollins.

Saper, J., & Magee, K. (1995). *Freedom from headaches.* New York: Simon & Schuster.

Saraceno, J. (1996, October 11). Still the greatest. *USA Today,* p. A1.

Scherer, M. (1993). *Living in a state of stuck: How technology impacts the lives of people with disabilities.* Cambridge, MA: Brookline Books.

Schmitt, A. (1994). *Brilliant idiot: An autobiography of a dyslexic.* Intercourse, PA: Good Books.

Schneider, J. (1990). Disability as moral experience: Epilepsy and self in routine relationships. In M. Nagler (Ed.), *Perspectives on disability: Text and readings on disability* (2nd ed., pp. 618–628). Palo Alto, CA: Health Markets Research.

Schumann, J. (1993). The brain looks at diversity. *Journal of Multilingual and Multicultural Development, 14,* 321–328.

Shafritz, L. (1994). *Face value*. (Available from Linda Shafritz, Post Office Box 45-5854, Los Angeles, CA 90045)

Shapiro, J.P. (1994). *No pity: People with disabilities forging a new civil rights movement*. New York: Times Books.

Shaywitz, S.E., Escobar, M.D., Shaywitz, B.A., Fletcher, J.M., & Makuch, R. (1992). Evidence that dyslexia may represent the lower tail of a normal distribution of reading ability. *New England Journal of Medicine, 326*, 145-150.

Sheffer, H.L. (1997, June/July). [Letter to the editor]. *Mainstream, 9*.

Shuman, R. (1996). *The psychology of chronic illness: The healing work of patients, therapists, and families*. New York: HarperCollins.

Singer, J.A. (1997). *Message in a bottle: Stories of men and addiction*. New York: Free Press.

Spinal Cord Injury Information Network. (1998, October 5). *Frequently asked questions* [On-line]. Available: http://www.spinalcord.uab.edu/frames/faq/html

Stanzel, S.M. (1996). Academic accommodations: A personal view. In S.C. Cramer & W. Ellis (Eds.), *Learning disabilities: Lifelong issues* (pp. 95–98). Baltimore: Paul H. Brookes Publishing Co.

Stine, G. (1998). *AIDS update 1998: An annual overview of acquired immunodeficiency syndrome*. Upper Saddle River, NJ: Prentice Hall.

Strauss, K.P. (1993). Implementing the telecommunications provisions. *Milbank Quarterly, 69*, 25–54.

Stuttering Foundation of America. (1989). *Did you know?* Memphis, TN: Author.

Suss, E. (1993). *When the hearing gets hard: Winning the battle against hearing impairment*. New York: Bantam Doubleday Dell.

Sylwester, R. (1995). *A celebration of neurons: An educator's guide to the human brain*. Alexandria, VA: Association for Supervision and Curriculum Development.

Updike, J. (1989). *Self-consciousness: Memoirs*. New York: Alfred A. Knopf.

U.S. Congress, Office of Technology Assessment. (1990, July). *Confused minds, burdened families*. Washington, DC: Author.

U.S. Department of Health and Human Services, National Center for Health Statistics. (1994). *Data from the 1990–91 National Health Interview Survey* (Series 10, Number 188). Rockville, MD: Author.

Van der Klift, E., & Kunc, N. (1994). Beyond benevolence: Friendship and the politics of help. In J.S. Thousand, R.A. Villa, & A.I. Nevin, *Creativity and collaborative learning: A practical guide to empowering students and teachers* (pp. 391–401). Baltimore: Paul H. Brookes Publishing Co.

Vaughn, S. (1997, July 13). Cancer patients battle not only disease but also workplace bias. *The Los Angeles Times*, p. D5.

Virvan, B. (1991, January/February). You don't have to hate meetings—Try computer-assisted notetaking. *SHHH Journal*, 25–28.

Ward, I.M., & Associates. (1994). The 10 commandments of communicating with people with disabilities [Videotape]. (Available from Program Development Associates, 5620 Business Avenue, Suite B, Cicero, New York 13039; 800-543-2119)

Weathers, B. (1997, September 29). Days of reckoning: Surviving Everest—barely: A doctor finds new meaning in life. *People*, 92.

Wendell, S. (1996). *The rejected body: Feminist philosophical reflections on disability.* New York: Routledge Press.

Willmuth, M.E., & Holcomb, L. (Eds.). (1993). *Women with disabilities: Found voices.* Binghamton, NY: Haworth Press.

Wright, J. (Ed.). (1997). *The New York Times 1998 almanac.* New York: Penguin USA.

World almanac and book of facts. (1998). Mahwah, NJ: World Almanac Books.

INDEX